CLOUD COMPUTING

FOR LAWYERS AND EXECUTIVES

A GLOBAL APPROACH

2ND EDITION

THOMAS J. SHAW

CLOUD COMPUTING

FOR LAWYERS AND EXECUTIVES

A GLOBAL APPROACH

2ND EDITION

The materials contained herein represent the opinions of the author and should not be construed to be the views or opinions of the companies he is associated with or employed by.

Nothing contained in this book is to be considered as the rendering of legal advice for specific cases, and readers are responsible for obtaining such advice from their own legal counsel. This book is intended for educational and informational purposes only.

Printed in the United States of America.

ISBN: 978-1-70781-130-4

CONTENTS

PREFACE

To provide all necessary computing capabilities, just like utilities provide water or power, from an outlet easily connected to, with high quality at low rates for metered usage: that, simply put, is the promise of cloud computing. Its aim is to make information technology (IT) just another utility to be plugged into and in essence forgotten about, because it is a commodity that we purchase based on its price and (perhaps) quality of service. For too long, IT has been the tail that has wagged the business dog instead of the other way around. Cloud computing now intends to reorient that dynamic by taking us on a journey, one that when combined with other enabling technologies, frees users from all the complexities and specialties that IT has become. Is it really that simple? Can we just connect our access device to a network and receive our IT utility service without further consideration *a la* power and water?

The answer, in mid-2013, as it was in mid-2011 when I wrote the first edition of this book, is a qualified "yes," but much still needs to be done. Many of the complexities are manageable by the providers of cloud computing services (generally referred to as CSPs — cloud service providers) without the need to expose all of the intricacies to the consumers of cloud computing services. As with any public utility, there may be occasional service outages that must be planned for.[1] The most discerning consumers of cloud computing services know that they must fully understand the general risks involved with what cloud computing can currently provide, what capabilities cannot be provided, and what steps must be taken to assess and mitigate the specific risks of utilizing services from prospective CSPs.

The cover of this book depicts clouds, but not all are the bright pillowy stacks of monolithic cumulus clouds so typically depicted when accompanying marketing descriptions of cloud computing. Instead, the real cloud environment today is as shown on this book's cover, with disparate cloud islands, promising to perhaps amalgamate into an easily understood whole. There is the threat of rain in these clouds and the day may be ending soon but behind it all is the lurking blue sky, holding out the promise that all things positive may be forthcoming. To make that a reality, cloud consumers must be able to pull together the different types of cloud iterations, dodge the rain of service outages, survive the night with unknown CSPs, ground the lightning of cloud information risk, and find the sunshine of reliable cloud services.

This book is written from the perspective of the organization as consumer of cloud computing services. More specifically, it targets the lawyers and others inside and outside international and domestic organizations (in corporations, law firms, and government) who are providing legal and technical advice to these entities on how best to deploy (or not) cloud computing services. Before looking at the substantive aspects of legal obligations and technical and legal risk, the book starts by explaining just what cloud computing is. It then discusses the benefits by answering why use cloud computing. Not all organizations or workloads are a good match for cloud computing at the current time, so next is a discussion of when to utilize these services. And then financial evaluation criteria of the cloud computing services are discussed, so that lawyers have a solid understanding of the cost factors involved, leading to the calculations of return on investment and payback periods essential to evaluating competing CSP proposals and obtaining approval from the organization's executives.

The book starts its substantive discussion by looking first at the legal obligations implicated by use of the cloud. Because this book is written by

---

1. *Amazon EBS failure brings down Reddit, Imgur, others*, Network World (Oct. 22, 2012).

an author internationally situated, a global perspective will be maintained throughout, with both non-U.S. as well as U.S. legal obligations examined. Many of those obligations address the national protection of personal information through the appropriate use of privacy and information security policies and procedures, so data protection statutes are given significant coverage in the book. But it also addresses statutes and regulations that restrict the flow of personal information across borders, both in business and litigation, and discusses certain legal powers that governments have globally that should be of concern to cloud consumers when evaluating CSPs hosted in or legally accessible from various countries.

Information security and privacy safeguards are probably the most important aspects of cloud computing for organizations to rigorously address in outsourcing to the cloud. This includes not only the assessment of the risk management processes of the CSP but also those of the organization that will be utilizing the cloud. In a survey of over 100 CSPs, a majority did not list "cloud computing security as one of their most important responsibilities" but believed that it was "their customer's responsibility to secure the cloud."[2] As such, significant coverage is given to information security and privacy risks of cloud computing and the various frameworks that have been developed to address these risks. Due to its leading position in setting the tone for cloud computing, the efforts of the U.S. federal government are examined at length.

For the cloud to really take off and be accepted by a majority of organizations, internationally accepted standards are essential. So the various cloud standards groups and the few standards that have been accepted to date are introduced. Adherence to standards will become an increasingly important matter as the cloud matures. It is also essential for organizations to stay in compliance with statutes, regulations, standards, and contracts. Organizations remain legally liable for their compliance obligations after outsourcing to the cloud, so the area of cloud audits is discussed next. How business continuity planning is impacted by the cloud is then presented, as is an overall approach to risk management in the cloud.

---

2. Ponemon Institute, *Security of Cloud Computing Providers Study* (Apr. 2011).

Other areas of special significance in the cloud are discussed next. These include how to address a data breach in the cloud that impacts the organization, including the use of insurance. Civil litigation and government investigations will be accompanied by demands/requests for data being processed by CSPs ("processing" is a term of art that includes all IT-related activities involved with data, including acquisition, storage, retrieval, use, transmission, backup, deletion, etc.). These are covered under the general litigation-related categories of electronic discovery and forensics in the cloud. This will include discussing how civil law countries respond to discovery requests from common law countries with extensive evidence discovery regimes.

The book then turns to addressing how to negotiate and contract with CSPs, broken down into two broad topics: the contractual provisions themselves and then how these provisions are used in a number of real-life situations, including well-known CSPs providing the different types of cloud services. A survey done by University of London's School of Law identified significant differences in the terms offered by U.S. and European CSPs (offering all three service models).[3] Looking at almost twenty different categories, the study identified how the majority of CSPs of varying types tended to look at choice of law, jurisdiction, and mandatory arbitration provisions from the perspective of what was better for the CSP (e.g., familiar laws).

The survey showed that many CSP contracts state that the CSP can implement changes to the terms of the agreement through posting on its website. Concerning data integrity, a majority of CSPs either disclaim ultimate responsibility or do not mention it at all and are not consistent on when or how they delete customer data at the end of the relationship. Some have lower requirements for what constitutes the type of compelled disclosure they will respond to. Most do not provide data location transparency or assurances of transmission protections when the data is transferred. And almost all try to limit their liability and any warranties on the service they provide.

To make all of these explanations practical for lawyers, the examples of two different kinds of organizations are presented in Chapter 8. The

---

3. Queen Mary University of London, School of Law, Legal Studies Research Paper No. 63/2010.

two cases are those of the multinational organization and of the domestic small and medium enterprise (SME). These are analyzed against a defined methodology that includes assessing first the organization and then the CSP, from both the perspectives of information security and privacy risks and the legal provisions necessary for success in cloud outsourcing. Before moving to the cloud, all organizations must first ensure that they are ready and able to handle this transition, by having rigorous programs in place to oversee these services.

The use of the cloud raises a number of ethical issues for lawyers, including the duty to keep their clients' data confidential when utilizing cloud services such as storage. This area is examined in light of the most recent ethics opinions issued by the ABA and state bar associations. The other type of client that lawyers may advise on cloud computing is the individual cloud consumer, whose differences with organizational cloud consumers are discussed. The book concludes with a summary of the steps that lawyers must go through to prepare themselves for the eventuality of their organization turning to cloud computing services, and some closing thoughts. The appendix lists many of the standards and guidance organizations that are endeavoring to provide direction on the cloud for public and private sector entities.

To make the book accessible to non-lawyer executives, at the start of each chapter, a listing of "Executive Takeaways" is presented. These are meant to allow a busy executive to gather many of the key areas upon which her or his organization should be focused in considering cloud use (or for lawyers to be ready to answer at least those queries). At a minimum, executives should read the entire first chapter in addition to these bullet point summaries in the Executive Takeaways. Other professionals in the organization, such as risk managers, CIOs, CISOs, CPOs, CFOs, auditors, data owners, and IT managers and their counterparts at CSPs will find at least some parts of the book applicable to their current roles.

Throughout the book, there are frequent uses of a small number of acronyms or phrases. Rather than repeat the full phrase or definition in each chapter or section, it may only be defined once in the entire book, but the reader will become familiar with these acronyms and phrases as they proceed through the chapters. These commonly used acronyms include **CSP** (Cloud Service Provider, the entity providing the various services in the cloud to the cloud consumer); **VM** (Virtual Machine, the representation of a physical IT environment that most organizations are familiar with); **Data Subject** (this comes from EU law and implies the owner of the data, whom the data is about); **OS** (Operating System, the software that controls the device), infosec (information security), SW (software); HW (hardware); **API** (Application Programming Interface, defining how information is passed between different processes), and **Processing** (any and all activities performed on data, as defined above).

In writing this second edition of the book two years later, I have gone back and reviewed not only the text but the references. Where I deemed it appropriate, I have left the original writing. I have updated the writing and references to incorporate new statutes, standards, cases, and thinking. I have tried to maintain the overall structure of the first edition, while adding sections and new technologies and factors for analysis as necessary. This book continues to address how the lawyer can help facilitate their clients' successful use of cloud computing services, but it deliberately does not go into great depth regarding the technical details of data protection or cybercrimes that organizations face, which can be gained from my other books.

Since the publication of the first edition of this book in May 2011, I have authored two more legal books, one on the history of law during World War II (*World War II Law and Lawyers: Issues, Cases, and Characters*) and another on protecting children on the Internet (*Children and the Internet: A Global Guide for Lawyers and Parents*). To fully understand the scope of the issues involved in cloud computing in more depth, I recommend reading these new books, plus my information security and privacy book (*Information Security and Privacy: A Practical Guide for Global Executives, Lawyers and Technologists*). All have been published within the last two years and provide greater detail on topics such as cybercrime, the historical context, and information security and privacy legal obligations and exposures, all from a global perspective.

Much has been added to the cloud computing canon in the last two years. I have tried to address as much of that change as possible, with the understanding that this book is about cloud computing risk, privacy, security, and legal issues, not principally a technical book. Some of the cloud topics that are newly mentioned or expanded in this second edition include: personal clouds, bring your own device (BYOD), critical infrastructure, cyber insurance, Big Data, health IT, and cloud taxation. There are a seemingly infinite number of topics related to the cloud; I hope that I now have covered all of the important ones for cloud consumer consideration.

The promise of cloud computing is quite limitless. Combined with the tablets, mobile devices, virtual worlds, speech recognition, wireless computing, social networks and other technologies that further remove computer users from the fixed-location, single-path access to computing resources, cloud computing provides a back-end counterpart that likewise frees users from being concerned with where they are located (or where their data or applications are located). Data and applications will be available anywhere the user can access them, at any time and in any volume, just by plugging the access device into an access port of the cloud computing utility. To successfully utilize this promise, lawyers must understand how to appropriately structure the relationships and evaluate the services that CSPs have on offer.

Thomas J. Shaw, Esq.
April, 2013

DEDICATION

My inspiration for this book, as for all of my writings and all that I do, is my daughter. Without her smiles, humor, creativity, singing, dancing, drawing, and nonstop but endearing talking while I wrote this book's first and second editions, it would all not seem so special. And it is for her youthful strength in the face of so many difficulties during the catastrophic earthquake, tsunami, and nuclear crisis in Japan during which I wrote the first edition. I hope that she is inspired to one day follow creatively in my footsteps.

ABOUT THE AUTHOR

Thomas J. Shaw, Esq., Attorney at Law, CPA, CRISC,
CIP, CIPP, CISM, ERMP, CISA, CGEIT, CCSK

Thomas J. Shaw, Esq., is an attorney in Asia and frequent author and speaker on legal topics from a global perspective, including cloud computing. He is the author of the 2013 book *World War II Law and Lawyers: Issues, Cases and Characters*, author of the 2012 book *Children and the Internet: A Global Guide for Lawyers and Parents*, author of the 2011 book *Cloud Computing for Lawyers and Executives—A Global Approach,* and lead author/editor of the 2011 book *Information Security and Privacy—A Practical Guide for Global Executives, Lawyers and Technologists*. He is also the author of the forthcoming 2014 book *World War I Law and Lawyers—Issues, Cases and Characters.*

Mr. Shaw writes extensively on the law and has published dozens of legal articles in many periodicals, including numerous articles on cloud computing. He has created and taught a workshop on cloud computing risk. He is also the editor/founder of two American Bar Association periodicals: the *Information Security & Privacy News* and the *EDDE Journal*. In addition to legal authoring and publishing and raising his daughter, Mr. Shaw works with organizations on Internet, Information, and International law, compliance, information governance, audit, contracts, new technologies, and risk. He runs CloudRisk Asia, which assesses risk for private- and public-sector organizations and cloud service providers (www.cloudriskasia.com). He also spends significant time helping to make children safe on the Internet. He can be reached at thomas@tshawlaw.com.

Chapter 1

INTRODUCTION TO CLOUD COMPUTING

Cloud computing is literally everywhere. The image of white cumulus clouds against a blue sky is seemingly omnipresent in the media, in the marketing of service, hardware, and software organizations, in the strategic planning and pilot projects of IT departments and business units, and in its physical points of presence across the world. Although it is apparently everywhere, it is by no means monolithic or risk-free. In beginning the process to evaluate the use of cloud computing services, there are a number of decisions that the potential consumer of cloud computing services must make. While for the individual consumer this decision may be rather easy, and basic black is acceptable, for the organization a more thorough understanding of the many and varied colors of risk under the cloud computing rainbow is necessary.

As noted by the International Conference on Data Protection and Privacy Commissioners, cloud computing "is attracting increasing interest due to promises of greater economic efficiency, lower environmental impact, simpler operation, increased user-friendliness and a number of other benefits,"[1] but it "may magnify certain risks inherent in data processing, such as breaches of information security, violation of laws and principles for privacy and data

---

1. 34th International Conference on Data Protection and Privacy Commissioners, *Resolution on Cloud Computing* (Oct. 26, 2012).

protection, and misuse of data stored in the cloud." Before discussing the steps in the methodology that is explained in the following chapters on how to identify and address the legal, business, security, privacy, litigation, compliance, and ethical risks involved in cloud computing, a firm foundation is required in the features and functions of this new paradigm.

This chapter will provide that initial understanding by explaining:

- What cloud computing is
- Why use cloud computing
- When to use cloud computing
- Financial considerations of cloud computing

Executive Takeaways

- Understanding of the defining characteristics of cloud computing
- Various cloud computing service and deployment models
- When to use cloud computing
- Financial criteria to evaluate cloud computing use

1.1 What Is Cloud Computing?

Cloud computing is defined in several ways in different forums. In essence, from the consumer perspective, it is a form of IT outsourcing and involves many of the same processes and management oversight that any service outsourcing requires. But it does have its own set of unique features. The most common definition (although vendors and countries trying to differentiate themselves using different terms or models) is that provided by the U.S. National Institute of Standards and Technology (NIST).[2] NIST defines

---

2. NIST, SP 800-145, *The NIST Definition of Cloud Computing* (Sept. 2011).

three areas of cloud computing: its essential characteristics, the service models commonly used, and the deployment models. As will be explained shortly, even as this definition has become firmly established, new concepts have arisen that would supplement this definition. The essential characteristics of cloud computing, with additional explanations, follow.

Essential Characteristics

- *On-Demand Self-Service*: A consumer of cloud computing services is able to obtain ("provision") the capabilities of the cloud, including computing, storage, and network services, without needing to contact each CSP individually, but can obtain these services from all necessary providers automatically through a single interface.
- *Broad Network Access*: The access to the cloud services are provided essentially through the Internet, using whatever network access devices consumers currently use. This implies that there should be no limitation for users anywhere, anytime, to be able to receive the necessary cloud services. Access devices of all kinds, wired and wireless, handheld and desk bound, will connect users to the cloud.
- *Resource Pooling*: All of the non-people IT resources are pooled together, including those from multiple CSPs, to give the impression of a large group of resources that can be utilized, irrespective of the actual physical implementation. This is done through resource virtualization, where an abstracted view of multiple physical resources is presented to the cloud computing consumer. Virtualization is not a new concept to IT. Virtual operating systems have been around for decades, but virtualization is an essential concept in cloud computing, where storage, network, operating systems, and computing (processing and memory) resources are bundled together and offered to multiple clients. Virtual resources should be independent of the physical devices or software implementation, location, and provider and so can be dynamically allocated, deleted, migrated, or reconfigured.
- *Rapid Elasticity*: The cloud computing resources can be added or subtracted when and as needed. This is especially valuable to cloud computing consumers in their production environment, to handle peak workloads without having to purchase the additional hardware and

software otherwise necessary, and in their testing environments, where multiple different stages of development can be added and deleted as needed.

- *Measured Service*: The cloud computing services are provided in only the amounts needed and the usage of the resources is then monitored, reported on, and billed for, just as any utility (e.g., power or water) would be. The metering function may consolidate various types and levels of cloud computing resources into a single charge or bill for each resource type and level directly at the lowest level of granularity.

There has been much discussion on whether any of this is actually new or whether these characteristics are just being recycled with a new marketing approach. Individually, some of these capabilities have been around in some form for decades, such as virtualization, Internet access, and metering. Perhaps what is actually new is combining the latest technological improvements in these areas with the concepts of automatic provisioning and elasticity of so many types of resources across so many providers and physical locations. So the unique characteristic of cloud computing is most easily defined as taking the latest technological and process capabilities in each of these areas and molding them into a single simplified view for the cloud computing consumers.

Service Models

NIST has defined three service models, which speak to what layer of the cloud architecture is being used. A number of IT architecture models depend on the concept of a stack of layers. For example, the TCP/IP architecture uses four layers, starting with the hardware/datalink (e.g., optical and Ethernet) layer, to the network layer (e.g., IP) to the transport layer (e.g., TCP) to the application layer. Similarly, NIST is using a five-layer stack, consisting of the facility, the physical hardware, the virtualized architecture, platform development, and application. The virtualized architecture would include not only the virtualization management system but also the virtual machines containing operating systems used by cloud computing consumers. All layers would include necessary APIs to communicate with them in a standardized manner. NIST's three service models are:

- *Software as a Service (SaaS)*: The CSP provides the application, which may or may not have modules, settings, or extensions that may be modifiable by the cloud computing consumer. In a SaaS service model, the facility, hardware, virtualized architecture and the platform development below the application are all controlled by the CSP. Typically, though not always, the interface is a simple Internet browser, which may be supplemented by various browser apps and by various security features.
- *Platform as a Service (PaaS)*: The CSP provides the development platform, which can be entirely a software development environment and related software development tools or it may include middleware for various kinds of message processing or session control or database and data file capabilities. The cloud computing consumers should be able to modify or extend these capabilities. In a PaaS service model, the facility, hardware and virtualized architecture below the platform development and application are all controlled by the CSP. APIs must be provided to the non-development tool capabilities, such as the middleware or database access.
- *Infrastructure as a Service (IaaS)*: The CSP provides the virtualized environment, likely as the virtual machines that include the operating systems and access to the virtualized resources like storage. The cloud computing consumers may be able to modify or extend operating capabilities and certain virtualized settings in their own environment, but in a multi-tenant environment should not be allowed access to the virtualization management system or direct access to the underlying hardware, network, and software. In an IaaS service model, the facility, hardware and the described parts of the virtualized architecture below the platform development and application are all controlled by the CSP.

There are a few points to clarify from these explanations. One is that not every service model offering fits neatly into these descriptions and there may be overlap between these models. A second point is that these descriptions have been supplemented with additional service models that target more specific needs. Among the more common of these are:

- *Data as a Service (DaaS)*: This service gained some traction through standards currently being promulgated, as discussed in Chapter 5. The possible offerings include both standard data offerings for space to be used by cloud consumers in the manner they choose and offerings that include full-featured databases, including both SQL and NoSQL options.
- *Identity as a Service (IDaaS)*: This service allows users or applications to be able to have their various identity management functions, such as identity provision, authentication of the requestor, and authorization to use requested resources, handled by a third party provider, which may be an existing CSP or a discrete SaaS, PaaS, or IaaS provider.
- *Security as a Service (SecaaS)*: This service can take a number of different forms and may encompass parts of IDaaS. The features available from these offerings range from extending malware protections to more widely-dispersed end-user devices to services that focus on offering network, application, spam and email filtering, and website security in the cloud. This is further discussed in Chapter 5.

Other service models envisioned include business process as a service, network as a service, communications as a service, testing as a service, management as a service, and so on, which all can be grouped under XaaS, which stands for everything as a service.

Deployment Models

NIST also defines the several ways that cloud computing services may be deployed. This categorizes by the degree of exposure the respective cloud deployments (or groupings of CSPs and service resources) have to the general public. At one end are the clouds that have no exposure to the public and at the other end are those cloud deployments that are open to anyone to use, even though the risk of this exposure is limited by virtualization techniques so that users are kept segregated from each other.

- *Private Cloud*: This grouping of cloud resources would be handled inside a single organization. It is typically a first step for larger organizations, moving from their internal-only infrastructure to one that provides some of the characteristics of a cloud, such as deploying resource virtualization. It is important to understand the private cloud as a series of implemented capabilities that move from a less to a more robust private cloud, instead of being concerned with crossing a line at which it is deemed a private cloud. For example, organizations can automate the creation of VMs based upon a scheme that groups them based upon the amount of CPU time and random access memory (RAM) made available. Although there is no direct use by the general public, this cloud deployment may not be located (partly or wholly) in the organization's facilities or even operationally managed by the organization, as some or most parts of the service management and hosting may be outsourced.
- *Community Cloud:* This grouping of cloud resources is handled inside a group of several related organizations, industry peers, or other types of business associations or consortia. This model requires common security policies and procedures and agreements on liability exposure among all of the members of the community. This deployment model should also have no direct exposure to the general public and may not be located (partly or wholly) in any organizations' facilities and some or most parts of the service management may be outsourced.
- *Public Cloud:* This grouping of cloud resources is owned by the CSPs and is provided to the general public. This may be the first step for smaller- and medium-sized organizations, which do not have the extent of compliance requirements that larger multinationals might. The primary attraction is the lower rates and standardized services possible with the significant volume from the general public. This cloud deployment model will of course be located outside the organization's facilities, but the CSPs themselves may outsource any part of their service to others. Because it is exposed to the general public, this model is the one that

requires the most stringent risk assessment and risk treatment controls, as discussed in Chapters 4 and 5.

- *Hybrid Cloud*: This grouping of cloud resources combines any of the above three deployment models into a new configuration. As there will be many parties responsible, due diligence, security controls, and contractual protections are vital. Based on the final configuration, there may be some exposure to the general public. This cloud deployment may not be located (partly or wholly) in the organization's facilities or even operationally managed by the organization, as some or most parts of the service management may be outsourced or in another organization's facilities. Given that some organizations, especially larger ones with more resources available for IT or those who use IT as a strategic differentiator, the hybrid cloud may be the final destination for their use of the cloud. Clearly, trade secrets and other key information may never be placed in the public cloud, while non-differentiating processing and most software testing should move to the cloud, implying the hybrid cloud model may become the predominant deployment model. Private clouds may also need to use the public cloud for "bursting" at peak times and so form a type of hybrid cloud.

Beyond these deployment models are cloud aggregators and brokers. These firms act as middlemen between CSPs and cloud consumers. The cloud brokers can present a large number of CSPs offering different deployment and service models in a unified manner, perhaps based on the ability to choose service levels, pricing or even geographic locations. The cloud aggregators can provide a location where CSPs sell excess capacity in any of their services and where buyers can purchase this excess capacity, hopefully at reduced rates, but with perhaps lesser guarantees of defined service levels and unknown assurances on information security and privacy protections.

Another common term that has come into use is the "personal" cloud. Unlike the deployment models above, this one is less about push from the CSP than about pull from the cloud consumers. Much as users perceive their data by their relationships to the data rather than by its actual physical attributes, so a personal cloud is the cloud consumer's individual view of their cloud-based data and the cloud services and applications that act upon that data. Tied closely to the emergence of mobile wireless access devices such as tablets and smart phones and BYOD, organizations will need to be able to deliver these personal cloud views in line with their customers' and employees' expectations, while understanding that these views are dynamic and likely to change in any direction with no notice.

Reference Architecture

NIST released its Reference Architecture in 2011.[3] This document defines five cloud computing actors: cloud consumer, cloud provider, cloud broker, cloud auditor, and cloud carrier (for networks). The document also describes the activities of CSPs, including service orchestration and cloud service management. Service orchestration refers to three layers, starting with the service models described above, which sit on top of the virtualization (resource abstraction) layer, which in turn sits atop the physical resource layer. Cloud service management consists of the other functions the CSP must perform to support its business model, including: business support, provisioning/configuration (e.g., metering and SLAs), portability of data, applications and systems from one CSP to another, and interoperability between services between CSPs. The reference architecture provides a useful high-level view of cloud computing depicting how each actor interfaces with the others.

1.2 Why Use Cloud Computing?

There are many reasons for organizations to use cloud computing services. The potential benefits include:

- *Lower unit cost for IT services*: This includes the costs of hardware, network, software, IT staff, and facility leasing. Even if all of these costs were exactly the same for the CSP as the organization using the cloud services, the fact that the CSP can spread these costs over many organizations implies a lower per unit cost when provided back to the organization, even allowing for CSP margins. One study showed benefit to cost ratios ranging from 5:1 to as high as 25:1 for the cloud when moving from a

---

3. NIST, SP 500-292 *Cloud Computing Reference Architecture* (Sept. 2011); supplemented by NIST, SP 500-299 *Cloud Computing 5 Security Reference Architecture* (June 2013).

traditional non-virtualized datacenter, with the total cost over the long term "as much as two-thirds lower,"[4] with the best benefit to cost ratios and the fastest payback periods realized with utilization of the public cloud over the hybrid or private deployment models.

- *Avoiding investment in IT resources solely to handle peak periods*: Every organization hosting its own IT processing is required to purchase additional hardware and software to handle peak periods (e.g., monthly payroll, end of quarter financial close, and reporting). During non-peak periods, those fixed investments are primarily unused. With cloud computing, such resources can be acquired as needed on a per-unit basis, rather than a whole-device purchase or lease or software license basis.

- *Access to skilled resources that the organization may not have in-house*: The centralization of computing resources and data also implies the centralization of the necessary IT human resources. Bringing together people, expertise, and physical resources will inevitably draw the better-skilled people wanting to gain exposure to such opportunities. Given the need to implement leading-edge controls to ensure their business success in a competitive commodity market, CSPs are going to have to attract, train, and retrain the top skill sets. This match between the needs of the CSPs and the desires of skilled people resources should make the CSPs a vital source of skills that organizations can tap.

- *Better security practices than the organization may otherwise deploy*: For much the same reasons, the CSPs will be required to have leading edge security practices, including organizational and individual security certifications, rigorous risk assessment and management programs, independent audits and assessments, connections to industry knowledge forums, and highly effective monitoring, measuring, reporting, and remediation processes. Leading CSPs will have to become centers of expertise in security and privacy to differentiate themselves with customers.

- *Built-in business continuity facilities*: By definition, with connections to multiple servers, sites, and CSPs, and automatic provisioning and rapid elasticity, the cloud provides an easy way to have a business-continuity

---

4. Booz Allen Hamilton, *The Economics of Cloud Computing – Addressing the Benefits of Infrastructure in the Cloud* (2009).

capability ready at any time. Instead of having to determine the type of such BCP facility one is going to invest in, such capabilities may now be available without additional investment. While business continuity plans are still required, the specialized facilities will not be, and the time spent in recovery should be positively affected by use of the cloud (as discussed in Chapter 5). In addition, the disaster recovery plan required to bring facilities back after a disaster is likely unnecessary, as organizations will just move to another site connected to their original CSP.

- *Improved network access:* Instead of being limited to various proprietary network protocols, the open Internet-based connections to the cloud provide the ability to always access the needed IT resources. The emphasis on openness demands rigorous security techniques to keep the access safe, and the use of authentication protocols must envision this open network approach (as discussed in Chapters 4 and 5). But organizational uses that previously required special network configuration when employees traveled, new offices started, or employees worked from home, can now be more easily addressed with a common methodology for all users.

- *More and better application development tools*: The organization can utilize the platform development tools made available by the CSPs. These tools may be more standardized and at later release levels than what is available inside organizations. The tools provide a way for the cloud service consumer to avoid investing in software that in itself is not a competitive differentiator. The organization can instead focus on the best utilization of those tools for its business. This may also provide the rigor to develop better coding standards and write standards-based APIs where possible.

- *Common platform for multi-organization projects*: For various multi-organization projects, such as consortiums, and along supply chains, there is a need to have a place where data can be interchanged and common processing done. With a CSP as a neutral host enforcing strong privacy controls, there is less risk of the confidential data of one organization being disclosed to another. Joint development projects may also be done in the cloud as well as hosting for messages passing between the organizations in a supply chain or consortium.

- *Ability to quickly start up in any location globally*: By combining the open network access with the ease of provisioning, new locations should not require the investments and time delay so typical when having to put up local servers and other devices in each new office. Now only an Internet connection should be a requirement to bring any office up with its needed IT resources. As access devices are already mobile with wireless access, even new network connection needs may be minimal for new offices.

- *Minimizing the need for application development environment setup*: The typical application development lifecycle requires a development environment and one to four test environments before having new code that is ready to place in the production system. With virtualization, there is no longer any need for separate physical environments to handle the different versions of programs and data. Clean virtual machines can be rapidly started up for each new iteration of the testing phases.

- *Reducing and re-focusing existing IT resources*: The organization will retain some if not most of its IT human resources after outsourcing to the cloud (the lack of personnel transitions is one way that cloud outsourcing differs from traditional IT outsourcing). These resources can now be re-deployed away from commodity-type IT functions and moved into roles that bring higher value for the organization. The benefits will differ by organization but may include: developing additional industry expertise, focusing on developing e-commerce or other applications that produce revenue for the organization, assisting with efforts to standardize the organization's global approach to IT, facilitating knowledge intake from and participation in IT specialist forums, becoming more focused on the skills to achieve IT compliance with security and privacy statutes, better oversight and governance rules of outsourcers, and greater awareness of new and emerging information-related threats and vulnerabilities.

- *Better protecting key organizational secrets and confidential data*: Data that resides on access devices of any kind is at risk not only from theft or loss, for which there are numerous countervailing safeguards, but also from governments around the world. Data may be seized under various guises by governments — not only data that is physically located within their borders but also data entering into the country.[5] By not allowing employees to carry sensitive organizational data on laptops but instead requiring them to access it as needed from the cloud, the risk of disclosure of business secrets is greatly reduced.

- *Reducing time spent and risk in IT procurement planning process*: Organizations spend time justifying, budgeting, and planning for IT purchases. With the cloud, that need is greatly reduced. The effort will instead focus on how much IT resources will be used, just as it is for other utilities. The cloud also reduces the risk of being wrong about assumptions on business growth, IT usage, economic life of IT purchases, and technology obsolescence. In addition, less time has to be spent on technical assessments of new IT equipment to be purchased, as the equipment will be provided by the CSP.

Cloud computing provides at least these and probably more reasons to use its capabilities, including the reasons explained in the next section. But the use of the cloud and all of its underlying technologies and processes brings with it a number of risks for organizations. As such, Chapters 4 and 5 are dedicated to exploring those risks, especially the risks to information security and privacy in the cloud. In Chapter 6, additional risks are explored, including risks originating in obligations arising from litigation and investigations. Chapters 2 and 3 describe the compliance requirements for organizations operating in the cloud. The last section in this chapter addresses another type of evaluation necessary when considering use of cloud computing services: the financial assessment of cloud computing versus existing options.

1.3 When to Use the Cloud

When determining if the cloud is right for an organization, there are other considerations that are not based on legal and security factors. This section looks at cloud computing as a business decision informed by IT, moving beyond the marketing to clearly articulate why cloud use may or may not make sense for an organization from a business perspective. It is important

---

5. Electronic Frontier Foundation, *EFF's Guide to Protecting Electronic Devices and Data at the U.S. Border* (2010).

to understand that the decision to use the cloud (or not) may be different at different points in time, for different groups within an organization, and for different applications, tools and infrastructure. It may not be a single decision but a series of much smaller analyses carried out multiple times in the organization. This discussion includes looking at the basic decision to use the cloud or not in light of an organization's particular situation, both now and in the future.

To assist in this analysis is a matrix-based methodology from the Open Group (which is introduced in Chapter 5) that facilitates an organization's decision-making process on cloud use and determines which service models might be most appropriate. The Cloud Buyer's Decision Tree[6] asks ten different cloud-specific "yes" or "no" questions, and based on the answer to each, a different path through the matrix is created. Each path creates a unique scenario, which is then evaluated as being an appropriate situation for a private cloud, the public cloud, or non-cloud outsourcing. There are thirty-one possible paths through this matrix.

For example, an organization that is considering the cloud but has specialized hardware requirements or application tailored to its specific business processes may not be a good candidate for either SaaS or IaaS cloud services, while those organizations with standard hardware and with business processes abstracted from the underlying application could be good candidates, dependent on other factors. For those business processes in-scope for potential cloud computing outsourcing, the following are the path-generating questions, in a modified form, with additional explanations.

- *Are there inter-dependencies between the organization's business process, application, platform, and infrastructure layers?* If there are interdependencies, it is more complex and perhaps impossible to be able to take one part of the organization's architecture stack and move it to the cloud. For example, if an application is highly customized for a unique business process, it may be very difficult to find an application from a cloud SaaS provider that provides all of the same functionality.

---

6. Open Working Group, *Cloud Buyer's Decision Tree - A Proposal for Discussion* (2010).

- *Are these business processes integral to the organization's competitive advantage?* Any business process that significantly impacts the organization's ability to stand out from its competitors is something that needs to be guarded closely. Trade secrets of all manners would be common examples. As the disclosure of such processes would imperil the ability of the business to generate revenue and may even raise going-concern issues, the use of the cloud may implicate a risk that cannot be sufficiently reduced.

- *Are there any impediments to outsourcing?* There are many cases where the desire to outsource and the ability to do so may not be in sync. Some examples provided include: labor contracts (that specify what work will be done, by whom, and how); long-term leases (that lock in the costs of datacenter facilities); switching costs (these costs may overwhelm the benefits of using the cloud); fixed assets with depreciation value (because these must be carried over into financial analysis of outsourcing even though they may not be productive assets after outsourcing); business culture (not all businesses are equally open to or able to deal with outsourcing, including differences in national or regional practices); geographic location sovereignty rules (as explained in Chapter 3, there are limits to what data can be sent where in many countries); industry regulation (such rules, as discussed in Chapter 2, place restrictions on outsourcing); and compliance audit rules (as explained in Chapters 2 and 5, use of the cloud implicates compliance reporting requirements).

- *Are there impediments to cloud adoption?* Once outsourcing is considered viable, it must be determined if an organization has any issues with moving to use of the cloud. Some of the items that could prevent such adoption include factors both on the part of the organization and on the part of the CSP. The organization may have customized software or hardware that is meeting its needs and no financial advantage can be derived by moving such a workload to the cloud. The CSP may not be able to provide the necessary cloud services or the required service levels needed for cloud adoption.

- *Is the primary business driver cloud-compatible?* There is typically one primary driver businesses consider in their use of cloud computing services. If this matches with the cloud paradigm, the use of the cloud may be indicated, while those that are not compatible may indicate the opposite. Some examples of cloud-compatible business drivers include: to reduce medium and/or long-term total cost of ownership; to improve cash flow and shift funds from capital expenditures to operating expenditures; to improve SLA metrics and/or quality of service; to get access to certain functionality and expertise; to leverage people resources; and to be able to scale fixed asset capacity up/down. Examples of cloud-incompatible business drivers include: to minimize short-term costs; to shift funds from operating expenditures to capital expenditures; and to shift assets, either owned or leased, and the personnel providing the operations functions, to the CSP.

- *Are the layers below the application/business process layers (middleware, operating system (OS), hardware, network, facilities and operations management) able to be standardized and shared among all of the organization's IT services?* The purpose is to understand at what level in the cloud architecture stack standardization and sharing can be implemented, as cloud computing relies on providing similar standard offerings to many. For example, the PaaS service model would look for standardization in OS, hardware, network, facilities and operations management (i.e., those functions below the PaaS layer).

- *Can the business processes be abstracted from the underlying applications (or do changes in business processes require changes in the applications)?* Business processes that are capable of abstraction can utilize the more generic applications offered by various CSPs. Changes can be made to the technical aspects of the application without impacting the business process and changes can be made by non-technical people to the business processes that do not require countervailing changes to the application.

- *Is IT a key enabler in the organization's competitive business advantage?* If the architecture or use of IT is part of the competitive advantage, it again may not be something that can be easily replicated in the cloud. It may not be something that the organization would want disclosed to external parties, even CSPs under non-disclosure. It is the more commoditized services that are the best early candidates for migration to the cloud.

- *Are both the hardware/OS and the application customized?* If both of these components are customized, it would be difficult to achieve the benefits of the cloud, which derives its key characteristics from providing unlimited amounts of resources based on a limited set of possible variations. Completely customized solutions would have difficulty matching available CSP service offerings.
- *Is the hardware/OS customized/specialized?* Some specialized or highly customized hardware (e.g., supercomputers) and OSs may not be able to find these same services provided by CSPs in their specific configurations and are better run inside the organization instead of the cloud.

1.4 Financial Consideration of Cloud Use

To make the decision to utilize cloud computing services, the legal and security risk assessments must proceed at the same time as the financial assessment. This analysis should identify the financial benefits and financial costs, derive a net financial benefit per each future time period, discount these as cash flows back to the present with an appropriate discount rate based on the organization's weighted average cost of capital (WACC), derive the return on investment (ROI) from the net benefits of the investment, and also determine the payback period (when the annual financial benefits will equal to the cost of the investment). This analysis must be done for each option, whether it concerns deciding between multiple CSPs or involves the decision to use cloud services outsourcing versus retaining the in-scope services inside the organization's control.

In addition to the financial benefits and costs, other factors in calculating a cloud financial model should include a quantification of the impacts of the cloud deployment on both financial risk and on additional capabilities. Risk has many possible components but includes the risk that the planned cloud deployment will not meet the needs or stated requirements of the organization and so not realize its projected benefits. Additional capabilities involve the new opportunities that cloud deployment provides the organization that were not previously available, just by existing in its particular cloud space. An example of this is using just part of a SaaS provider's application suite and then having the ability to take advantage of more of the suite's applications or other provided capabilities (e.g., database) that are or become available from the provider. Another would be collaboration with other organizations in the same space.

This section will focus on the financial benefits and costs of cloud computing as the starting point of the analysis to derive the comparative total costs of ownership for these options. Starting with the financial benefits of cloud computing use, these include:

- Reducing purchases of normal-use hardware and software, with a savings also in the reduced organizational planning time used to justify capital expenditures
- Reducing purchases of peak-use hardware and software
- Reducing purchases of business-continuity hardware and software
- Minimizing the energy costs and facilities costs through virtualization of (and therefore reduction in the number of) physical servers
- Minimizing disposal costs of hardware, including the ability to upgrade with technology changes instead of retaining assets during the financial depreciation cycle
- Reducing the costs of IT personnel in administering the IT systems
- Reducing the costs of IT and other personnel by utilizing provisioning systems instead of people
- Increasing the productivity of other employees through the use of rapid provisioning (less wait time)
- Avoiding investment in failed IT deployments and projects
- Avoiding technological obsolescence
- Increasing revenue through cloud-based applications and tools providing increased exposure, faster time to market, or functionality not otherwise available
- Increasing revenue through cloud-based infrastructure providing faster provisioning, larger scaling, and ability to reach community-based customers and vendors

An analysis of these factors will include both a baseline of the current situation and the proposed architecture of the cloud computing system. The use of different service models will find the savings in different levels of the system architectural stack. The delta (differential) will include the cost of the various hardware servers (if SaaS, PaaS or possibly IaaS) and software (application software if SaaS, development tools if PaaS, possibly operating systems if IaaS), IT personnel rates, hardware disposal costs, the energy and facilities costs, and the management costs of the people and devices. While there are clearly some new costs involved in the use of the cloud, such as the virtual machine software and the virtual management and provisioning systems, these will be spread out as an operating expense (OPEX) and not a capital expense (CAPEX). And more importantly, such costs will presented to the cloud consumer on a "pay as you go" basis, instead of requiring the consumer to incur the whole cost of procuring a system architecture built for maximum utilization levels but only rarely (peak times, disasters) actually reaching them.

A comparison between the alternatives of the organization continuing to provide the various IT services or outsourcing these services to a CSP requires identifying and summing up the costs. These include hardware (either as a direct expense or as a recovery expense like depreciation or amortization) for production systems, test systems for resiliency and for business continuity, software for the same systems, telecom/network, maintenance, facilities rent and build-out, utilities, staffing, training, business continuity facilities, asset procurement/management, and the appropriate management allocations. While it is quite variable among vendors, in the most general terms CSPs will charge, based on the service model and the specific services on primarily a pay-as-you-go monthly fee, for virtual machine instance hours, data storage or transfer quantities, or the number of application or platform users, plus any combination thereof, plus charges for starting up and for specialized services.

The following template shows a simplified cost-identification methodology using several options. The first option (organization-hosted private cloud) uses only infrastructure (servers) and development tools operating in an organization's facility and operated by the organization. The second option (public cloud) has these resources being provided by a CSP providing IaaS and PaaS. A third option (CSP-hosted private cloud) uses the capabilities of the CSP to provide a private cloud, so would use the first option's costing factors for those parts of the organization's infrastructure and tools inside the private cloud but the second option's costing factors for the infrastructure and tools provided by the CSP. A fourth option (hybrid cloud) combines many or all of the factors from the first three options, for example for using a cloud for occasionally-used extra capacity. The template shows the factors of the first two options.

All in-scope hardware costs are assumed to be capitalized over a three-year economic life rather than expensed, and all in-scope software leased instead of purchased. Cloud consumer-developed software would be amortized or expensed in either case and is not part of this incremental analysis. The costs of end-user devices (hardware and software) should not be affected by the deployment model used, as all necessary security controls should be built in regardless of where the servers are located. This should include bring your own device (BYOD) scenarios, but outsourced services may imply a greater need for user security identity and authentication requirements (discussed below).

The organization should not incur additional costs (e.g., new APIs) when doing development work in the cloud, as all application interfaces will remain the same at this time. The organization maintains a hot site for business-continuity purposes and so provides the disaster and incident response by itself. If there are any one-time startup charges from the CSP, those should be included in the respective IaaS or PaaS costs in the first year. This template does not contain every possible expense but is merely representative, so organizations will want to customize it for their own situations. It also assumes that all users migrate to the cloud service at once (not in a staged migration where some of the financial benefit is lost). It does not include service-termination costs, as those should be part of the model for the follow-on cloud deployment.

Tax implications on net profits (income tax) or on revenue (sales tax) are not considered but may have a significant impact on certain business models.[7] At least in the United States, the states are still trying to determine what they should do about Internet taxation, which may impact organizations as cloud consumers.[8] There may also be other taxation issues, like whether a business creates a taxable nexus by operating in the cloud in a

---

7. *See e.g. Amazon, Overstock Lose Challenge to N.Y. Web Sales Tax*, Bloomberg (Mar. 29, 2013).

8. *See e.g.* MA Dept. of Rev., Letter Ruling 12-8: Cloud Computing (July 16, 2012).

country that it is not physically present in or if transfer pricing is applicable to a multi-jurisdictional corporate private cloud, which are beyond the scope of the discussion here but need to be investigated when creating the cloud financial analysis.

Cloud service using customer site & operation	Year 1	Year 2	Year 3	Total
HW Depreciation – Production				
HW Depreciation – Test				
HW Depreciation – BCP				
SW Expense – Production				
SW Expense – Test				
SW Expense – BCP				
HW Maintenance				
NW – ISP, telecom, etc.				
Datacenter facility – rent				
Datacenter facility – utilities				
BCP facility – rent				
BCP facility – utilities				
Other offsite costs – backups/mirrors				
Operations staff – costs				
Development staff – costs				
Technical and awareness training				
Compliance – Regulatory and Infosec				
Internal SLA measurement/reporting				
Asset procurement/management				
Management oversight				
Non-discounted cash flows				

Cloud service using CSP site & operation	Year 1	Year 2	Year 3	Total
VM Instance Hours – Production				
Data storage – Production				
Bursting capability – Production				

Cloud service using CSP site & operation	Year 1	Year 2	Year 3	Total
VM Instance Hours – Test				
Data storage – Test				
Periodic data extraction				
Development tools – PaaS				
Development staff – costs				
NW – ISP, telecom, etc.				
IdAM – joining CSP's scheme				
Awareness training				
Management oversight				
Integration of incident response				
Vendor oversight				
Non-discounted cash flows				

In this example, the various individual costs of the infrastructure are moved from the organization to the CSP. As such, there are no costs for hardware or (base) software for the production or test environments. In addition, the costs of the server-operations staff have been moved to the CSP (this may or may not be part of the service offering from the CSP and may be priced separately). Without ownership of hardware, there is no hardware maintenance expense. The need for a separate business continuity site and related hardware and software is removed, as this should be a default characteristic of cloud use. But the business continuity response plans and normal incident response will need to be integrated with the procedures and contact lists of the CSP. The rent of the data center facilities and related utilities is also removed (assuming leases can be easily unwound). And the asset procurement function and the need to manage these assets will no longer be needed for these types of assets. The same is true of the supervisors and managers of the operations staff, who can be redeployed into new functions or teams.

What would be newly charged are the monthly costs from the CSP, in the form of the virtualized-infrastructure charges, the database-related changes, and the use of the CSP's development tool environment. There may also be a charge to periodically extract the organization's data from the CSP, which it should do both for its own reasons of data preservation and portability. There may also be costs in joining the identity and authentication management (IdAM) scheme of the CSP, such as the cost of digital certificates, new authentication techniques, identity verification software, etc. Remaining are the costs of the development staff, the network charges that allow them to utilize the CSP, and the management of the development staff. There would need to be a new CSP oversight function, which should have multiple levels (including technical, legal, risk, compliance, and audit) and include both personnel costs and perhaps software costs (for certain monitoring/reporting /analysis tools). What are not shown are any efficiency improvements in the utilization of other staff through the cloud's capabilities (e.g., developers no longer have to wait for a test environment to be set up).

This financial model greatly simplifies the real world. In reality, moving some in-scope servers does not reduce the rental costs of the data center to the organization and will not completely reduce those respective utilities. Staff costs will not be completely eliminated, in that at least for some period, the organization will need to retain that technical expertise in-house and may choose to retain a permanent monitoring function. The choice was shown as all new server equipment versus outsourcing but that is rarely the case, as equipment will likely have varying net book values. Equipment that is no longer needed has disposal costs, salvage value, and possibly remaining economic life. And organizations may stage the implementation through several phases, increasing certainty but also increasing the cost of deployment.

One other consideration in cloud financial models is the use of non-standard cloud services purchase options, available either through cloud brokers or from CSPs. An example of this is the AWS EC2 Spot service, which allows cloud consumers to bid for use of extra capacity at the CSP. Based on winning bids for hourly use of the services, these rates may be 10 percent of standard CSP rates.[9] These types of spot instance services can be used by those cloud consumers who have heavy data analysis needs, for application

---

9. *Amazon Cloud Revenue Heads Higher as Google Plays Catch-Up: Tech*, Bloomberg (Mar. 8, 2013).

Chapter 2

U.S. STATUTES

There are a number of provisions in U.S. laws that impact cloud computing. These include consumer data privacy protection statutes, privacy legislation focused on specific types of information or devices, general or specific provisions addressing information security, data breach rules, and rules concerning the use of IT subcontractors. These exist at both the state and federal level. Some laws and regulations apply only to specific industry sectors, while others are more far reaching and apply to all organizations involved in a business activity (e.g., e-commerce). Besides those that apply to the private sector, there are a series of statutes and regulations that apply to the U.S. federal government in its use of the personal data of citizens. These rules, while not directly affecting most private sector businesses not doing business with the government, are nonetheless important to understand given the large role the U.S. government is playing in trying to push for the wide-spread acceptance of cloud computing. There are also other statutes that are of special interest to cloud consumers in their choices of CSPs. These statutes allow governments to use different surveillance and evidence-gathering powers to examine the data hosted in and messages transmitted through the cloud.

The discussion in this chapter includes three sections, starting with U.S. laws directly relevant to use of the cloud. To make the comparisons between countries easier, the discussion of each country/region in these two statutory chapters (including Chapter 3) will look at the same five areas: privacy regime, cross-border data transfer restrictions, information security and data breach rules, blocking statutes, and cloud-computing-specific laws, cases, and activities. The section on the U.S. federal government looks at both its activities in promoting cloud use and the statutory privacy, infosec, and records obligations of federal agencies. The final section includes not only U.S. surveillance statutes but, as a bridge to the next chapter on international statutes, selected surveillance laws from other countries.

The number of U.S. federal statutes and regulations that potentially applies to cloud computing services is significant, and includes quite an alphabet soup of names (the acronyms will be defined shortly): HIPAA,[1] HITECH,[2] GLBA,[3] FCRA,[4] FACTA,[5] SOX,[6] FTCA,[7] plus COPPA,[8] DMCA,[9] CFAA,[10] FERPA,[11] and a variety of industry-specific rules, such as in the securities, commodities, and telecommunications industries. This chapter will focus on the statutes listed above before the "plus," which are significant for the obligations of private-sector organizations utilizing cloud computing. The remaining statutes apply more specifically to obtaining relief for various types of violations that occur in cyberspace, CSP obligations, or specific industry regulations.[12] In addition, there are a variety of U.S. state laws dealing with data breach, data disposal, information security, encryption, spyware, phishing, online privacy, and more. These will be highlighted with leading state examples.

Beyond the statutes discussed below, there are a number of different issues inherited from the cloud's use of the Internet as an enabling platform. These legal issues have been addressed in U.S. statutes and court decisions across the last several decades and include issues such as determination of

---

1. Health Insurance Portability and Accountability Act, of 1996, Pub. L. 104-191.

2. American Recovery and Reinvestment Act of 2009, Pub. L. No.111-5, Division A: Title XIII—Health Information Technology and Division B: Title IV—Medicare and Medicaid Health Information Technology; Miscellaneous Medicare Provisions.

3. Gramm-Leach-Bliley Act of 1999, Pub. L. No.106-102.

4. Fair Credit Reporting Act of 1970, Pub. L. No. 91-508.

5. Fair and Accurate Credit Transactions Act of 2003, Pub. L. No. 108-159.

6. Sarbanes-Oxley Act of 2002, Pub. L. No. 107-204.

7. Federal Trade Commission Act of 1914.

8. Children's Online Privacy Protection Act of 1998, Pub. L. No. 105-277.

9. Digital Millennium Copyright Act of 1998, Pub. L. No. 105-304.

10. Computer Fraud and Abuse Act of 1984, Pub. L. No. 98-473.

11. Family Educational Rights and Privacy Act of 1974, Pub. L. No. 93-380.

12. *See* Thomas J. Shaw, *Children and the Internet – A Global Guide for Lawyers and Parents* (2012), chap. 4.

personal jurisdiction over defendants whose only contacts with the forum may be through the Internet.[13] There are liability issues for service providers when the information that they are holding might violate obscenity standards but not as a publisher of customers' content.[14] There are also the intellectual property violations of copyright and trademark rights through linking and other Internet-specific techniques.[15] There are statutes that protect digital technologies.[16] And there are the consumer protection issues such as junk mail/spam laws that have been passed to address that[17] and issues related to domain names[18] and the protection against unauthorized use of computers,[19] all related to use of the Internet.

Executive Takeaways

- Private sector statutory obligations impacting cloud computing services
- Public sector activities in promoting cloud use
- Issues raised in cloud computing-specific cases
- U.S. and international laws of concern (surveillance) for cloud computing consumers

---

13. *See e.g. Zippo Mfg. Co. v. Zippo Dot Com, Inc.*, 952 F. Supp. 1119 (W.D. Pa. 1997); *Yahoo! Inc. v. La Ligue Contre Le Racisme et l'antisemitisme*, 433 F.3d 1199 (9th Cir. 2006); *Attaway v. Omega*, No. 11A01-0712-cv-608 (Ind. Ct. App. 2009).

14. *See* Communications Decency Act of 1996, Pub. L. No.104-104, §230.

15. *See* Digital Millennium Copyright Act (1998); *A&M Records, Inc. v. Napster, Inc.*, 239 F.3d 1004 (2001); *MGM Studios, Inc. v. Grokster, Ltd.* 545 U.S. 913 (2005).

16. *See* Digital Millennium Copyright Act of 1998, Pub. L. No. 105-304.

17. *See* Controlling the Assault of Non-Solicited Pornography And Marketing (CAN-SPAM) Act of 2003, Pub. L. No. 108-187.

18. *See* Anti-Cybersquatting Consumer Protection Act of 1999, Pub. L. No. 106-113.

19. *See* Computer Fraud and Abuse Act of 1986, Pub. L. No. 99-474.

2.1 U.S. Private Sector Laws

Privacy Framework: Federal and State Statutes

Health Care Data Privacy

The Health Insurance Portability and Accountability Act (HIPAA) Privacy Rule requires that protected health information (PHI) be safeguarded in its use and disclosure. PHI is information in all mediums that is received from an individual by or created by a covered entity (CE) (e.g., health care provider, plan, or clearinghouse), that relates to the (past, present, or future) physical or mental health or condition, provision of or payment for health care of or to an individual that identifies or can reasonably be used to identify the individual. When disclosing PHI for the purposes of collection, the covered entities should disclose the minimum amount necessary to achieve its purpose, and safeguard and keep track of these disclosures.

The Health Information Technology for Economic and Clinical Health Act (HITECH) extends the Privacy Rule to business associates (BAs), which are persons or entities that perform "certain functions or activities that involve the use or disclosure of PHI on behalf of, or provides services to, a covered entity." The CE is required to obtain satisfactory assurance from the BA of compliance with the Privacy Rule in writing, typically via a contractual agreement. This now includes all subcontractors who "create, receive, maintain, or transmit" PHI.[20] CEs and BAs may use cloud computing services and their CSP should sign the business associate agreement, subjecting them to the HIPAA/HITECH rules and regulatory oversight. Incentives and penalties for the "meaningful use" of certified Electronic Health Record technology and the implementation of Health Information Exchanges should significantly increase the utilization of the cloud to process and store electronic PHI (ePHI). The increase in cloud use may also impact the rise in

---

20. Modifications to the HIPAA Privacy, Security, Enforcement, and Breach Notification Rules Under the Health Information Technology for Economic and Clinical Health Act and the Genetic Information Nondiscrimination Act; Other Modifications to the HIPAA Rules, 78 Fed. Reg. 5566 (Jan. 25, 2013).

data breaches of ePHI,[21] some of which happen with government agencies as well,[22] although new guidelines may help.[23]

Financial Data Privacy

The Gramm-Leach-Bliley Act (GLBA) Privacy Rule requires financial institutions to keep the personal information of their customers private. It also requires these institutions to provide notice to their customers in the form of an annual privacy notification that describes the institution's privacy practices. It gives consumers the right to limit ("opt out" of) some of the information-sharing practices of the financial institutions to unaffiliated organizations, but not data processing outsourcing or legally required disclosures. There is a differentiation between "consumers" who are typically only in a short-term relationship with the financial institution and receive notice based on sharing with unaffiliated firms and "customers" who are in a longer term relationship (e.g., getting a loan) and get annual privacy notices. The Fair Credit Reporting Act (FRCA) requires consumer reporting agencies to safeguard consumer credit information and provides the ability to opt out of sharing a consumer's credit information with affiliates of the financial institution. The Fair and Accurate Credit Transactions Act (FACTA) requires financial institutions and creditors (generally, any firm that ordinarily sells on credit) to set up identity-theft detection programs (the "Red Flags Rule").[24] The use of Social Security numbers on checks is now prohibited by federal law.[25]

Financial Reporting/Compliance

The Sarbanes-Oxley (SOX) Act is concerned with the accuracy of financial reporting for publicly listed companies. In this context, it is primarily concerned with the internal controls used to provide those financial results. But in at least a few areas it does look to provide privacy obligations for

21. Ponemon Institute, *Third Annual Benchmark Study on Patient Privacy & Data Security* (Dec. 2012).

22. HHS Office of the Inspector General, *CMS Response to Breaches and Medical Identity Theft* (Oct. 2012).

23. HHS OCR, *Guidance Regarding Methods for De-identification of Protected Health Information in Accordance with the Health Insurance Portability and Accountability Act (HIPAA) Privacy Rule* (Nov. 2012).

24. 72 Fed. Reg. 63718-63775 (Nov. 9, 2007).

25. Social Security Number Protection Act of 2010, Pub. L. No. 111-318.

organizations. One is that the audit committee of the organization is required to deal with "confidential, anonymous submissions" by employees on matters of "questionable" accounting or auditing.[26] In another, retaliation against informants is a criminal offense and so the information provided by these informants must remain confidential.[27] These provisions have caused concern for possible conflicts with other countries' data privacy laws, impacting organizations' subsidiaries operating in the U.S. or their companies that are listed on U.S. stock exchanges.[28] In addition, while there was already a program in place for reporting of violations of such statutes as the Foreign Corrupt Practices Act,[29] (which also has provisions for internal controls related to books and records of transactions)[30] new rules have further emphasized the need for effective whistleblower/compliance programs where privacy is assured. The Dodd-Frank Act entitles whistleblowers reporting to the SEC with rewards based on a percentage of the enforcement action penalty,[31] while the revised Federal Sentencing Guidelines incentivize organizations to have an effective compliance and ethics program in place to be eligible for a reduction in sentencing. The organizations should have mechanisms for "anonymity or confidentiality, whereby the organization's employees and agents may report or seek guidance regarding potential or actual criminal conduct without fear of retaliation."[32]

State Privacy Laws

U.S. states have a variety of different types of laws protecting privacy, including those that address consumers' credit history, spam, phishing, spyware, social security numbers, and online privacy. For example, the state of Minnesota requires data be subject to approval before Internet service providers

---

26. Sarbanes-Oxley Act §§ 301(4)(B).
27. *Id.* at §§ 1107.
28. Article 29 Data Protection Working Party, Opinion 1/2006 on the application of EU data protection rules to internal whistleblowing schemes in the fields of accounting, internal accounting controls, auditing matters, fight against bribery, banking and financial crime.
29. Foreign Corrupt Practices Act of 1977, Pub. L. 95-213.
30. *Id.* at 15 U.S.C. § 78m (b).
31. Dodd-Frank Wall Street Reform and Consumer Protection Act, Pub. L. No. 111-203, § 922.
32. Federal Sentencing Guidelines Manual § 8B2.1(b)(5)(c) (Nov. 1, 2010).

can disclose information about the Internet sites their subscribers have visited.[33] Nebraska prohibits false statements in online (and other) privacy policies where personal information is collected.[34] In Hawaii, it is a felony to fraudulently obtain control of a password through phishing activities.[35] In Maryland, prospective employers cannot require that employees or job candidates provide their personal social media credentials.[36]

Under New Hampshire law, it is a violation to copy onto a consumer's PC or use a spyware program that takes control of, modifies settings on, or collects personal information from a consumer's PC.[37] In Texas, users of the radio frequency identification (RFID) in driver's licenses must ensure that transmitted information is encrypted, and biometric and other information cannot be sold.[38] California law prohibits the public display of Social Security numbers (SSNs), as well as requiring an SSN for access to, for example, an Internet site.[39] In Illinois, it is now illegal to make employment decisions on a credit report or credit history.[40] In Iowa, it is a crime to falsify routing information and initiate unsolicited bulk electronic mails (junk emails) to a certain number of recipients within a 24-hour period.[41]

Cross-Border Data Transfers

There generally are no express material restrictions on cross-border transfers of personal information under U.S. law,[42] beyond compliance with those security and privacy requirements listed in this section. Organizations must keep in mind that the country they are transferring the data to from the United States will likely have more stringent requirements on cross-border transfers and it may not be possible to easily transfer the data back to the United

---

33. Minnesota. Stat. § 325.M.01 to M.09.
34. Nebraska. Stat. § 87-302(14).
35. Hawaii. Rev. Stat. § 708-891.5.
36. Maryland, An Act Concerning Labor and Employment – User Name and Password Privacy Protection and Exclusions (2012).
37. N.H. Stat. § 359 H1-H6.
38. Texas. Trans. Code § 521.032 (c).
39. California. Civil Code § 1798.85.
40. Illinois. Public Act 096-1426 (2010).
41. Iowa Code § 716A.1-A.7.
42. White & Case, *Data Transfer Laws In 22 Major Jurisdictions Surveyed And Analyzed* (2003).

States (i.e., the U.S. may not be deemed to have sufficiently rigorous data protection standards relative to those in the receiving country). The entire round-trip of data movement is important to understand, in the cases when data is intentionally moved abroad, when the cross-border data movement may not be intended (e.g., for business continuity), or when it is clearly not intended by the organization (e.g., under data mobility).

The United States and the EU have reached an agreement under which the personal information located within the EU may be transferred to the United States if a number of conditions are met. This Safe Harbor Privacy Principles agreement is discussed in more detail in the EU's cross-border data transfer section in Chapter 3. The Commerce Department has released clarifications on the Safe Harbor framework and cloud computing.[43]

Information Security and Data Breach Notification
Health Care Information

The HIPAA Security Rule requires the covered entities to establish policies and procedures for administrative, physical and technical safeguards over electronic PHI (ePHI). These include *administrative*: access to ePHI, employee training, audits, management oversight, and business continuity; *physical*: facility access controls and pass lists, access to hardware and software, addition and removal of equipment to a network, and secure deletion of retired equipment; and *technical*: risk analysis and management, system access controls, encryption, authentication, and integrity. Subcontractors must have in place programs to comply with the Security Rule.

The HITECH Act extended the Security Rule to business associates. It also introduced the requirement for data breach notification to affected individuals and the government by covered entities, business associates and related entities for a breach of unencrypted ePHI to unauthorized entities ("an impermissible use or disclosure"). This now requires the covered entity or business associate to demonstrate that "there is a low probability" that the PHI "has been compromised."[44] In addition to statutory requirements,

---

43. U.S. Dept. of Commerce, Clarifications Regarding the U.S.-EU Safe Harbor Framework and Cloud Computing (April 2013).

44. Modifications to the HIPAA Privacy, Security, Enforcement, and Breach Notification Rules Under the Health Information Technology for Economic and Clinical Health Act and

health information security has its own standard, beyond those described in Chapters 4 and 5.[45]

Financial Information

The GLBA Safeguards Rule requires financial institutions to institute an information security program that protects the "security and confidentiality of customer information" (nonpublic personal information) by implementing administrative, physical, and technical safeguards. Subsequent regulations require management oversight of the information security program (both internal and outsourced) and risk assessments, in addition to appropriate risk-based security controls.[46] Further regulations cover data breaches in its systems or those of its outsourcers, after which financial institutions are required to notify affected customers and regulators.[47] Other regulators such as the FTC and the SEC have also issued similar rules that expand the number of firms covered by these requirements.[48] The SEC has offered guidance regarding data breaches pertaining to the disclosure of cybersecurity risks and incidents as a possible material event.[49] FRCA/FACTA require the implementation of specific appropriate controls, such as on the use of consumer financial identifiers and secure disposal of credit reports. The FTC, under section 5 of the FTC Act, is given the authority to address unfair or deceptive trade practices, which it has used to deal with firms who have unreasonable information security practices or whose practices are different than its stated public policies. Under the Dodd-Frank law, the new Consumer Financial Protection Bureau will have powers similar to the FTC's

the Genetic Information Nondiscrimination Act; Other Modifications to the HIPAA Rules, 78 Fed. Reg. 5566 (Jan. 25, 2013).

45. ISO, 27799, Health informatics — Information security management in health using ISO/IEC 27002 (2008).

46. *Interagency Guidelines Establishing Standards for Safeguarding Customer Information,* 66 Fed. Reg.8616 (Feb. 1, 2001).

47. *Interagency Guidance on Response Programs for Unauthorized Access to Customer Information and Customer Notice (Incident Response Guidance),* 70 Fed. Reg. 15736 (Mar. 29, 2005).

48. SEC Final Rule: Privacy of Consumer Financial Information, Regulation S-P (2000), for brokers, dealers and investment advisers and FTC Final Safeguards Rule, 67 Fed. Reg. 100 (May 23, 2002) for "any other financial institution or other person that is not subject to the jurisdiction of any [other] agency or authority [charged with enforcing the statute]."

49. SEC, Division of Corporation Finance, CF Disclosure Guidance: Topic No. 2, *Cybersecurity* (Oct. 13, 2011).

"unfair and deceptive" trade practices standard and a new standard to deal with "abusive" acts and practices.[50]

Financial Reporting/Compliance

SOX section 404 requires the management of a publicly held organization to represent the state of the internal controls over financial reporting. External financial auditors will then provide their opinion about this management representation and also provide their own opinion about the state of internal controls, including the information security policies and procedures used by the organization or any of its IT outsourcers who perform controls having a material impact on financial reporting. The audit of third party outsourcing organizations such as CSPs is further discussed in Chapter 5. Under section 302, the organization's CEO and CFO are required to certify that there are no material misstatements in these reports about internal controls used in financial reporting. Under the Federal Sentencing Guidelines, the effectiveness of the organization's compliance and ethics program must be periodically evaluated.

State Information Security Laws

U.S. states have a variety of different types of laws addressing information security, including general security requirements, secure disposal, secure transmission/storage, and data breach. For example, Rhode Island has enacted a law on data disposal that requires a business to take reasonable steps to destroy a customer's personal information within its custody or control when it is no longer needed by the business.[51] New York now has a law requiring information on procedures for the destruction or data wiping of all hardware containing personal or confidential information before recycling.[52] Nevada has enacted a law that generally requires any entity that transmits personal information outside a secure network or moves storage devices containing personal information to utilize appropriate encryption techniques, including safeguarding and management of the cryptographic keys.[53] It also requires

---

50. Dodd-Frank Act at § 1031.
51. R.I. Gen. Laws § 6-52-2.
52. N.Y. Electronic Equipment Recycling and Reuse Act (2010).
53. Nev. Rev. Stat 603A.215.

data collectors utilizing card payment systems to comply with the Payment Card Industry Data Security Standard (PCI DSS).[54]

California was the first state to enact a data breach law[55] that requires notice to the affected state resident of the breach of their unencrypted personal information (name plus SSN, driver's license number, financial account or credit/debit card numbers, medical or health insurance information) to any unauthorized person. Massachusetts has enacted perhaps the most sweeping general security rules, which apply to personal information of Massachusetts residents, regardless of where the information resides.[56] Each entity that collects personal information is required to implement and maintain a comprehensive information security program that has appropriate technical, administrative, and physical safeguards. These include risk assessments, security policies, overseeing service providers, preventing terminated employee access, incident handling, regular monitoring, annual reviews, secure authentication and access controls, up-to-date patching, use of network firewalls, and encryption for wired or wireless network transmissions of personal information or storage on portable devices, malware protection, and employee training on computer system security.

Blocking Statutes

Rather than have blocking statutes, it is the United States whose laws, especially its liberal pre-trial discovery process, other countries seek to block. The U.S. federal courts will allow discovery on "any nonprivileged matter that is relevant to any party's claim or defense" and this relevant information "need not be admissible at the trial if the discovery appears reasonably calculated to lead to the discovery of admissible evidence."[57] And the U.S. courts will typically not recognize the blocking statutes of other countries as a reason to disallow evidence in a U.S. court.

For example, while U.S. federal courts would proceed under the Federal Rules of Civil Procedure for evidence gathering rules, countries that have

---

54. *Id.*
55. Cal. civ. code § 1798.82.
56. Mass. 201 CMR 17.00.
57. Fed. R. Civ. P. 26(b)(1).

ratified the Hague Evidence Convention[58] are able to enact statutes refusing to comply with common law discovery requests,[59] which many countries have done. The Hague Evidence Convention requires letters of request be sent to the high court authority in the country where the requested data is located.[60] The U.S. Supreme Court has held that the Hague Evidence Convention is an optional supplement for use in obtaining data held abroad, not the exclusive procedural rule to follow.[61] In a separate case, the Court held that a party responding to a discovery request cannot use a foreign data protection statute to resist discovery.[62] This analysis is rather complex, requiring all factors from statutes and cases in a four-phase detailed approach.[63]

Cloud-Computing Specific

The activities of the U.S. government are described in the next section, so this section will only look at cloud rules and cases. As an example of cloud-specific rules, the Federal Financial Institutions Examination Council (FFIEC) provided guidance regarding outsourced cloud computing.[64] Pointing to the risk analysis practices in its IT Examination Handbook (see Chapter 5), it noted several areas of focus, including due diligence, vendor management, audit, information security, business continuity, and legal, regulatory, and reputational considerations.

Through early 2013, there still have only been a small number of court cases that have directly dealt with cloud computing by name. Of course, there have been numerous cases dealing with IT outsourcing but few that have named cloud computing specifically. The following are U.S. court decisions that have dealt with the cloud directly in some manner. There are other

---

58. Hague Convention on the Taking of Evidence Abroad in Civil or Commercial Matters, Mar. 18, 1970, 23 U.S.T. 2555 (1972).

59. *Id.* art. 23.

60. *Id.* art. 1-2.

61. Societe Nationale Industrielle Aerospatiale v. U.S. District Court for Southern District of Iowa, 482 U.S. 522, 524 (1987).

62. Societe Internationale Pour Participations Industrielles et Commerciales S.A. v. Rogers, 357 U.S. 197, 205 (1958).

63. *See* Thomas Shaw, *International E-Discovery – U.S. Litigation Exposure for Asia/Pacific Corporations*, EDDE Journal (newsletter. of the ABA Section. Science & Technology Law) Vol. 1 Issue 1 (Winter 2010).

64. FFIEC, Outsourced Cloud Computing (July 10, 2012).

cases that are related to the Internet proper but not specifically discussing the cloud. There have also been a number of cases involving the rights of privacy for users putting their data in the cloud, which are covered in the discussion on e-discovery in the cloud in Chapter 5.

These cases looked at the following varied issues in use of the cloud:

- Cloud hosting as a factor in trademark likelihood-of-confusion analysis
- Use of the cloud to retrieve otherwise deleted forensic data in enforcement action
- Non-loss of privacy rights in data hosted by others (e.g., in the cloud)
- Requirements under FISMA to use a private cloud
- Market power of cloud SaaS provider leveraged into cloud IaaS services
- Impact of cloud access of supporting document location in transfer of venue
- Potential impact of the cloud in seeking damages under CSA
- Lack of liability of CSPs for subscribers' acts under the Communications Act

The first cloud case was a trademark case that used the fact that both parties used cloud computing to support the likelihood-of-confusion factor regarding proximity of the goods or services offered by the two parties.[65] The court held that use of the same type of computing platform (in this case it was SaaS applications) should not be a significant issue in determining whether the products or services offered are similar. The second cloud case involved the FTC's enforcement action against a company charged with violating section 5 of the FTC Act[66] for unfair or deceptive trade practices and subsequent destruction of computer-based evidence.[67] The information purportedly destroyed was found to be mostly duplicated on Salesforce.com servers, so even though the evidence had been deleted and "scrubbed" from local servers, the FTC was able to retrieve sufficient evidence from the cloud for the defendant to present a defense.

---

65. Rearden LLC v. Rearden Commerce, Inc., 597 F. Supp. 2d 1006, (N.D. Cal. 2009).
66. 15 U.S.C. § 45(a).
67. FTC v. First Universal Lending LLC, Case No. 09-82322-Civ (S.D. Fla. 2011).

The third cloud case involved an appeal regarding suppression of evidence motions by a defendant charged with possession of child pornography. One issue was whether the rights of privacy in electronic information diminish based on the storage medium where it is held (in this case the cloud, but that is not part of the facts of the case).[68] The court held that "privacy rights in electronically stored personal information" is not lost because that data is "retained in a medium owned by another" (e.g., CSPs).

Although not a case involving an organization's rights in the cloud, the battle between two significant cloud participants (Google and Microsoft) over the awarding of a U.S. government cloud computing services contract may provide some insights on CSPs.[69] In this complaint, from which an injunction was issued by the court, Google argued that the requirements as laid out in an RFQ issued by a government agency specified the products of its competitor (Microsoft), who was awarded a contract for almost 90,000 users based on the RFQ. Beyond the sole sourcing dispute, another issue was the government agency's requirement for use of a private cloud for security. Google stated that a private cloud was "not a requirement under FISMA" and that the agency "could address its security requirements by requiring the contractor to provide security controls that are confirmed to meet the security standards."

A fourth case was that involving two competing real property managers who provided "vertically integrated cloud computing services."[70] The court noted the difficulty in switching these cloud applications, due to "high switching costs associated with moving the customer's data to a new system, the cost of new licensing fees, and the disruption of day-to-day business attendant to re-aligning IT systems and transferring data." For these firms, this may include accounting, maintenance, leasing, revenue management, payment processing, and background screening applications. The plaintiff alleged that defendant used its industry-leading cloud-based back office accounting application to intimidate clients not to host the defendant's cloud application on any cloud service except the defendant's.

---

68. State v. Bellar, 217 P. 3d 1094 (Ore. App. 2009).
69. Google, Inc. v. the United States, Cmplt. No. 10-743 C (Fed. Cl. 2010).
70. RealPage, Inc. v. Yardi Systems, Inc., Case No. cv-11-00690, (C.D. Cal. 2012).

The court ruled that there was potentially an illegal negative tying arrangement, because the purchase of the application required non-purchase of cloud services from the plaintiff. The court rejected the fact that application purchasers could self-host as an alternative as a defense to a negative tying claim. The court also found that the defendant had market power (the power to "force a purchaser to do something that he would not do in a competitive market"), which is less than having monopoly power. But the court refused to dismiss the potential of a monopoly claim, given that the two parties were the only significant players in this cloud market segment and that the defendant attempted to use its leading position in one part of the cloud market (industry-specific application) to dominate in another part of the cloud market (hosting for integrated-industry specific applications).

A fifth case looked at a request for transfer of venue. The court stated that it must evaluate both "the fair and efficient administration of justice" and factors applicable to the parties.[71] Among these private-party factors is "the relative ease of access to sources of proof." One of the defendants stated that most of its applicable documents in this case were in California, not Texas. Another defendant countered that this defendant had the documents in a cloud computing system with locations in Texas and the documents could be easily accessed through the cloud. The court, quoting from a federal circuit case, noted that "the ability to conveniently transport documents electronically 'does not render this factor superfluous.'"[72] It did note though that not every circuit concurred and that cloud access could "render this factor superfluous."

In a sixth case, the plaintiff was seeking damages for the theft of a self-taken nude image that was copied from her mobile phone during servicing by the defendant company.[73] The plaintiff was seeking, inter alia, punitive damages under the Stored Communications Act, because the source of the photos could have been a cloud-based system and so discovery was warranted to determine this. The defendants had stated that a "personal cellular telephone is not a communications facility under the Stored Communications Act," leading the plaintiff to try to amend the complaint. The magistrate

---

71. Gemalto *SA v. HTC Corp.*, Case No. 6:10CV561, (E.D. Tex. 2011).
72. In re Genentech, Inc., 566 F.3d 1345-46 (Fed. Cir. 2009).
73. Navarro v. Verizon Wireless, *LLC*, Case No. cv-12-1958, (E.D. La. 2013).

judge had not allowed the amendment, based on another recent case[74] that held that "'[a]n individual's personal cell phone does not *provide* an electronic communication service just because the device *enables* use of electronic communication services,' and that information that an individual stores on her cellular telephone is not electronic storage under the statute." As there was no clear evidence of cloud use, the court denied the motion to overturn the magistrate judge's decision on the amended complaint.

In the seventh case, the plaintiff alleged trademark and copyright infringement against the defendant, who operates websites allowing users to stream or broadcast live video across the Internet to other subscribers.[75] The plaintiff also alleged claims under the Communications Act, asserting that the use of the defendant's service and servers by potential violators of the trademark and copyright laws brought the defendant's service within its scope. The court was not willing to allow liability for "mere receipt" of its users' video streams, as it would then "have to allow similar Communications Act claims against scores of cloud computing service providers such as Microsoft, Apple, Google, Amazon.com, Dropbox, Box.net and others."

2.2 U.S. Public Sector Laws and Activities
Activities
The U.S. federal government is a leader in pushing for the use of cloud computing, perhaps in contrast to some other leading governments.[76] The federal CIO has articulated the vision for the federal government's use of the cloud.[77] Twenty-five percent ($20 billion) of the U.S. federal IT spending is estimated to be something that could migrate to the cloud. To help set the stage for this massive shift migration, the federal government promotes a number of activities, as follows:

- Leveraging cloud computing accelerators
- Ensuring a secure, trustworthy environment
- Streamlining procurement processes

---

74. Garcia v. City of Laredo, Tex., Case No. 11-41118 (5th Cir. 2012).
75. Zuffa, LLC v. Justin.TV, Inc., 838 F.Supp.2d 1102 (D. Nev. 2012).
76. European Governments Staying Out of the Cloud, N.Y. Times (Nov. 20, 2012).
77. U.S. CIO Vivek Kundra, *Federal Cloud Computing Strategy* (Feb. 2011).

- Establishing cloud computing standards
- Recognizing the international dimensions of cloud computing
- Laying a solid governance foundation

This can also be seen by the following schedule, which outlines the migration strategy at the federal government level for implementing cloud computing solutions (either new or migrating existing capabilities). Under the Office of Management and Budget (OMB) guidance, federal agencies are required, when submitting their IT budgets, to complete an alternatives analysis that includes a cloud computing alternative, on the following schedule:[78]

- By September 2011 for all newly planned or performing major IT investments/acquisitions
- By September 2012 for all IT investments making enhancements to an existing investment
- By September 2013 for all IT investments in steady-state

To facilitate the move of government agencies into the cloud, NIST has developed the *Cloud Computing Technology Roadmap,* to foster adoption of cloud computing by federal agencies and support the private sector; reduce uncertainty by improving the information available to decision makers; and, facilitate the further development of the cloud computing model. Individual documents in the Roadmap series include one to help define, communicate, and recommend "strategic and tactical requirements that must be met for U.S. government agencies to further cloud adoption and the interoperability, portability and security standards, guidelines, and technology that need to be in place to satisfy these requirements."[79] A second volume provides further information, such as use cases,[80] while a third volume provides some of the

---

78. Federal CIO Council, *State of Public Sector Cloud Computing* (2010).

79. NIST SP 500-293 (draft), *U.S. Government Cloud Computing Technology Roadmap vol. I - High-Priority Requirements to Further USG Agency Cloud Computing Adoption,* Rel. 1.0 (Nov. 2011).

80. NIST SP 500-293 (draft), *U.S. Government Cloud Computing Technology Roadmap vol. II - Useful Information for Cloud Adopters,* Rel. 1.0 (Nov. 2011).

factors for use cases and interoperability for those planning or implementing cloud projects.[81]

In July 2012, the Government Accountability Office produced a report looking at the results to date of the "Cloud First" policy of the OMB, which requires federal agencies to implement cloud-based solutions whenever a "secure, reliable, and cost-effective cloud option exists" and to migrate three technology services to a cloud solution by June 2012.[82] The report reviewed seven major federal agencies'[83] efforts and found that they had key missing requirements, including retiring the legacy systems left behind when migrating functionality to the cloud.

Seven common challenges were identified in this report:

- Meeting federal security requirements (e.g., real-time monitoring, physical inventory)
- Obtaining guidance (e.g., implementation guidelines)
- Acquiring knowledge and expertise (e.g., lack of staff cloud expertise)
- Certifying and accrediting vendors (e.g., before FedRAMP becomes operational)
- Ensuring data portability and interoperability (e.g., difficulties in extracting data)
- Overcoming cultural barriers (e.g., risk aversion based on prior data leaks)
- Procuring services on a consumption (on-demand) basis (e.g., budgeting for variable-cost services)

The government has also been a leader in showing how to obtain cloud computing services under the Federal Risk and Authorization Management Program (FedRAMP) (see Chapter 4) and in defining standards under NIST (see Chapter 5). Finally, the federal government's Big Data Research

---

81. NIST SP 500-293 (draft), *U.S. Government Cloud Computing Technology Roadmap vol. III - Technical Considerations for USG Cloud Computing Deployment Decisions*, Rel. 1.0 (Nov. 2011).

82. Government Accountability Office, *Information Technology Reform, Progress Made but Future Cloud Computing Efforts Should be Better Planned* (July 2012).

83. Departments of Agriculture, Health and Human Services, Homeland Security, State, and Treasury; the General Services Administration, and the Small Business Administration.

and Development Initiative[84] will not only make large amounts of data from federal agencies (e.g., (NSF) National Science Foundation, Department of Health and Human Services (HHS)/ National Institute of Health (NIH), Department of Energy (DoE), Department of Defense (DoD), Defense Advanced Research Projects Agency (DARPA), and and the U.S. Geological Survey (USGS)) publicly available, it will do so by utilizing the public cloud resources of private-sector CSPs. NIH made 200 terabytes of data on the human genome publicly available through Amazon Web Services.

The Department of Defense has authored its own strategy for implementing its DoD Enterprise Cloud Environment.[85] With its particular situation, the Department has recognized that in utilizing cloud computing, it has "challenges that require careful adoption considerations, especially in areas of cybersecurity, continuity of operations, information assurance (IA), cybersecurity, and resilience. Additional challenges include service acquisition and funding sustainment, data migration and management, and overcoming network dependence at the tactical edge (disconnected, intermittent and low-bandwidth (DIL) users." Despite these requirements, it intends to go forward with cloud transitioning to a cloud enterprise environment through four concurrent steps: fostering cloud adoption, data center consolidation, establishing a DoD cloud infrastructure, and delivering cloud services.

Statutes

When implementing cloud computing, the federal agencies are still required to follow a number of federal statutes and standards, principally FISMA for information security, the Privacy Act, and records-related rules. This section provides an overview of some key statutes and standards, while specific information security and privacy risks and requirements of cloud use for the U.S. government are further discussed in Chapters 4 and 5.

---

84. Executive Office of the President, Office of Science and Technology Policy, *Obama Administration Unveils "Big Data" Initiative: Announces $200 Million in New R&D Investments* (Mar. 29, 2012).

85. Dept. of Defense CIO, *Cloud Computing Strategy* (July 2012).

Information Security

Part of the E-Government Act,[86] the Federal Information Security Management Act (FISMA) has as its objective to provide a "comprehensive framework" that addresses risk and information security controls for federal government systems and information.[87] In turn, the heads of federal agencies are required to provide safeguards that are "commensurate with the risk and magnitude of the harm" for unauthorized processing of those systems and information for which they are responsible.[88] The agency head must implement an information security program across the agency that includes periodic risk assessment, information security policies and procedures, security awareness training, periodic testing, incident handling and remedial actions, and business continuity.[89] There is also a requirement for an annual independent evaluation.[90] As part of this act, NIST is given the responsibility for information security standards and guidelines that provide "adequate information security for all agency operations and assets," including minimum standards.[91]

To obtain approval for information systems, federal government agencies are required to go through a six-step process as outlined in NIST SP 37A.[92] This Risk Management Framework starts with categorizing the information system, utilizing Federal Information Processing Standard (FIPS) 199,[93] which is further explained in Chapter 5. The second step is to select the security controls and the third step to implement the controls, using FIPS 200,[94] NIST SP 800-53,[95] and NIST SP 800-53A.[96] The fourth step is to assess the

86. E-Government Act, Title III, §301 (2002).

87. 44 U.S.C. § 3541.

88. 44 U.S.C. § 3544(a)(1)(A).

89. 44 U.S.C. § 3544(b).

90. 44 U.S.C. § 3545.

91. E-Government Act, Title III, § 303(a)(3).

92. NIST, SP 800-37 rev. 1, *Guide for Applying the Risk Management Framework to Federal Information Systems - A Security Life Cycle Approach* (2010).

93. FIPS Publ. 199, *Standards for Security Categorization of Federal Information and Information Systems* (2004).

94. FIPS Publ. 200, *Minimum Security Requirements for Federal Information and Federal Information Systems* (2006).

95. NIST, SP 800-53 rev. 4, *Security and Privacy Controls for Federal Information Systems and Organizations* (Feb. 2013).

96. NIST, SP 800-53A rev. 1, *Guide for Assessing the Security Controls in Federal Information Systems and Organizations - Building Effective Security Assessment Plans* (2010).

security controls using NIST SP 800-53A. The fifth step is to authorize the system and the final step is to monitor the security controls. The risk assessment and treatment processes for federal systems under cloud computing is discussed in Chapters 4 and 5.

Privacy

The Privacy Act requires U.S. federal government agencies to maintain records on individuals only relevant and necessary to accomplish the purpose of collection[97] and not to disclose records about individuals except with certain limited exceptions.[98] The data subject is provided with the rights to access and to request corrections to these records about herself/himself.[99] Agencies need to maintain these records to ensure their "accuracy, relevance, timeliness, and completeness."[100] Each agency is required to establish the appropriate "administrative, technical and physical safeguards to insure the security and confidentiality of records and to protect against any anticipated threats or hazards to their security or integrity."[101] This is further discussed in Chapter 4. Any contractors used by a federal agency (e.g., CSPs) must comply with the provisions of this act.[102] In many other countries, the data protection statutes discussed in Chapter 3 also apply to government agencies, or there is a similar data protection statute that does, sometimes with more rigorous provisions.

Records

U.S. federal agencies are required to maintain a program of records management under the Federal Records Act.[103] The Act also requires that they "establish safeguards against the removal or loss of records."[104] When they receive a valid request for these records, they are required to provide this data in the requested format under the Freedom of Information Act,[105] but

---

97. 5 U.S.C. § 552a(e)(1).
98. 5 U.S.C. § 552a(b).
99. 5 U.S.C. § 552a(d).
100. 5 U.S.C. § 552a(e)(5).
101. 5 U.S.C. § 552a(e)(10).
102. 5 U.S.C. § 552a(m).
103. 44 U.S.C. § 3102.
104. 44 U.S.C. § 3105.
105. 5 U.S.C. § 552.

with the ability to delete information for reasons of privacy[106] and other listed exceptions, such as trade secrets, medical information and law enforcement data.[107] The National Archives and Records Administration (NARA) is responsible for the "custody, use, and withdrawal of records" transferred to it.[108] NARA has issued both an FAQ[109] and a Bulletin[110] about records management and cloud computing. The earlier FAQ (revised by the later bulletin) described the following records management "implications":

- As many applications do not include record disposition schedules, the cloud may not meet federal electronic records management requirements[111]
- CSPs must be made aware of records retention schedules for data in all locations, so that agencies can control record deletions
- CSPs must also ensure that records are accessible so as to ensure "agency responsiveness to discovery, or FOIA/Privacy Act, or other access requests"
- There is a lack of formal technical standards governing how data is stored and manipulated in cloud environments, threatening the "long-term trustworthiness and sustainability of the data"
- A lack of portability standards may result in difficulty removing records for recordkeeping requirements or complicate the transition to another environment
- Vendors' terms of services may not sufficiently address federal contracting standards
- Agencies are responsible for complying with records management regulations wherever records are created and stored and addressing what to do in the case of CSP bankruptcy

---

106. 5 U.S.C. § 552(a)2(E).
107. 5 U.S.C. § 552.(b).
108. 44 U.S.C. § 2108.
109. NARA, Frequently Asked Questions About Managing Federal Records In Cloud Computing Environments (2010).
110. NARA Bulletin 2010-05, *Guidance on Managing Records in Cloud Computing Environments* (2010).
111. 36 C.F.R. 1236.

The later bulletin provided some guidelines, including the following:

- Determine if federal records in a cloud environment are covered under an existing records retention schedule
- Determine how all records will be captured, managed, retained, made available to authorized users, and retention periods applied
- Include instructions to periodically test transfers of federal records to other environments, including agency servers, to ensure the records remain portable
- Determine how data will be migrated to new formats, operating systems, etc., so that records are readable throughout their entire life cycles
- Resolve portability and accessibility issues through good records management policies and other data governance practices

The United States is not the only country with records management laws. For example, in Australia, there are similar laws that establish the government's obligation to preserve records[112] and the ability of citizens to then request access to those records.[113] In the United Kingdom the law requires the government to select and preserve appropriate public records[114] and to allow access to these records.[115] In continental Europe, there are numerous laws dealing with records management including the data protection statutes described in Chapter 3. France also has a law allowing access to government records[116] and Germany has federal and numerous state laws.[117] Canada also has federal

---

112. Australia, Archives Act (1983).

113. Australia, Freedom of Information Act (1982).

114. U.K., Public Records Act (1958) and National Archives Act (2002).

115. U.K., Freedom of Information Act (2000).

116. France, Law on Access to Administrative Documents, Loi 78-753 du juillet 1978 portant diverses mesures d'amélioration des relations entre l'administration et le public et diverses despositions d'ordre administratif, social et fiscal (1978), revised for EU Directive 2003/98/EC in 2005.

117. Germany, Federal Freedom of Information Act, Gesetz zur Regelung des Zugangs zu Informationen des Bundes (2005).

and provincial laws,[118] while there are similar laws in Japan,[119]India,[120] and Mexico;[121] in Brazil, data privacy is a constitutional right.[122]

2.3 Surveillance Laws

Beyond the laws directly relating to the obligations of organizations and their respective CSP's security and privacy practices, there are a series of laws that influence the risk analysis of cloud computing consumers. For those outside the United States, the USA PATRIOT Act is a statute to consider for any data that may be subsequently processed within the United States as part of the cloud network of a CSP and its hosting subcontractors. It is also important to note that while this statute demonstrates the expanded powers available to the U.S. government, most every government around the world has similar powers, either by statute or otherwise, and so similar considerations must be evaluated by all cloud consumers of each applicable jurisdiction's ability to compel disclosure of organizational information.

For example, in Europe the EU Data Retention Directive must be part of the risk analysis for data processed in that region, and in China, the various state secrets and security laws and regulations that give the government significant investigatory powers must be fully understood. These laws are sometimes intertwined with but mostly separate from governments' attempts to block or shape Internet content (more than 35 countries are currently involved in such activities).[123] In addition, governments have potential access to cloud-based data inside their borders through traditional methods such as search warrants or common law grand jury subpoenas.

It is important to understand that governments also potentially have access to cloud data physically residing outside of their borders through Mutual Legal Assistance Treaties (MLATs). These are bilateral agreements between governments to help each other during criminal investigations, allowing indirect requests to CSPs over whom a foreign government may

---

118. Canada, Access to Information Act (1985).
119. Japan, Law Concerning Access to Information Held by Administrative Organs (1999).
120. India, Right to Information Act (2005).
121. Mexico, Federal Law of Transparency and Access to Public Government Information, Ley Federal de Transparencia y Acceso a la Information Publica Gubernamental (2002).
122. Brazil, Constitution art. 5.
123. *See* OpenNet Initiative country profiles.

not otherwise have personal jurisdiction (e.g., no local offices). For example, in 2003, the U.S. and the EU and all 25 member states entered into MLATs.[124] Regarding the difference in data protection regimes between the two parties: "generic restrictions with respect to the legal standards in the requesting State for processing personal data may not be imposed by the requested State as a condition... to providing evidence or information...[T]he fact that the requesting and requested States have different systems of protecting the privacy of data does not give rise to a ground for refusal of assistance, and may not as such give rise to additional conditions...Such refusal of assistance could only arise in exceptional cases in which, upon balancing the important interests involved in the particular case, furnishing the specific data sought by the requesting State would raise difficulties so fundamental as to be considered by the requested State to fall within the essential interests grounds for refusal."[125]

United States

USA PATRIOT Act

The Uniting and Strengthening America by Providing Appropriate Tools Required to Intercept and Obstruct Terrorism Act (PATRIOT Act)[126] as amended, gives the government an expanded ability to perform electronic surveillance. This is a complex set of changes to more than a dozen statutes. Among the changes are those impacting Foreign Intelligence Surveillance Act (FISA) Orders and National Security Letters (NSLs). Orders under FISA[127] were expanded to include documents for investigations to "protect against international terrorism and clandestine intelligence activities."[128] This does not require a probable cause showing (only relevance to an investigation into international terrorism or clandestine intelligence activities) in the ex parte proceeding before the FISA court but does include a gag order on CSPs who receive this order, meaning cloud consumers may not know that

---

124. Agreement on Mutual Legal Assistance Between the United States of America and the European Union (June 25, 2003)
125. Explanation of art. 9(2)(b), U.S. Senate Treaty Document 109-13.
126. U.S.A.P.A.T.R.I.O.T. Act (PATRIOT Act), Pub. L. No. 107-56 (2001).
127. Pub. L. No. 95-511 (1978).
128. *Id*. at § 215.

their cloud-based data was accessed by the government.[129] FISA amendments creating the ability to perform surveillance on the data of non-U.S. citizens in public clouds outside of the United States has caused great concern in the EU,[130] although European law enforcement also makes requests for cloud data in the United States.[131] These orders have not been heavily used (1,674 requests in calendar 2011).[132]

NSLs have been much more heavily used (16,511 requests in calendar 2011).[133] Previously authorized by several acts such as the Right to Financial Privacy Act,[134] FCRA (see section 2.1), and ECPA (see below), the scope of NSLs was expanded by the Patriot Act from having to do with foreign powers to the purposes of protecting "against international terrorism or clandestine intelligence activities."[135] These cover telephone transactional records, financial records, and consumer reports. There was initially no judicial review of these mostly Federal Bureau of Investigation-initiated administrative subpoenas, but this was addressed in a reauthorization act.[136] But the limited scope of the judicial review and the gag orders on the NSLs have recently caused the enabling law[137] to be struck down by a federal court.[138] At least one analysis by another government concluded that this law posed significant risks for the personal information of its citizens ("powers enacted by the USA Patriot Act to make orders for access to personal information located in Canada that is involved in outsourcing of public body functions to a US linked contractor") and recommended certain safeguards, including local statutes and contractual controls.[139]

---

129. *Id.*

130. European Parliament's Committee on Civil Liberties, Justice and Home Affairs, *Fighting cyber crime and*
  protecting privacy in the cloud, § 3.3-3.4 (Oct. 2012).

131. *See e.g.* Deutscher Bundestag, *Sicherheit, Datenschutz und Überwachung von Cloud-Daten* (Mar. 8, 2013).

132. U.S. Dept. of Justice Office of Legislative Affairs, 2011 FISA Report to Congress (Apr. 30, 2012).

133. *Id.*

134. Pub. L. No. 95-630 (1978).

135. *Id.* at § 505.

136. Pub. L. No. 109-177 (2006).

137. 18 U.S.C. § 2709.

138. In re National Security Letter, Case No. 11-02173 (N.D. Cal. 2013).

139. *Privacy and the USA Patriot Act - Implications for British Columbia Public Sector Outsourcing*, Information & Privacy Commissioner for British Columbia (2004).

The recent revelations[140] about the PRISM program and its collection of data from online service providers by the U.S. National Security Agency (NSA) has raised concerns about the 2008 revisions to FISA[141] and the types and scale of data now collected under FISA section 702.[142] The U.S. director of national intelligence, while admitting the existence of this and related collection programs, reiterated its primary role in national security endeavors and also the legislative approvals of Congress and the ongoing oversight by both Congress and the FISA courts.[143]

Electronic Communications Privacy Act

The Electronic Communications Privacy Act (ECPA) is made up of three distinct and somewhat overlapping laws, the Wiretap Act,[144] the Pen Register Act,[145] and the Stored Communications Act (SCA).[146] In very simplified terms (the analysis of this law is very complex, involving numerous often conflicting court decisions), the Wiretap Act is concerned with the privacy of electronic communications in transit while the SCA is concerned with the privacy of electronic communications in storage. Regarding data that is stored in the public cloud, the analysis of legal protections (again very simplified) is based on whether the CSP is deemed as providing an electronic communications service (e.g., sending/receiving email), remote computing services (storage and processing) or neither, in which case the statute does not apply and standard Fourth Amendment protections apply to governmental requests for access.

The ability of the government to gain access to such information in the cloud is complicated under the ECPA. Using the example of a cloud-resident email message, government access to it requires either a search warrant (if it is an unopened email or is in transit) or a subpoena (if it is an opened email or if an unopened email over 180 days old), although some courts

---

140. *Pub. L.* No. 110-261, *FISA Amendments Act (2008)*.

141. *In Secret, Court Vastly Broadens Powers of N.S.A.*, N.Y. Times (July 6, 2013).

142. Procedures for Targeting Certain Persons Outside the United States Other than United States Persons.

143. *U.S. Confirms That It Gathers Online Data Overseas*, N.Y. Times (June 6, 2013).

144. 18 U.S.C. § 2510.

145. 18 U.S.C. § 3121.

146. 18 U.S.C. § 2701.

have limited the latter.[147] These rules apply to the location of the data (in the U.S.) and not necessarily the citizenship of the recipient.[148] Data residing in the cloud are likewise accessible through a subpoena or court order if relevant to an investigation. Possibly complicating this already uncertain and jurisdiction-specific analysis is the decision that corporations do not have a right of personal privacy.[149] The government can compel production of, or the CSP can voluntarily provide, non-content-related data under the SCA, such as customer-identifying information.

Google, in its 2012 Transparency Report, stated that during the period from July 1 to December 31, 2012, it had received over 20,000 requests for data from various governments around the world. Over 8,000 of these came from the United States under ECPA, with the vast majority being subpoenas, followed by search warrants, then court orders. According to Google's own Legal Process FAQ, it will only allow user content (e.g., Gmail) to be obtained through a search warrant, not a subpoena or a court order, due to the lower standards of proof and judicial review involved in the latter. Google stated that it would notify the user if such a request was made unless the user had closed its account or was legally prohibited from doing so. In addition, more than 1,000 requests each came from the governments of Brazil, Germany, France, the United Kingdom, and India. Google also revealed that it had received between 0 and 999 NSLs. Microsoft's 2012 Law Enforcement Requests Report showed over 70,000 requests were received globally, with just of 2 percent resulting in disclosure of user content. But over 50,000 of these requests did result in the disclosure of non-content (subscriber/transactional) data. France, Germany, and the United Kingdom were again the near the top in requests, exceeded only by the United States and surprisingly, Turkey.

---

147. United States v. Warshak, Warshak and TCI Media, Inc., Case Nos. 08-3997, 08-4085, 08-4087, 08-4212, 08-4429, 09-3176 (6th Cir. 2011).

148. Suzlon Energy Ltd. v. Microsoft Corp., Case No. 10-35793 (9th Cir. 2011).

149. Federal Communications Commission. v. AT&T Inc., USSC No. 09–1279 (2011), at least for exemptions under the Freedom of Information Act.

Communications Assistance for Law Enforcement Act

The Communications Assistance for Law Enforcement Act (CALEA)[150] of 1994 was created to give law enforcement the ability to tap into U.S. telephone networks as necessary. Originally targeting voice communications, it now deals with all kinds of voice, image, and data traffic on the Internet. Telecommunications carriers and equipment makers are required to assist law enforcement in complying with legal orders for content and caller information. This now applies to voice over IP (VoIP) providers, broadband Internet access providers, and ISPs. Although expressly excluding information service providers, the applicability of this statute to CSPs is not yet settled.

International

EU Data Retention Directive/Cybercrime Convention

The European Parliament passed the Data Retention Directive, which requires the EU members to pass national laws that require providers of publicly available electronic communications services to retain information about Internet traffic, including IP addresses for up to two years.[151] This is true even though the data subject may not be a suspect in a crime. It does not include access to the contents of the communications. It does include Internet access, Internet email and Internet telephony. Appropriate safeguards are required for the collected data, which are to be destroyed at the end of the retention period. There has been substantial resistance to implementing this directive but all member states were required to do so by May 2011. The data retained under this directive can be used with the procedural rules in the EU Convention on Cybercrime.[152] This convention addresses a series of online crimes (illegal access and interception, data and system interference, misuse of devices, computer-related forgery and fraud, child pornography, copyright), and the procedures for real-time interception, preservation and partial disclosure of traffic data, the preservation, search and seizure of stored

---

150. Pub. L. No. 103-414 (1994).

151. Directive 2006/24/EC of the European Parliament and of the Council of 15 March 2006 on the retention of data generated or processed in connection with the provision of publicly available electronic communications services or of public communications networks and amending Directive 2002/58/EC.

152. Council of Europe Convention on Cybercrime European Treaty Series - No. 185 (2001).

computer data, and real-time interception of content data. In addition, member states all have their own surveillance laws.[153]

China's State Secrets Law

China's State Security Law[154] requires both citizens and organs of the state to protect the "security, honor and interests" of the country. To carry out this function, the appropriate government security authorities may enter any site and examine "related files, materials and articles." As appropriate, "technological reconnaissance" may be utilized. Organizations and individuals cannot refuse to provide relevant information. The State Secrets Law requires public and private organizations, as well as citizens to guard state secrets, which are defined as those that have a bearing on "state security and national interests."[155] In addition to the usual national security information, state secrets is held to include information related to national economic and social development, science and technology, and "other matters that are classified as state secrets." It is the possession of the secrets, not the harm caused, that is criminally punishable.

In October 2010, a revised version of this law went into effect. Under this revised law, Internet and telecommunications operators and service providers have to discover, report to the government, keep records, and potentially remove information transmitted on public information networks that involve disclosure of state secrets. A previous law[156] had already made all ISPs subject to the state Public Security Bureau and required implementing security and regular reporting and assistance with investigations into any violations of the law. And the revised law does not allow systems containing state secrets to be connected to the Internet or to pass such information without adopting "protective measures."

---

153. *See e.g.,* France, Loi relative à la sécurité quotidienne (2001); Germany, Telekommunikations-Überwachungsverordnung (2005).

154. China, State Security Law of the People's Republic of China (1993).

155. China, Law on Guarding State Secrets of the People's Republic of China (1989).

156. China, Computer Information Network and Internet Security Protection and Management Regulations (1997).

Other Countries

Most countries have some sort of electronic communications monitoring capability, which includes not only the ability to intercept the communications but the storage of the message and any related attachments.[157] These are under the guises of national security, anti-terrorism or criminal statutes but many are broadly or vaguely worded, meaning that pretty much all data is susceptible to covert perusal by government operatives across the world. Given the agreements by technology companies to provide some manner of backdoor access to their secure communications as required by sovereign entities,[158] organizations should seek detailed and up-to-date analysis of the surveillance possibilities of each country where their data may be hosted or legally reached. For example, in India, the country that is host to so much of the new outsourcing activity over the last few decades, the revised information technology law[159] allows the government to "intercept, monitor or decrypt ... any information generated, transmitted, received or stored in any computer resource."

But beyond the laws of the country hosting the physical location of data in the cloud, companies must consider the extraterritorial reach of governments. MLATs and the ability of governments to reach defendants through normal personal jurisdiction techniques or through more complex rules of reaching parent companies of locally-situated subsidiaries provide a number of ways for governments to obtain data in the cloud. It may be the result that if the choices of cloud-hosting countries from a CSP are all OECD (Organization for Economic Co-operation and Development) members at similar levels of privacy protection and statutory development with enforced MLATs, any one such country may not have significant legal advantage over another in regards to data hosting location.

---

157. *See e.g.* Canada, Anti-Terrorism Act of 2001; Australia, Surveillance Devices Act of 2004.

158. See e.g. EFF, Colombia Adopts Mandatory Backdoor and Data Retention Mandates (Dec. 17, 2012).

159. India, Information Technology (Amendment) Act (2009).

Chapter 3

INTERNATIONAL STATUTES

All organizations operating globally must understand the laws of each country in which they do business, including statutes and regulations involving use of the Internet and cloud computing. If organizations are processing their customers' personal information, then this will include the data protection statutes in those countries where the processing is done or where their consumers are located, even if the organization has no presence there. Cloud computing adds a new twist, as data mobility and the use of multiple layers of subcontractors may cause the organization's information to migrate to a host in a country in which the organization neither does business nor has customers nor intended processing. So the list of potential countries whose laws the organization is responsible to comply with can become quite large.

In each of these countries, the national or local statutes will create new obligations for the organization, its CSPs and the CSP's subcontractors. These obligations may be part of data protection statutes that protect consumers and therefore mandate or suggest certain privacy and information security controls. These controls typically require oversight of any third-party subcontractors who are processing organization data that include personal information. The obligations may be part of blocking statutes that prohibit export of data for purposes of common law discovery. They may also be part of trade secrets laws, procedural discovery rules, or industry-specific regulations. Organizations need to fully understand the impact that international statutes and regulations have on cloud computing. This chapter first looks at cross-border agreements in general, then at international statutes in the three major economic regions of the world: Europe, Asia/Pacific and the Americas, using the same five-part analysis of privacy regime, cross-border data transfer restrictions, information security and data breach rules, blocking statutes, and cloud computing specific rules and activities.

Executive Takeaways

- How cross-border agreements differ from domestic outsourcing agreements
- Why organizations may be subject to international laws in the cloud
- Statutory information security and privacy obligations in Europe, Asia, and the Americas
- Cloud-specific international rules and activities

3.1 Cross-Border Agreements

International Outsourcing

To understand the implications of international statutes on outsourcing such as CSP agreements, it is useful to first understand what basic provisions should be included in such agreements (this is discussed in more detail in Chapters 7 and 8). All outsourcing agreements, domestic and international, should have at least the following provisions related to information security and privacy. The outsourcer must implement and comply with one of a number of international information security standard sets of controls, such as International Organization for Standardization (ISO) 27002,[1] PCI DSS,[2] or ISACA's COBIT.[3] Beyond standard provisions for confidentiality

---

1. ISO/IEC 27002, *Information Technology—Security Techniques—Code of Practice for Information Security Management* (2005).
2. Payment Card Industry, *Data Security Standard Requirements and Security Assessment Procedures* ver. 2.0 (2010).
3. ISACA, *Control Objectives for Information and Related Technology 5* (June 2012).

and intellectual property protection, there will be specific security controls concerning sensitive personal information (e.g., employee health or payroll data) or confidential or secret corporate data (e.g., strategic planning documents or trade secrets). There will be specific security procedures for how to dispose of or return data in the normal course of business or at the termination of the agreement. There must be timely and periodic risk assessments and monitoring of the effectiveness of information security controls. Timely response and appropriate escalation to all security incidents must be mandated, as well as reporting on the remedial steps taken to both isolate and resolve the problem, and the follow-on steps to ensure non-reoccurrence. Organizations will also demand the right to audit or to receive appropriate audit reports from an independent third party auditor. Compliance with all applicable laws must be mandatory.

International outsourcing by organizations of their data and processes to third party vendors requires several additional considerations when dealing with foreign laws. Although provisions can be written that supersede foreign laws or implement something close to domestic statutes for the purposes of the agreement, if for some reason the outsourcing agreement is unenforceable, does not contain the required provisions, or involves a non-party to the agreement (e.g., a third party or subcontractor), the organization may have to deal with the differences in laws between the originating country and other countries where the data is processed or where the organization's customer is located.

The types of issues to address in an international outsourcing agreement include:

- Jurisdiction/forum—what court in which country will hear any dispute?
- Governing law—what law will be used to interpret any dispute and what role do the respective conflict of law rules play?
- Dispute resolution—will foreign judgments or arbitral awards be enforced?

- Cross-border insolvency—what processes are used to protect the viable party and is there a local law based on UNCITRAL's cross-border insolvency model law?[4]
- Export controls—are there restrictions on the movement of goods and services?
- Bribery controls—are there restrictions on the actions of corporations (e.g., FCPA (Foreign Corrupt Practices Act)?
- Foreign laws: are conflicts of laws (data protection, evidence, data retention, breach) between the countries or industries involved?
- Discovery: which party has what responsibility (e.g., preservation) in litigation?
- Compelled disclosures: how will the service provider deal with such requests?
- Multi-country business continuity/disaster recovery: what impacts are there for multiple telecom providers, certificate authorities, utilities companies, etc.?

Cloud Computing Considerations

Cloud computing adds new considerations beyond those just described for international outsourcing. Typical international outsourcing is across borders to a known vendor in a known location. When an organization outsources its processes and data under the cloud computing paradigm, the location of the processing and data may no longer be known in advance, as being able to add flexibility means the additional on-demand resources may come from a source not known in advance. Just like a user of electricity does not know if its power came from the same province or country or came from across the border, the utility-like nature of cloud computing means a potentially unknown provider in an unknown country. And so organizations could find their data located in a jurisdiction with unknown laws or known but unfavorable laws. For example, could foreign governments gain access to corporate secrets now located on servers hosted inside their borders? Can civil litigants now perform discovery on corporate emails?

---

4. United Nations Commission on International Trade law (UNCITRAL) *Model Law on Cross-Border Insolvency* (1997).

In addition, cloud computing raises a series of potential risks, which are described at length in Chapter 4. From the international outsourcing to the cloud perspective, there are new risks that bear special consideration, as follows:

- Can all subcontractors used by the CSP in each country (hosting companies, telecom companies, ISPs, off-site data storage vendors) be reached legally (or even known) if the CSP goes out of business?
- Does flowing through the cloud make organizational information subject to each country's surveillance laws (e.g., in the U.S., the PATRIOT Act enhancements)?
- Do countries have specific limitations on the use of certain encryption levels used by the organization for data confidentiality, integrity and user authentication?
- Do digital certificates issued in affected countries have the same level of trust?
- Are federated identify management and authentication techniques available in all countries?
- Can data required in civil or criminal litigation and/or investigation have its integrity and authenticity ensured under all countries' rules of evidence?
- Can data inside a country now be exported without being blocked by local statutes?
- Do local consumer protection statutes have similar rules on limitations of data use by data processors, such as prohibitions on secondary usage?
- Are local rules for handling data breaches, data retention, and data disposal similar?
- Will hosting in certain countries make the data a more likely target for hackers, criminals, and state-sponsored actors to try to gain access to the organization's data?

An additional perspective on international cloud computing is provided by a report from the BSA (originally the Business Software Alliance, now just the Software Alliance). This is a trade group representing large technology companies, such as Adobe, Apple, Intel, Microsoft, Oracle, Siemens, etc., that looks into violations of intellectual property rights and attempts to break down barriers to competition and foster innovation. With a clear desire to see the global expansion of cloud computing, this report[5] evaluates countries' laws and economics that promote the cloud, including those pertaining to data privacy, security, cybercrime, intellectual property rights, standards and international harmonization of rules, promoting free trade, and its broadband network and information and communication technology (ICT) deployments. It ranked 24 countries that make up 80 percent of the global ICT market. From top to bottom, the countries in this year's rankings are: Japan, Australia, United States, Germany, Singapore, France, The United Kingdom, Korea, Canada, Italy, Spain, Poland, Malaysia, Russia, Mexico, Argentina, India, Turkey, China, South Africa, Indonesia, Brazil, Thailand, and Vietnam.

3.2 European Union

As a collection of 27 countries,[6] the European Union (EU) requires the lawyer to look first to the EU regional directives and then to individual country laws. Two significant areas of laws in the use of cloud computing services are those involving the protection of personal information, which focuses on an EU regional directive, and blocking statutes, which are set up in certain civil law countries to discourage or prohibit responding to litigation-related discovery requests from common law countries. In addition, there are rules emerging that are specific to cloud computing.

Privacy Framework: Data Protection Directive

The EU's 1995 Data Protection Directive (DPD)[7] sets the tone for all data-protection related rules in this region. This model law set a floor of minimum requirements that EU member states must turn into laws at a national level by a certain date. But due to individual statutes in each country, there will be

---

5. BSA, *2013 Global Cloud Computing Scorecard – A Clear Path to Progress* (Mar. 2013).

6. Austria, Belgium, Bulgaria, Cyprus, Czech Republic, Denmark, Estonia, Finland, France, Germany, Greece, Hungary, Ireland, Italy, Latvia, Lithuania, Luxembourg, Malta, The Netherlands, Poland, Portugal, Romania, Slovakia, Slovenia, Spain, Sweden, and the United Kingdom.

7. EU Data Protection Directive, Directive 95/46/EC of the European Parliament and of the Council of 24 October 1995 on the protection of individuals with regard to the processing of personal data and on the free movement of such data.

some differences that organizations must take into account. The DPD also applies to the three other members of the European Economic Area[8] and serves as a model for other countries in Europe, such as Switzerland. Within these countries, data protection authorities (DPAs) are responsible for investigations and the imposition of penalties.[9] The Article 29 Working Party on the Protection of Individuals with regard to the Processing of Personal Data is an independent advisory body[10] that handles questions, provides guidance, and looks into uniform implementation of the DPD.[11]

The DPD applies to commercial processing of "personal data," relating to a natural person ("data subject") identified or identifiable from the data.[12] Processing is defined as "any operation or set of operations which is performed upon personal data, whether or not by automatic means, such as collection, recording, organization, storage, adaptation or alteration, retrieval, consultation, use, disclosure by transmission, dissemination or otherwise making available, alignment or combination, blocking, erasure or destruction."[13] Processing may only be done with unambiguous consent or in the performance of a contract or legal obligation, or when in the data subject's vital interest or the public interest.[14] Sensitive data may require additional restrictions.[15]

Beyond the data subject, to whom the personal information relates, the key roles are the data processors[16] and data controllers.[17] In simple terms, the organization that is a custodian of the personal information and that alone or jointly with others directs the processing of the data is the data controller while an organization and any of its outsourcing subcontractors who cannot control how the processing is performed are the data processors. Data processors are not only required to process the data only as directed by the

---

8. Iceland, Liechtenstein, and Norway.
9. DPD art. 28.
10. *Id.* art. 29.
11. *Id.* art. 30.
12. *Id.* art. 2(a).
13. *Id.* art. 2(b).
14. *Id.* art. 7.
15. *Id.* art. 8.
16. *Id.* art. 2(e).
17. *Id.* art. 2(d).

data controller but to secure it by appropriate "technical and operational measures."[18]

Because the roles of data controller and data processors are not unique and can both apply to the same entity, it is important in the cloud computing context to consider who has which roles, and which role determines compliance obligations, applicable law, and legal liability.[19] CSPs who believe they are only data processors may find that they are considered to be data controllers, if they process personal data. An example of this is the placing of cookies on a user's PC or the processing of log data tracking the individual's activities.[20]

The data controller is primarily responsible for ensuring that the respective data protection laws in each country are complied with.[21] Compliance with the national law is required where "processing takes place" in the local establishment of the controller.[22] Compliance with the local law is also required if there is processing using local equipment but the controller is not established in the territory, unless such processing is only for the purpose of transit of the data through the territory.[23] This processing and equipment may be as simple as leaving a cookie on a user's PC or utilizing Java.[24]

Given the data mobility principle, it is important to understand which national law is applied. The applicable law under the DPD is that of the controller's establishment(s),[25] except that the security of the processing ("appropriate technical and organizational measures to protect personal data") is to be done under the national law of the processor.[26] A UK court ruling that may have impact on cloud computing said the law that should be applied is where data is transmitted from (i.e., the country where the server

---

18. *Id.* art. 17(3).

19. *See* Article 29 Data Protection Working Party, *Opinion 1/2010 on the concepts of "controller" and "processor"* (2010).

20. *See* Article 29 Data Protection Working Party, *Opinion 1/2008 on data protection issues related to search engines* (2008).

21. DPD art. 4.

22. *Id.* art. 4.1(a).

23. *Id.* art. 4.1(c).

24. *See* Article 29 Data Protection Working Party, *Working Paper 56 on determining the international application of EU data protection law to personal data processing on the Internet by non-EU based web sites* (2002).

25. DPD art. 4.

26. *Id.* art. 17(3).

is located), similar to the "emission theory" used in television broadcasting,[27] implying that the law of the jurisdiction of the cloud hosting sites may be implicated instead of the law of the customer in a receiving country.

The controller is responsible for ensuring that personal data is:[28]

- processed fairly and lawfully
- collected for specified, explicit, and legitimate purposes and not further processed in a way incompatible with those purposes
- adequate, relevant, and not excessive
- accurate and up to date
- used to permit identification of data subjects for no longer than is necessary

The rights of data subjects includes notification of both data about the data subject collected from the data subject and from other sources,[29] and the right of access and rectification, erasure, or blocking of not only data but the processing done on that data.[30]

The controller "must implement appropriate technical and organizational measures to protect personal data against accidental or unlawful destruction or accidental loss, alteration, unauthorized disclosure or access, in particular where the processing involves the transmission of data over a network."[31] But importantly for cloud services, the controller must use a processor that provides "sufficient guarantees in respect of the technical security measures and organizational measures"[32] This relationship must utilize a written agreement stating these requirements, including the technical and organizational measures listed above.[33]

---

27. Football Dataco Ltd.. et. al. v. Sportradar GmbH and Sportradar *AG* (2010) EWHC 2911 (Ch).
28. DPD art. 6.
29. *Id*. art. 11-12.
30. *Id*. art. 13.
31. *Id*. art. 17(1).
32. *Id*. art. 17(2).
33. *Id*. art. 17(3)-(4).

The EU is committed to continuing to look at its data protection regime. In a document issued in 2010,[34] the European Commission (EC) highlighted a number of data protection areas that it intended to consider, including: the impact of new technologies, data breach notification (discussed below), protections for children, data subject rights, clarifying consent, widening the definition of sensitive data, data protection rule harmonization, simplified and harmonized controller notification procedures, implementing privacy enhancing technologies, privacy certifications, improving the procedures for international data transfers (discussed next), and adequacy determinations.

In early 2012, the EC issued a draft regulation (it still must go through the legislative process) as an update to and replacement of the DPD.[35] It is being issued in regulation form instead of directive form, so that it may immediately apply in a uniform format to all member states and not have to await enabling legislation in each country. This regulation is intended in part to deal with new technologies. "In particular, cloud computing—where individuals access computer resources remotely, rather than owning them locally—poses new challenges for data protection authorities, as data can and does move from one jurisdiction to another, including outside the EU, in an instant. In order to ensure a continuity of data protection, the rules need to be brought in line with technological developments."[36] It also is supposed to deal with "[t]he current situation—fragmentation and incoherence."[37]

The regulation's provisions require faster reporting of data breaches, direct regulation of data processors, more express-consent requirements, and replacing data controller registration with internal policies, documentation, and external audits. The provisions apply to those processing EU residents' data, regardless of where the data controller is located. They also call for a single DPA for multinational corporations to deal with instead of many,

---

34. *A comprehensive approach on personal data protection in the European Union*, Communication from the Commission to the European Parliament, the Council, the European Economic and Social Committee and the Committee of the Regions (2010).

35. EC, Proposal for a Regulation of the European Parliament and of the Council on the protection of individuals with regard to the processing of personal data and on the free movement of such data (General Data Protection Regulation) (Jan. 25, 2012).

36. EC, How will the EU's reform adapt data protection rules to new technological developments?

37. EC, The Proposed General Data Protection Regulation: The Consistency Mechanism Explained (Feb. 6, 2013).

based on their "main establishment" in Europe. The right to be forgotten requires deletion of published information based on the data subject's request.

The EU's Article 29 Working Party released its opinion on 28 aspects of the new data protection regulation.[38] The Working Party has expressed support for the more precise definitions leading to better harmonization of applicability of the law and therefore freer movement of data. It recognized benefits of greater rights for individuals, greater accountability for data controllers (including the calls for data protection by design and by default), increased legal grounding of data processors data security obligations, and powers for DPAs. It expressed concern that there may not be the same level of protection for individuals if their data is processed by a micro-, small-, or medium-sized business. Besides concerns about definitions and certain political and procedural aspects, the Working Party expressed concern for: exceptions given to public entities, the actual implementation issues of the right to be forgotten (e.g., what if third parties don't honor the request for deletion?) and against profiling, increased accountability (e.g., when data protection impact assessments are required), and data breach (e.g., evaluating the severity of the breach against objective criteria). It further clarified its opinion later in the year.[39]

In the EU, whistleblower programs fall under the data protection regime. The Article 29 Working Party issued guidance about how to assess these programs for compliance with the data protection requirements: legitimacy of whistleblowing systems; application of the principles of data quality and proportionality; provision of clear and complete information about the scheme; rights of the incriminated person; security of processing operations; management of whistleblowing schemes; transfers to third countries; and compliance with notification requirements.[40] The French data protection authority CNIL revised its self-authorization scheme,[41] which now allows

---

38. Article 29 Data Protection Working Party, Opinion 01/2012 on the data protection reform proposals (Mar. 23, 2012).

39. Article 29 Data Protection Working Party, Opinion 08/2012 providing further input on the data protection reform discussions (Oct. 5, 2012).

40. Article 29 Data Protection Working Party, Opinion 1/2006 on the application of EU data protection rules to internal whistleblowing schemes in the fields of accounting, internal accounting controls, auditing matters, fight against bribery, banking and financial crime.

41. Délibération n° 2010-369 du 14 octobre 2010 modifiant l'autorisation unique n° 2005-305 du 8 décembre 2005 n° AU-004 relative aux traitements automatisés de données à caractère

for whistleblowing schemes in finance, accounting, banking, fight against corruption, anti-competitive practices, Japanese Financial Instruments, and Exchange Act[42] compliance and U.S. SOX compliance.

Cross-Border Data Transfers

Chapter IV of the DPD addresses personal data transfers to third countries. With data mobility, this is a key issue for cloud computing. In general, transfers to third countries of personal data are only allowed if that country provides for an "adequate level of protection."[43] There are a number of exceptions to this, such as when a data subject's unambiguous consent is obtained, performance of a contract or legal obligation requires transfer, or a transfer is in the data subject's vital interest or the public interest.[44] Transfers to third countries may also occur if there are sufficient safeguards, such as provided for in contractual provisions,[45] including standard contractual clauses.[46] As only a dozen countries have been found to date to have adequate levels of protection,[47] this contractual exception has been seen as a critical component for multinational corporations to transfer the data they hold outside of the EU as needed.

Beyond agreements needing DPA approval as to the adequate levels of protection, two types of methods may be employed. One is Model Contract Clauses and the other Binding Corporate Rules (BCR). BCR are an alternative to signing agreements each time data is transferred, are used for transfers within the organization, have to be specifically tailored to the organization, and must follow the DPD's principles. The Model Contract Clauses bind all signatories to the agreement and may require approval of the respective local DPA but can be used for transfers to third countries outside an organization. There are two types of these model clauses: those for transfers

---

personnel mis en œuvre dans le cadre de dispositifs d'alerte professionnelle.
42. Japan, Financial Instruments and Exchange Act (Act No. 25 of 1948).
43. DPD art. 25(1).
44. *Id.* art. 26(1).
45. *Id.* art. 26(2).
46. *Id.* art. 26(4).
47. Andorra, Argentina, Australia, Canada, Faeroe Islands, Guernsey, Isle of Man, Israel, Jersey, New Zealand, Switzerland, and Uruguay.

between controllers (in two sets)[48] and clauses for transfers between controllers and processors.[49] These latter model clauses cover the obligations of the parties, rights of the data subjects to proceed against the data controller, the data processor, and any sub-processors for any breaches of their obligations causing harm to the data subjects, and the right to choose venue, mediation, and termination. When utilizing this mechanism to transfer data to third countries, the data controller remains liable to the data subject but the data processor is liable to the data controller for the performance of the sub-processor's obligations.

There is one other exception, which is use of the Safe Harbour Privacy Principles. The EU has an agreement with the U.S.[50] (Switzerland has a similar one), which organizations regulated by the U.S. Federal Trade Commission (FTC) or Department of Transportation can join. An organization must do two things to join the safe harbor; claim that it adheres to and complies with the Privacy Principles (e.g., notice, choice, onward transfer, security, data integrity, access, enforcement) in its publicly available privacy policy, and self-certify with the Department of Commerce that it complies with the Principles.[51] The former clause allows the FTC to enforce the Principles under section 5 of the FTC Act for unfair or deceptive trade practices.

The EU, represented by the Article 29 Working Party and the Asia Pacific Economic Cooperation (APEC), is looking into how data flows between Europe and the Asia/Pacific region could work.[52] A reconciliation between

---

48. Commission Decision of 15 June 2001 on standard contractual clauses for the transfer of personal data to third countries, under Directive 95/46/EC; Commission Decision of 27 December 2004 amending Decision 2001/497/EC as regards the introduction of an alternative set of standard contractual clauses for the transfer of personal data to third countries.

49. Commission Decision on standard contractual clauses for the transfer of personal data to processors established in third countries under Directive 96/46/EC of the European Parliament and of the Council (2010).

50. Commission Decision 520/2000/EC of 26 July 2000 pursuant to Directive 95/46 of the European Parliament and of the Council on the adequate protection of personal data provided by the Safe Harbour Privacy Principles and related Frequently Asked Questions issued by the US Department of Commerce.

51. European Commission Staff Working Document, *The implementation of Commission Decision 520/2000/EC on the adequate protection of personal data provided by the Safe Harbour privacy Principles and related Frequently Asked Questions* issued by the US Department of Commerce.

52. CNIL, *International data transfers: towards an articulation of data flow systems between Europe and the Asia-Pacific area?* (Feb. 21, 2013).

the EU's BCR approach and APEC's Cross-Border Privacy Rules (CBPR, discussed in the following section) is underway. As both systems are based on organizational codes of conduct and a priori approval by regulators or approved agents, a set of tools for multinational companies to utilize in mapping BCR-CBPR is planned.

Information Security and Data Breach Notification

DPD Article 17 more specifically states that the risk-adjusted technical and organizational measures that must be taken are to protect the personal data against "accidental or unlawful destruction or accidental loss, alteration, unauthorized disclosure or access, in particular where the processing involves the transmission of data over a network, and against all other unlawful forms of processing." The data controller must ensure that the data processor follows these principles. The e-Privacy Directive[53] supplements the DPD by requiring public electronic communication services to similarly take appropriate risk-adjusted measures. Encryption is specifically mentioned as one of the potential safeguards.[54] National laws may have specific security requirements. For example, there are specific information security controls specified in the revised German Federal Data Protection Act, including a preference for encryption.[55]

While there is no EU-level data breach notice requirement, some DPAs believe this may be inferred from the notice principle. The e-Privacy Directive requires notice of the risks of a breach.[56] The e-Privacy Directive, as amended, requires communications service providers to report data security breaches to the applicable national authority and if a likelihood of adverse impact on the personal data or privacy of a subscriber exists (i.e., it is encrypted or otherwise made unintelligible), the communications service provider must

---

53. Directive 2002/58/EC of the European Parliament and of the Council of 12 July 2002 concerning the processing of personal data and the protection of privacy in the electronic communications sector (Directive on privacy and electronic communications).

54. *Id.* at Whereas (20).

55. Germany, Annex, Federal Data Protection Act (BDSG) last amended by Article 1 of the Act of 14 August 2009 (Federal Law Gazette I, p. 2814).

56. *Id.* art. 4(2).

also notify the affected subscriber.[57] The Article 29 Working Party has recommended expansion to all sectors and types of data.[58]

Blocking Statutes

Twenty-seven (27) members of the EU/EEA plus Switzerland have joined the Hague Evidence Convention.[59] Certain countries in the EU also have blocking statutes. For example, France has a blocking statute[60] that prohibits communications of a commercial or technical nature to foreign public officials[61] and communications of a commercial or technical nature for use in foreign judicial proceedings,[62] both subject to international agreements, such as the Hague Convention.[63] This blocks the effect of foreign procedural discovery rules locally and forces those involved in litigation in common law countries to use the Hague procedure. There are also blocking statutes in Switzerland,[64] the United Kingdom, the Netherlands, Norway, Sweden, and Belgium. U.S. courts tend not to heed blocking statutes,[65] as demonstrated by repeated court decisions ordering discovery in spite of European laws that one party claimed blocked the transfer of such data for use in common

---

57. Directive 2009/136/EC of the European Parliament and the Council of 25 November 2009 amending Directive 2002/22/EC on universal service and users' rights relating to electronic communications networks and services, Directive 2002/58/EC concerning the processing of personal data and the protection of privacy in the electronic communications sector and Regulation (EC) No. 2006/2004 on cooperation between national authorities responsible, art. 2.4(c).

58. Article 29 Data Protection Working Party, Working Document 01/2011 on the current EU personal data breach framework and recommendations for future policy developments (Apr. 5, 2011).

59. Bulgaria, Cyprus, Czech Republic, Denmark, Estonia, Finland, France, Germany, Greece, Hungary, Iceland, Italy, Latvia, Lichtenstein, Lithuania, Luxembourg, Malta, Netherlands, Norway, Poland, Portugal, Romania, Slovakia, Slovenia, Spain, Sweden, and the United Kingdom.

60. France, Loi 80-538 of July 16, 1980.

61. *Id.* art. 1.

62. *Id.* art. 1-*bis*.

63. Hague Convention of 18 March 1970 on the Taking of Evidence Abroad in Civil and Commercial Matters.

64. Switzerland, Penal Code arts. 271, 273.

65. Thomas Shaw, *International E-Discovery – U.S. Litigation Exposure for Asia/Pacific Corporations*, EDDE Journal (newsletter. of the ABA Section. Science & Technology Law) Vol. 1 Issue 1 (Winter 2010).

law proceedings,[66] and despite ABA calls upon courts in the United States to give more credence to foreign data protection laws.[67]

Cloud Computing Specific Rules

Certain rules that focus only on cloud computing are emerging. For example, a German DPA in the state of Schleswig-Holstein issued a legal opinion that personal data should not be sent to the cloud without more stringent safeguards.[68] This opinion stated that CSPs located outside the EU, even those located in countries determined adequate under the DPD, were not lawful data importers unless they utilize one of DPD's mechanisms for transfer to a third country, such as Model Contract Clauses and BCRs (even though BCRs are typically used within a corporate group), employed in tandem with compliance with section 11 of the German Federal Data Protection Act. Under this view, the safe harbors such as the one between the U.S. and the EU would also violate the law without these further requirements.

The Article 29 Working Party has issued its opinion on cloud computing in regards to the DPD and the e-Privacy Directive.[69] It expressed concern with the lack of control of personal data, the transparency of subsequent processing of the data, and the transfer of data outside the protection of these directives. It identified the cloud consumer as fulfilling the role of data controller in most cases and the CSP the role of data processor, and if either or both is located in the EEA, then the EU's data protection regime applies. The Working Party's opinion is that consent by the data controller is required for the data processor to subcontract any work in the cloud. It also requires that the data processor facilitate the data controller in delivering all rights of the data subjects and opines in the proposed regulation

---

66. *See e.g.*, Trueposition, Inc. v. LM Ericsson Telephone Co., Case No. 11-4574 (E.D. Pa. 2012), Crystal Cruises, Inc. v. Rolls-Royce PLC, Case No 10-24607 (S.D. Fla. 2011), Metso Minerals Industries, Inc. v. Johnson Crushers Int'l, Inc., Case No. 10-C-0951 (E.D. Wis. 2011), In re SNP Boat Service SA, Case No. 453 BR 446 (Bankr. S.D. Fla. 2011), AccessData Corp. v. Alste Technologies GmbH, Case No. 2:08cv569 (D. Utah 2010).

67. ABA House of Delegates, Resolution 103 (Feb. 6. 2012).

68. Cloud Computing und Datenschutz, Independent Center for Privacy Protection of the State of Schleswig-Holstein (Jun. 18, 2010).

69. Article 29 Data Protection Working Party, Opinion 05/2012 on Cloud Computing (July 1, 2012).

that a data processor who does not follow the data controller's instructions becomes a co-data controller, with those inherent responsibilities. Various European DPAs (e.g., Germany, France, Italy, UK) have also issued guidance on cloud computing.[70]

The Article 29 Working Party has also suggested (its work is advisory and influential but not mandatory) to using the concept of binding corporate rules for CSPs (as data processors). In much the same way it developed BCRs for data controllers to have an international transfer of personal data, "BCR for Processors aim to frame international transfers of personal data that are originally processed by the company as Data Processor according to the external instructions of Data Controllers (such as outsourcing activities)." To do so, it has provided the processor BCRs factors for CSPs.[71] Some of these include that the CSP must grant third-party rights to data subjects to enforce the agreement if the data controller disappears, that the service agreement must be binding on the data controller, that the application form (to the DPA) explain how the BCR is binding on the members of the CSP group and on employees, that the CSP must accept liability for its members outside the EU or external subcontractors, that the CSP has the burden of proof for breaches of the BCR and must clearly state the relationship of national laws to the BCR.

Activities

There are a variety of national and regional efforts that have been started to push cloud computing at the government level in the EU, such as the G-Cloud (government cloud) in the UK, Trusted Cloud in Germany, Andromede in France, and EuroCloud (pan-European business cloud network). There is also the work of ENISA[72] (see Chapter 5), ETSI, and the EU's

---

70. Datenschutzbeauftragten des Bundes und der Länder, *Datenschutzkonforme Gestaltung und Nutzung von Cloud-Computing* (Sept. 29, 2011) and *Orientierungshilfe – Cloud Computing* (Sept. 26, 2011); CNIL, *Recommandations pour les entreprises qui envisagent de souscrire à des services de Cloud computing*; Garante della Privacy, *Cloud Computing - Proteggere i dati per non cadere dalle nuvole*; ICO, *Guidance on the use of cloud computing, ver. 1.1.* (Oct. 2, 2012).

71. Article 29 Data Protection Working Party, Working Document 02/2012 setting up a table with the elements and principles to be found in Processor Binding Corporate Rules (June 6, 2012).

72. ENISA, *Security & Resilience in Government Clouds* (Jan. 2011).

Digital Agenda[73] Commissioner, plus vision documents for cloud use in Europe.[74] There have been a series of projects funded by the EU related to cloud computing, including TClouds (developing advanced cloud infrastructure), RESORVOIR (software to make available unused capacity), OPTIMIS (SMEs cloud use), and Conrail (making any company a potential CSP) projects. But the direction is not always toward the expansive use of cloud computing by the public sector. For example, the House of Lords in the United Kingdom recently slowed down a plan to let government agencies combine voter registration databases in the cloud, seeing it as too risky for now.[75]

To energize cloud computing at the government level, as part of its Digital Agenda, the EC rolled out the European Cloud Partnership (ECP) as part of the European Cloud Strategy, projecting a positive impact from cloud computing of up to €1 trillion by 2020 and the creation of 4 million jobs.[76] To achieve a Digital Single Market, several problems had to be addressed, including a fragmented legal regime, contractual uncertainties, and uncertain or missing standards. Three key actions are identified for the EC to launch:

- Creation of cloud standards and certification of cloud service to demonstrate their adherence to these standards
- Development of model terms for use by "professional cloud users," model terms and conditions for small firms and end-consumers of cloud services, and a code of conduct for CSPs
- Promotion of public sector procurement (but not building the infrastructure) to influence interoperability, standards, competitiveness, data protection, and service levels by forming the ECP at the member-state level and bringing the size of such massive spending power to bear on influencing the cloud

73. *A Digital Agenda for Europe,* Communication from the Commission to the European Parliament, the Council, the European Economic and Social Committee and the Committee of the Regions (2010).

74. EC Experts Group, *The Future of Cloud Computing – Opportunities for European Cloud Computing Beyond 2010.*

75. *European Governments Staying Out of the Cloud,* N.Y. TIMES (Nov. 20, 2012).

76. *Unleashing the Potential of Cloud Computing in Europe,* Communication from the Commission to the European Parliament, the Council, the European Economic and Social Committee and the Committee of the Regions (Sept. 27, 2012).

The ECP will be run by a steering committee, which has already begun to meet.[77] In addition, the European Data Protection Supervisor has weighed in on this direction.[78]

3.3 Asia/Pacific

Asia, unlike Europe, does not have a broad regional directive requiring member states to enact local data privacy laws conforming to certain principles. Instead, Asia has the APEC Privacy Framework,[79] which provides voluntary guidance to assist the passage of local statutes. So while organizations must consider the specifics of each country's statutes (just like they must for individual European country statutes) and how these laws protect local information, this common framework source means that Asian privacy laws are more similar than dissimilar, at least with respect to the privacy principles they follow. In a few cases, they are also heavily influenced by European privacy laws.

Privacy Framework: APEC

Asia-Pacific Economic Cooperation (APEC) is a forum for facilitating economic growth, trade, cooperation and investment in the Asia/Pacific region. The APEC member countries[80] have endorsed a framework for the use of personal data based on a single set of principles. The framework encourages "the development of appropriate information privacy protections ensuring the free flow of information in the Asia/Pacific region." It is generally consistent with the OECD's Guidelines[81] covering: collection limitation, data quality, purpose specification, use limitation, security safeguards, openness, individual participation and accountability.

---

77. Report from the European Cloud Partnership Steering Board meeting (Nov. 19, 2012).
78. Opinion of the European Data Protection Supervisor on the Commission's Communication on "Unleashing the potential of Cloud Computing in Europe" (Nov. 16, 2012).
79. APEC Secretariat, *APEC Privacy Framework*, 2005.
80. Australia, Brunei Darussalam, Canada, Chile, People's Republic of China, Hong Kong, Indonesia, Japan, Republic of Korea, Malaysia, Mexico, New Zealand, Papua New Guinea, Peru, the Philippines, Russia, Singapore, Chinese Taipei (Taiwan), Thailand, the United States, and Vietnam.
81. OECD. Guidelines on the Protection of Privacy and Transborder Flows of Personal Data (1980).

The nine APEC-endorsed Privacy Principles are as follows:

- *Preventing Harm* (P1): Individuals should be protected from the wrongful collection and misuse of their personal information.
- *Notice* (P2): The controllers of personal information should provide clear statements about their practices and policies, before or at time of collection.
- *Collection Limitation* (P3): Information should be lawfully collected and only if relevant to the purpose of collection.
- *Use of Personal Information* (P4): The only exceptions to the use of the information being different than the purpose of collection is if consent is given by the individual, or to provide a product or service the individual requested, or if required by law.
- *Choice* (P5): Individuals should be given a choice on the collection, use, and disclosure of their personal information.
- *Integrity of Personal Information* (P6): Data should be accurate, complete, and up to date.
- *Security Safeguards* (P7): Controls should prevent unauthorized data access, loss, use, modification, or disclosure and be proportional to these risks and information sensitivity.
- *Access and Correction* (P8): Individuals should be able to access and correct their personal information, unless the burden of doing so is disproportionate to the risk, for legal or corporate compliance reasons, or to avoid compromising another individual's privacy.
- *Accountability* (P9): The information controller is accountable and must ensure personal information transferred to a third party is protected in accordance with these principles.

There are a number of countries in the Asia/Pacific region with comprehensive data protection statutes but also many countries that don't take such a comprehensive approach.

Countries with Comprehensive Data Protection Statutes

Ten of the countries and territories in the Asia/Pacific region have express data protection statutes: Australia,[82] New Zealand,[83] Hong Kong SAR,[84] Taiwan,[85] South Korea,[86] Japan,[87] Macau SAR,[88] Malaysia,[89] the Philippines,[90] and Singapore[91] (which previously had only a voluntary code[92]). All adopt most if not all of the nine APEC Privacy Principles, with the exception of the preventing harm principle. But there a number of local protections added. There are principles having to do with the retention of data contained in the laws of New Zealand, Hong Kong, Singapore, Taiwan, Malaysia and Macau. Special controls for sensitive information are required in Australia, Malaysia, Macau, the Philippines, and South Korea. Controls over the disposal of data are required in the Philippines and Australia and over unique user identification numbers in Australia and New Zealand. Macau, with its European-influenced statute, additionally has principles for automatic decision making, combining of personal data, and professional secrecy. While most statutes are widely applicable, those in South Korea and Taiwan were historically industry-sector specific, but have been widened to be more inclusive.[93]

---

82. Australia, Privacy Act (1988), as amended by the Privacy Amendment (Enhancing Privacy Protections) Act (2012).

83. New Zealand, Privacy Act (1993).

84. Hong Kong, Personal Data (Privacy) Ordinance (1995), as amended by Personal Data (Privacy) (Amendment) Ordinance (2012).

85. Taiwan, Computer-Processed Personal Data Protection Law (1995), as amended by the Personal Data Protection Act (2010).

86. Republic of Korea, Act on Promotion of Information and Communication Network Utilization and Information Protection (2001), as amended by the Act on the Protection of Personal Data (2011) and the Act on Promotion of Information and Communications Network Utilization and Information Protection (Amendment) (2012).

87. Japan, Act on the Protection of Personal Information (2005).

88. Macao SAR, Personal Data Protection Act (2005).

89. Malaysia, Personal Data Protection Act (2010).

90. Philippines, An Act Protecting Individual Personal Information in the Information and Communications Systems in the Government and Private Sector, Creating for this Purpose a National Data Protection Commission, and for Other Purposes (2012).

91. Singapore, Personal Data Protection Act (2012).

92. Singapore, Model Data Protection Code for the Private Sector (2003).

93. For a more detailed look at each country's privacy principles, *see* Thomas Shaw, *Asia-Pacific Data Privacy Laws: Model Corporate Privacy Principles*, The Privacy Advisor (Mar. 2010).

Countries without Comprehensive Data Protection Statutes

For those Asian countries that do not have a comprehensive data protection statute, privacy is found in constitutional rights to privacy and Internet-related laws. For example, India has a constitutional basis for privacy protection and also, along with Indonesia and Vietnam, has privacy provisions in its e-commerce laws. Mongolia has had the Law on Personal Secrecy (Privacy Law) since 1995. Thailand has had a privacy law since 1997 that applies only to the government. In addition, a number of these countries have had privacy laws that have been drawn up and submitted to their legislatures over the past decade and are in various stages of being approved. As will be discussed below, there are commitments from some countries to complete privacy legislation based on sub-regional forums in the next several years. The following is a brief look at the privacy protections in some countries in Asia that do not have comprehensive data protection statutes at this time.

China

China does not have a comprehensive data protection law but provides protection through a large number of sources, including national and provincial statutes, industry regulations, and constitutional protections. There are various privacy protections in China's Constitution,[94] in criminal privacy sanctions,[95] new tort laws,[96] civil statutes covering privacy of personality and reputation,[97] provincial consumer protection regulations,[98] and sectoral regulations (covering e-banking,[99] outsourcing, employees,[100] management of computer information networks,[101] and the provision of email services[102]). For information security, regulations enacted in 2009 require companies in China providing outsourcing services to implement security measures to

---

94. China, Constitution, arts. 38, 40.

95. China, Seventh Amendment to the Criminal Law (2009).

96. China, Tortious Liability Law (2009).

97. China, Civil Code of the P.R.C.

98. More than a dozen provinces out of the 31 in China have enacted such statutes.

99. China, Banking Regulatory Commission, Measures Governing Electronic Banking (2006).

100. China, Administrative Regulations for Employment Services and Employment (2008).

101. China, Computer Information Network and Internet Security, Protection and Management Regulations (1997).

102. China, Measures for the Administration of Internet E-mail Services (2006).

protect confidential information received in the course of providing those services. The e-banking regulations require the use of firewalls, antivirus software, intrusion prevention, encryption technologies for confidentiality, and identity management.

China has from time to time floated information security guidelines in a draft format for comment. These draft guidelines[103] would apply protections to the processing of personal electronic information. The specifics include the right to receive notification and information concerning the nature of the processing, the ability to opt-out, prohibit use, or delete data, the rights to access and correction, confidentiality, and limitations on collection and use, including informed consent and not collecting non-relevant sensitive information. The transfer of personal information to other entities (e.g., outsourcing) will require data subject consent (there are not the usual exceptions for processing related to the requested service or for the benefit of the data subject). International data transfers outside the country are in essence prohibited unless there is a law allowing such. This latter principle obviously is a cause for concern in a public cloud environment if adopted as is and literally enforced.

China has also promulgated regulations regarding the commercial banks' use of credit cards. These include privacy rules, such as the requirement for banks to safeguard client information, to not disclose such information or use it for any secondary purposes such as marketing, to ensure that whole card numbers are not printed or otherwise disclosed, to ensure that card application information is protected and destroyed, and that in general minimum information is used where possible and not retained but deleted as necessary.[104] Banks also face additional rules to protect client data, including not off-shoring personal information of a financial nature.[105]

---

103. China, Information Security Technology - Guidelines for Personal Information Protection (2011).

104. China, Measures for the Supervision and Administration of the Credit Card Businesses of Commercial Banks (2011).

105. China, Notice Urging Banking Institutions to Protect Personal Financial Information (2011).

The Chinese Ministry of Industry and Information Technology has issued new rules for ISPs.[106] These rules cover standard privacy principles not covered comprehensively under the law, such as data subject consent before collection, notice, limitations on secondary usage, breach notice, security safeguards, and restrictions on disclosures to third parties and collections. In the absence of a comprehensive national privacy statute, provincial statutes in China take on greater significance, much like they do in the United States if there is no federal law. The Chinese province of Jiangsu has passed a new privacy regulation that is not industry-sector specific.[107] The requirement for private sector organizations is to obtain consent for the legal collection of personal data and to explain how it will be processed. The organizations must then obey these limitations and not disclose data to third parties or be subject to a variety of enforcement actions. Public sector agencies should not re-collect the same information.

At the end of 2012, a committee of the National People's Congress approved enhanced privacy rules for online users' data.[108] These included many of the standard privacy protections found elsewhere, such service provider identifying the purpose, scope, and means of collection of data, the data then only being used by the service provider for those purposes, consent from the data subject to a legal collection, sufficient security protections of the data subject's personal information, no selling or divulging of personal information, breach response and reporting to the government, and the right to delete personally identifiable information. Perhaps conversely, online users must utilize their true names in dealing with the service provider.

India

The privacy law has changed in India but is still somewhat unsettled. Historically, a right to privacy is found in India's Constitution[109] and protected

---

106. China, Ministry of Industry and Information Technology, Several Regulations on Standardizing Market Order for Internet Information Services (2011).

107. China, Jiangsu Province, Regulation of Information Technology (2011).

108. China, Decision of the Standing Committee of the National People's Congress to Strengthen the Protection of Internet Data (Dec. 2012).

109. India, Constitution art. 21.

under laws dealing with contracts,[110] criminal acts,[111] intellectual property,[112] civil rights,[113] and information technology. The Information Technology Act[114] prohibits unauthorized access to and theft of data from computers and networks, and addresses computer crime, hacking, damage of source code, breach of confidentiality, and viewing of pornographic material. With the lack of a privacy law, the outsourcing industry had set up best practices in data privacy and related contractual provisions to comply with the necessary privacy laws in other countries.

In 2011, the Indian Ministry of Communications and Information Technology issued rules that cover reasonable privacy (including sensitive data) and information security practices for data processed inside India that are in some cases more stringent than those of countries that might be sending data to India via outsourcing arrangements.[115] The privacy principles include limitations on personal data collection and use, rights of access, correction, and notice, and transfer and written consent requirements for sensitive information. These apply to any corporation that "collects, receives, possesses, stores, deals or handles" personal information.[116] These new obligations require a privacy policy, set limits on the collection and use of data, restrict the processing of sensitive personal data (including medical, biometric and financial information and passwords but not political or religious affiliation) and require consent before such data can be processed. It also allows for data subject access and correction, requires consent before disclosure to third parties (with the usual exceptions). It allows international transfers of sensitive data to recipients with at least the same level of data protection, requires notice to data subjects, and requires a reasonable information security program, including data breach response procedures. Compliance with ISO 27001 would be deemed a reasonable information security program.

---

110. India, Contract Act, No. 9 (1872).

111. India, Penal Code Act, No. 45 (1860).

112. India, Copyright Act (1957).

113. India, Specific Relief Act, No. 47 (1963).

114. India, Information Technology Act, No. 21 (2000).

115. India, Ministry of Communications and Information Technology, Information Technology (Reasonable Security Practices and Procedures and Sensitive Personal Data or Information) Rules (2011).

116. India, Information Technology (Reasonable Security Practices and Procedures and Sensitive Personal Data or Information) Rules 2011.

With the difficulty of getting a comprehensive data protection law passed, these rules were promulgated by the Indian government as regulations under the Information Technology Act of 2000. There are several points to note about these new rules. One is that they apply to private sector corporations, but not the government. Another is that, with the exception of sensitive data, data collection is not required to be lawful. The data retention limitations/deletion requirements only apply to sensitive data. And there is no requirement for the collector of data to keep it updated. These rules apply to data processed in India, even if it is not about Indian citizens or if it is collected and initially processed outside India.

Later clarifications were issued regarding who is subject to these rules.[117] The rules apply to both organizations ("body corporate") and persons within India. Any such organization that is doing processing under contract for either a local or overseas entity is not subject to rule 5, which restricts data collection and processing by requiring notice, disallowing secondary processing, and limiting processing to the purpose of collection. It is also not subject to rule 6, which places limits on sensitive data, requiring written consent before processing such information and limiting the duration of its retention. But an organization contracting directly with a data subject (as opposed to a legal entity for whom it collected the information) is subject to the rules.

The Ministry has also issued other rules covering the duties of intermediaries in privacy and security practices, including security incidents, and also information sharing with the government as required.[118]

---

117. India, Clarification on Information Technology (Reasonable Security Practices and Procedures and Sensitive Personal Data or Information) Rules 2011 Under Section 43A of the Information Technology Act, 2000, Ministry of Communications & Information Technology (Dept. of Information Technology) Press Information Bureau, Government of India, Bhadra 2, 1933, (Aug. 24, 2011).

118. India Ministry of Communications and Information Technology, Information Technology (Intermediaries Guidelines) Rules (2011).

Indonesia

There is a right to privacy under the Indonesian Constitution[119] and several statutes, including those dealing with human rights,[120] e-commerce law,[121] and medical rights,[122] penalize disclosure of confidential information.[123]

Russia

The Constitution of the Russian Federation provides a right of privacy.[124] The law "On Personal Data," after some revisions, requires registration and encrypting of personal information in databases[125] and there are other protections under the labor code.[126] Under these laws, international data transfers must be to countries with adequate safeguards unless the consent of the data subject is obtained, similar to safeguards required for data transfers within Russia.

Thailand

The Constitution of Thailand protects the right of privacy[127] and the government is subject to the Official Information Act (Private Sector).[128] This requires the implementation of appropriate safeguards to protect personal information stored in government agency systems. There are also protections under the regulations of telecom providers.[129]

---

119. Indonesia, Constitution, art. 28 G(1).

120. Indonesia, Human Rights Law, No. 39 (1999).

121. Indonesia, Electronic Information and Electronic Transactions Law, No. 11 (2008).

122. Indonesia, art. 2 of Act No. 6 (1963).

123. Indonesia, Criminal Code (art. 322.1).

124. Russian Federation, Constitution (1993), arts. 23-24.

125. Russia, Federal Law No. 152-F (2006).

126. Russia, Labor Code.

127. Thailand, Constitution (2007), Art. 35.

128. Thailand, Official Information Act (1997).

129. Notification of the National Telecommunications Commission Re Measures to Protect Telecommunications Subscribers, Data Privacy, Privacy Rights and Freedom of Communications (2001).

Vietnam

The civil code of Vietnam provides some limited privacy protections.[130] The electronic transactions law[131] provides protection for information on private and personal affairs. The IT law,[132] as supplemented,[133] does establish some information security requirements. A consumer protection law provides for the safeguarding of consumer information.[134]

Although the countries without comprehensive data protection laws will not be discussed further in this chapter, those that are members of ASEAN (Indonesia, Thailand, Vietnam) have made a commitment to harmonize their data protection laws by 2015,[135] so it is important for organizations to look for new national statutes implementing the APEC Privacy Framework.

Cross-Border Data Transfers

APEC has created "pathfinder" initiatives to promote trust and facilitate cross-border information flows. One such effort is Cross-Border Privacy Rules (CBPR); the rules are created by involved business parties and must comply not only with the APEC Privacy Framework but also with any applicable local privacy statutes. National privacy commissioners, non-regulator government agencies, and privacy trustmarks help to ensure that organizations comply with their privacy commitments.[136] Another outcome of this project is the APEC Cross-Border Privacy Enforcement Arrangement,[137] which is a framework for the voluntary sharing of information and assistance among the APEC Privacy Enforcement Authorities.

The leaders of APEC have endorsed the CBPR to both enhance the privacy of consumers and promote multi-country information flow and privacy regime interoperability.[138] While not privacy rules in themselves, this framework provides a method by which an organization can be certified by an accountability agent. The accountability agent will compare the

---

130. Vietnam, Law No. 33 (2005).
131. Vietnam, Law on E-Transactions, No. 51 (2005).
132. Vietnam, Law on Information Technology, No. 66 (2006).
133. Vietnam, Decree No. 63/2007/ND-CP.
134. Vietnam, Law on Protection of Consumer Interests, No. 59 (2010).
135. ASEAN, Roadmap for Integration of e-ASEAN Sector (2004).
136. APEC, *Data Privacy Pathfinder Projects Implementation Work Plan* (2008).
137. APEC, *Cross-border Privacy Enforcement Arrangement, Fact Sheet* (2010).
138. APEC Ministers, Ministerial Statements (Nov. 11, 2011).

organization's cross-border privacy rules against a baseline, and by being certified, the organization commits to following those rules. If it does not, it can be found in violation of a nation's privacy regime. There may be certain other existing privacy regimes whose followers may automatically be certified under the CBPR framework. The CBPR is not a replacement of the national privacy laws, only an additional commitment, albeit one that may operate as a higher (or lower) standard than local laws. Member states who utilize the CBPR need to be part of the previously established Cooperation Arrangement for Cross-border Privacy Enforcement.

Australia

Rather than the prior law's trans-border data flows, the amended act is concerned with the disclosure of personal information of Australians outside the country. Disclosing entities are required to ensure that the overseas recipient complies with the Australian Privacy Principles (APP) or is subject to a law that is substantially similar overall to the APP. There are exceptions, such as if consent is obtained or for performance of a contract that the individual is party to or has an interest in.

New Zealand

The Privacy Commissioner is now authorized to stop outbound transfers of personal information.[139] This prevents New Zealand from becoming an intermediary for data transferred from countries relying on New Zealand's safeguards that are subsequently transferred on to third countries with inadequate safeguards. The Act does not explicitly address cross-border enforcement cooperation arrangements. This law provides that personal information must be protected by security safeguards that are reasonable in the circumstances. It specifically requires government agencies handling personal information to ensure that the data are protected against loss, unauthorized access, use, or modification by implementing reasonable security safeguards.

---

139. New Zealand, Privacy (Cross-border Information) Amendment Act 2010, Pub. Act 2010 No. 113.

Hong Kong

Prohibition against transfer of personal data to place outside Hong Kong except in specified circumstances (art. 33): Personal data may not be transferred outside Hong Kong unless there is a reasonable belief in a substantially similar law, with exceptions including consent. This article has never come into force.

Taiwan

International Data Transfers (art. 21): Data transfers may be restricted by the government if the receiving country does not adequately protect the data subject's personal data (or involves certain national interests).

Korea

There are no stated statutory restrictions.

Japan

Restriction of Provision to a Third Party (art. 23): Personal data cannot be provided to third parties, except if the individual consents or for the individual's safety, children's welfare, public health, or compliance with laws or when the individual can opt-out. Outsourcing personal data that achieves the purpose (e.g., payroll outsourcing) is not considered to be provision to a third party.

Macao

Transfer of Data outside Macao (arts. 19-20): Data transfer must be only to jurisdictions that have appropriate levels of protection, unless consent is given or for performance of a contract, or it is in the public interest or the vital interests of the individual.

Malaysia

Transfer of Personal Data to Place outside Malaysia (art. 129): The transfer is prohibited unless approved by the government, which will consider whether there are substantially similar laws or controls in place. There are a number of exceptions, very similar to the exceptions in the EU's DPD.

Philippines

Extraterritorial Application (sec. 5): The provisions in the act apply to wherever personal information of Philippine citizens is processed if there are other links by the processor to the Philippines.

Singapore

Transfer of personal data outside Singapore (sec. 26): Personal data is not to be transferred outside the country unless it is to a location where there are similar protections.

Information Security and Data Breach Notification

A number of Asian countries have implemented information security provisions in their laws in accordance with the APEC Privacy Framework.[140] In Hong Kong SAR, the companies that control the collection, holding, processing, or use of personal data have to take "all practicable steps to protect the personal data held against unauthorized or accidental access, processing, erasure or other use."[141] Taiwan's initial data protection law had the requirement to appoint someone to prevent personal data from being subject to "burglary, alteration, destruction, extinction, or disclosure."[142]

South Korea's older law requires only that those corporations handling personal data take the "requisite technical and administrative steps."[143] A newer Korean consumer protection law requires that those corporations handling financial transactions abide by regulator standards for IT "manpower, facilities and electronic apparatus used to transmit or process electronic financial transaction information."[144] Japanese law requires corporations holding personal information to take the "necessary and proper measures" to exercise control over that data, which are set out by the regulatory agencies overseeing the various industries.[145] Australian law requires "reasonable steps" to protect personal information being held and to destroy or de-identify per-

140. APEC Secretariat, *APEC Privacy Framework*, 2005.

141. Hong Kong SAR, Personal Data (Privacy) Ordinance (1995), DPP 4.

142. Taiwan, Computer-Processed Personal Data Protection Law (1995), art. 17.

143. Republic of Korea, Act on Promotion of Information and Communication Network Utilization and Information Protection (2001), art. 28.

144. Republic of Korea, Electronic Financial Transactions Act (2006), art. 21.

145. Japan, Act on the Protection of Personal Information (2005), art. 20.

sonal information that is no longer needed.[146] New Zealand, Macao, and other countries have similar statutory security requirements, but Macao actually goes further in laying special requirements for controls over sensitive data.[147]

Due to the lack of specifics in the statutes, what is acceptable security practice is not certain, but judicial decisions in the region provide some insight. For example, in Hong Kong, customer data held by an insurance company was moved by its insurance agent from the company's server to a server at the agent's house. The commissioner held that the company's "alleged controls were substantially inadequate to guard against unauthorized access, transfer, storing and taking away" of customer data.[148] In another Hong Kong case, customer service terminals of a telecommunications provider customer were facing a public area and it was determined that the procedures used by the telecom provider did not prevent third parties from accessing customers' personal data, and thus failed to take all reasonably practicable steps to ensure that personal data were protected against unauthorized or accidental access by unrelated parties.[149]

In one Australian case, customers' personal information from Internet orders was visible to other Internet users.[150] The investigation found that the online software used by the company did not have appropriate security and that the company did not have adequate security testing, policies, and standards. The commissioner noted that reasonable security safeguards could include: physical security measures, secure storage and destruction facilities, computer and network security, intrusion and email interception security, and security protocols on staff access to and handling of personal information. While the company's security was not deemed adequate to protection the personal information, which included sensitive health information, it did respond rapidly to close down its webstore and address the breach.

---

146. Australia, Privacy Act as amended by the Privacy Amendment (Enhancing Privacy Protections) Act, APP 11.

147. Macao SAR, Personal Data Protection Act (2005), principle 16.

148. Hong Kong, PCPD Notes on Complaint & Enquiry Cases related to DPP4 - security of personal data, Case No.: 2006010.

149. Hong Kong, PCPD Notes on Complaint & Enquiry Cases related to DPP4 - security of personal data, Case No.: 2009009.

150. Australia, Own Motion Investigation v. Medvet Science Pty Ltd (2012).

In another case, customers were able to access personal financial information when calling a telecom company after only entering their mobile phone number. The commissioner believed that the mobile phone number was associated with a person and freely given out. As such, the telecom company had not taken reasonable steps to protect the personal information from misuse, loss and unauthorized access, modification, and disclosure. [151] In yet another case, personal data of airline passengers were displayed on the Internet when queried by another passenger. This was caused by a programming error in a secondary computer system. The commissioner held that because the airline promptly provided a fix upon notification, had in place key processes (computer testing, audits and adherence to system guidelines) and the system's security was compliant with international regulations and subject to annual compliance audits, its response was adequate.[152]

The number of countries in the region that have passed mandatory data breach notification provisions is still small but growing. Dealing with data breaches in the cloud has many aspects, including technical and business, but there is also a significant legal response that is required.[153]

Australia

Security of personal information (art. 11): The organization must use reasonable steps to avoid misuse, interference, loss, or unauthorized access, modification, or disclosure of data and it must destroy or de-identify personal information that it is no longer using for disclosed purposes.

While Australia has not yet enacted data breach legislation, the Office of the Australian Information Commissioner has published a voluntary guide to assist government agencies and private organizations on how to deal with data breaches of personal information.[154] It also released a discussion paper on the need for mandatory privacy breach notification in 2012.[155]

---

151. Australia, Own Motion Investigation v. Telecommunications Company, PrivCmrA 16 (2010).

152. Australia, Own Motion Investigation v. Airline, PrivCmrA 7 (2009).

153. Thomas J. Shaw, *Legal response to data breaches in the cloud*, IAPP Privacy Advisor (Oct. 2012).

154. Office of the Australian Information Commissioner, *Data breach notification: A guide to handling personal information security breaches* (2012).

155. Commonwealth of Australia Attorney-General's Department, *Discussion Paper: Australian Privacy Breach Notification* (2012).

New Zealand

Storage and Security of Personal Information (principle 4): Security safeguards must be in place to prevent against loss or unauthorized access, use, or modification.

While New Zealand has not yet enacted data breach legislation, the Privacy Commissioner has provided steps for government agencies to respond to breaches.[156]

Hong Kong

Security of Personal Data (principle 5): Steps must be taken to prevent unauthorized access, use, or loss.

There is no mandatory data breach reporting in Hong Kong, but the Office of the Privacy Commissioner has published data breach guidelines.[157] Businesses should notify the data subjects of a breach when a "real risk of harm is reasonably foreseeable." Organizations should also notify law enforcement, the Office of the Privacy Commissioner, and any relevant regulatory agencies. There is also a short template that can be used by organizations when providing data breach notice to the Commissioner.[158]

Taiwan

Security Measures (art. 27): Appropriate safeguards should be implemented to prevent data loss, modification or disclosure, including the disposal of data, in conjunction with the applicable government agency.

Data Breach (art. 12): When personal information is stolen, disclosed, or altered, notification is required to affected individuals of breaches that violate the statute.

---

156. New Zealand Privacy Commissioner, *Key Steps for Agencies in Responding to Privacy Breaches and Privacy Breach Checklist* (2008).

157. Hong Kong Office of the Privacy Commissioner for Personal Data, *Guidance on Data Breach Handling and the Giving of Breach Notification* (2010).

158. Hong Kong Office of the Privacy Commissioner for Personal Data, *Data Breach Notification Form* (2010).

Korea

Safeguards (art. 29): The personal information processor shall take such technical, managerial, and physical measures as necessary to ensure the safety so that personal information may not be lost, stolen, leaked, altered or damaged.

Data Breach Notification (art. 34): Data subjects are to be notified in case of a data breach, with a list of pre-described information, and if large, the authorities are to be notified as well.

Japan

Security Control Measures (art. 20): The business has to implement proper security controls to prevent loss, leakage, or destruction of the personal data.

Supervision of Employees (art. 21): The business has to exercise appropriate supervision over its employees who handle personal data.

Supervision of Delegates (art. 22): The business has to exercise appropriate supervision over its third party delegates who handle personal data.

There is no express provision in the law creating an obligation to notify data subjects and/or data authorities in the event of a data security breach. However, there are a number of guidelines issued by government ministries with industry oversight responsibility. Some guidelines (e.g., the Guidelines issued by the Financial Service Agency applicable to banking) create an obligation to notify data subjects and/or governmental authorities that issued the guidelines in the event of a data security breach.

Macao

Security of Processing (art. 15): The controller must take appropriate measures to ensure the personal data against unlawful access or loss, including transmission over networks. This also applies to any third party that is performing the processing for the controller.

There is no stated statutory data breach notification requirement.

Malaysia

Security (art. 9): Data must be protected, considering its nature, storage location, security measures, personnel, and data transfer measures. If data processors are used, they must provide sufficient guarantees of technical and organizational measures and take reasonable steps to ensure compliance with the measures.

There is no stated statutory data breach notification requirement.

Philippines

Security of personal information (sec. 18): The data processor is required to implement reasonable and appropriate organizational, physical, and technical measures intended for the protection of personal information against any accidental or unlawful destruction, alteration, and disclosure, as well as against any other unlawful processing.

The authorities and data subjects must be notified after a data breach, when unauthorized acquisition of such personal information is likely to give rise to a real risk of serious harm to any affected data subject.

Singapore

Protection of personal data (sec. 24): The organization in possession or control of personal information is responsible to make reasonable security arrangements to prevent unauthorized access, collection, use, disclosure, copying, modification, disposal, or similar risks.

There is no stated statutory data breach notification requirement.

Blocking Statutes

Six Asia/Pacific countries have joined the Hague Evidence Convention.[159] Australia has given the ability to the Attorney General to issue an order to prohibit the production "in a foreign court of a document" that is in Australia.[160] Many other countries require judicial approval, for either a direct request or a letter of request from a foreign court under the Hague Convention. For example, under New Zealand's Evidence Act, judges will determine if evidence can be gathered in New Zealand for use in an overseas tribunal.[161]

---

159. Australia, People's Republic of China, India, Republic of Korea, Singapore, and Sri Lanka.
160. Australia, Foreign Proceedings (Excess of Jurisdiction) Act of 1984, § 7(1)(a).
161. New Zealand, Evidence Act of 2006, § 185.

Cloud-Computing Specific

Rules

To facilitate the certainty of the cloud at the regional level, APEC has sponsored the CBPR. Various national efforts have also produced guidance for businesses and individuals. For example, New Zealand has generated a code of conduct for the CSP's services.[162] This voluntary code requires truthful disclosure of a variety of information by the CSP, including: CSP corporate identity, ownership of consumer data, security, data location, data access and use, backup and maintenance, geographic diversity, SLA and support, data breach notification, data transportability, business continuity, data formats, and application ownership. There are also questions on auditability, acceptable use, and privacy policies.

In Singapore, in an industry area with significant government regulation, the Monetary Authority of Singapore (MAS) issued in July 2011 a circular stating that it considered cloud computing to be outsourcing, requiring the completion of a Technology Questionnaire for Outsourcing. This circular stated: "As cloud computing service providers typically process data for multiple customers, financial institutions are instructed to pay attention to the cloud computing service providers' abilities to isolate and identify their customer data and other information system assets for protection. Financial institutions should retain the right to have all IT information and assets promptly removed or destroyed in the event of contract termination with the cloud computing service provider, notwithstanding the cause for such termination. Financial institutions are also advised to consider the resilience and safety of the cloud computing service provider's infrastructure to ensure that the outsourcing does not compromise their business continuity preparedness."

The Australian government has issued a better practice guide to help entities deal with the legal issues of cloud computing.[163] Targeted at government agencies, but also mostly generally applicable, the guide briefly covers the areas of protection of information (e.g., privacy, security, confidentiality, records management, and auditing), liability, performance management (e.g.,

---

162. New Zealand, Cloud Computing Code of Practice (2012).

163. Australia Information Management Office, *Negotiating the cloud – Legal issues in cloud computing agreements* (Nov. 2011).

services levels and business continuity), ending the arrangement with the CSP including termination by either party, dispute resolution, harmful code, change of control, and trans-border data issues. The guide also addresses managing the cloud computing agreement during its lifetime, including enforcing the SLA.

In South Korea, following on from 2011's "Strategies for Promoting Cloud Computing and Strengthening Competition" directive, the cloud computing law was proposed in 2012. This would include a focus on certification and registration of CSPs, require data breach reporting, promote model CSP contract clauses, provide notification of any storage of data outside the country, and permit use of cloud consumer data only for their intended purposes.

Activities

APEC has various cloud activities underway as part of its Telecommunications and Information Working Group. In its St. Petersburg Declaration, it noted how cloud computing could be vital in disaster response and recovery efforts.[164] Previously, there was some resistance to cloud computing, based on differing factors in the region, such as the government of New Zealand reminding companies there that "they must keep the original files containing financial information hosted onshore."[165] The Australian state of Victoria released a guide that discusses how cloud computing impacts the local privacy act,[166] which warned that "any cost savings in using cloud computing may be diminished if an organisation attempts to effectively de-identify the personal information it holds in order to use cloud services." Now, there are significant activities among Asian governments to promote cloud computing use among both government agencies and the private sector (even if regulators may be going more slowly).

In China, the national and regional governments are all involved in cloud-related projects. The national government in 2011 announced plans for cloud

---

164. 2012 APEC Telecommunications and Information Ministerial Meeting, *Building Confidence and Security in the Use of ICT to Promote Economic Growth and Prosperity* (Aug. 8, 2012).

165. *Cloud Computing Regulation: What Will the New Year Bring?*, Cloud Expo (Jan. 2011).

166. Office of the Victorian Privacy Commissioner, *Information Sheet: Cloud Computing,* Info Sheet 03.11, (May 2011). **(Is this a publication?)**

computing pilot projects in several major cities.[167] Regional governments are eager to fund cloud infrastructure projects to attract jobs and businesses but have had problems with issues such as the inconsistent availability of broadband networks nationally and inadequate planning and demand.[168] In September 2012, the national government rolled out, under its next five-year plan, the development of cloud technology in China.[169] The key points of this five-year plan include making key breakthroughs in cloud computing technology and standards, developing cloud server and storage systems with significantly higher capabilities, developing a multi-tenant, multi-application cloud O/S and high-availability management system, and focusing on regional and industry-oriented cloud applications and services. This should all target a community of hundreds of millions of end-users and small- and medium-sized enterprises (SMEs) and areas/industries like e-government, healthcare, culture and education, urban management, industrial design, and social services.

In Japan, the "Kasumigaseki" cloud is being promoted as a way for government agencies to drastically reduce their IT expenditures while at the same time increasing their capabilities. The Japan Smart Cloud Strategy focused on facilitating cloud service utilization, promotion of strategic research and development of next generation cloud technologies, and promotion of international consensus and global collaboration. The privatization of Japan Post has included the significant use of SaaS applications to sell financial services to the public, a market gained from the customers of more than 20,000 post offices across the country that also operate as a massive savings bank. The recent plan for Japan's renewal, including recovery from the 2011 earthquake/tsunami/nuclear disaster, is expected to help boost the need for cloud computing services. Japan's National Institute of Information and Communication has signed an agreement to collaborate with the Information Technology Laboratory of the U.S. National Institute of Standards and Technology on

---

167. China, Ministry of Industry and Information Technology and National Development and Reform Commission, *Notice on Implementing Pilot Projects to Promote the Innovation and Development of Cloud Computer Services* (2011).

168. *China's cloud deployment dampened by nascent enterprise demand*, ZDNet (Mar. 15, 2013).

169. China, Ministry of Science and Technology, Development of Cloud Technology in China, 12th Five-Year Plan (Sept. 2012).

projects such as the Cyber-Physical Data Cloud.[170] Japan's National Institute of Informatics and the U.S.'s National Aeronautics and Space Administration (NASA) will collaborate on interoperability between their respective cloud platforms for the benefit of international science.[171]

In India, the national government has announced plans to create a national backbone to a large cloud network that connects each of the state governments' data centers to it. To be called GI Cloud, it supports the National e-Governance Plan of India to make all government services accessible to citizens in their own locality.[172] The plan creates private clouds for each of the state governments and national government agencies. The government will publish guidelines for application development, security, and service delivery and run an application store.

The South Korean government in 2011 established a Government Cloud Computing Demonstration Center to encourage public sector agencies to adopt the cloud. It had previously developed plans to spend significant funds to build up its cloud computing capabilities. Taiwan likewise committed funds[173] and has set up the Taiwan Cloud Computing Consortium as a partnership among business, government, and academia to generate cloud opportunities.

The Australian federal government put out a strategic direction paper on how cloud computing could be used by the government, including use by agencies on unclassified government services, and a draft policy statement that the government "will choose cloud based services if they demonstrate value for money and are adequately secure."[174] In Singapore, the government has initiated the G-Cloud as the infrastructure to be used by the whole government, acting as a private cloud for the respective government agencies.

---

170. NICT Press Release, *Memorandum of Understanding was signed with ITL/NIST* (Feb. 8, 2012).

171. NASA Press Release, *NASA and Japan Announce Cloud Computing Collaboration* (June 4, 2012).

172. India, Dept. of Electronics and IT, *GI Cloud Adoption and Implementation Roadmap* (Feb. 2013).

173. Cloud Computing a Threat, and Opportunity, for Taiwan's PC Makers, International Herald Tribune (June 14, 2010).

174. Australian Office of Finance and Deregulation, *Cloud Computing Strategic Direction Paper - Opportunities and Applicability for Use by the Australian Government* (Apr. 2011).

3.4 Americas

The countries in North and South America outside the United States have promulgated some of the leading statutes on data protection, including two that are recognized as adequate by the EU. These statutes draw their influences from the Fair Information Principles, the EU's DPD and national laws, and a local regional concept called *habeas data*. Meaning "you should have the data," this right allows an individual to ask for a court's intercession to correct or destroy personal data that impinges upon her or his honor, image, or privacy. It is included in many constitutions and statutes in the region. While there are a number of statutory protections in countries like Chile,[175] Columbia,[176] Paraguay,[177] Costa Rica,[178] Peru,[179] and Uruguay,[180] this section will focus on four of the largest countries, Canada, Mexico, Brazil, and Argentina.

Privacy Frameworks: National Statutes
Canada

Canada, like the United States, the EU, and Australia, has both federal laws and state/territory data protection laws. The federal law for non-government organizations is the Personal Information Protection and Electronic Documents Act (PIPEDA)[181] and the Privacy Act applies to government.[182] There are data protection statutes in all of the major provinces[183] as well as

---

175. Chile, Law for the Protection of Private Life, Ley No 19628 de Protección de la Vida Privada (1999).

176. Columbia, Law dictating general provisions for the protection of personal data, Ley 1581 por el cual se dictan disposiciones generales para la protección de datos personales (2012).

177. Paraguay, Law on Information of Private Character, Ley No. 1682 de La Información de Carácter Privado (2001).

178. Costa Rica, Law on Protection of the Person Concerning Personal Data Treatment, Ley No 8968 de Proteccion de la Persona Frente al Tratamiento de sus Datos Personales (2011).

179. Peru, Personal Data Protection Law, Ley No 29733 de Protección de Datos Personales (2011).

180. Uruguay, Protection of Personal Data and Habeas Data Action, Ley No 18831 de Protección de Datos Personales y Acción de Habeas Data (2008).

181. Canada, S.C. 2000, Ch. 5.

182. Canada, The Privacy Act R.S.C. 1985.

183. An Act Respecting the Protection of Personal Information in the Private Sector R.S.Q. 1994 (Quebec), The Personal Information Protection Act S.B.C. 2003 (British Columbia), The Personal Information Protection Act S.A. 2003 (Alberta).

specialized statutes for protection of health data.[184] Because of the potential conflicts between federal and provincial laws, PIPEDA allows for the exemption from its application for "collection, use or disclosure of personal information that occurs within that province."[185] PIPEDA begins by limiting collection, use and disclosure of personal information, except in the stated circumstances.[186] It then includes the requirement to comply with the principles set out in the schedule.[187] These principles have been designated a National Standard of Canada by the Standards Council of Canada, the country's national accreditation body, and are based on the *Model Code for the Protection of Personal Information* from the Canadian Standards Association, an accredited standards development organization.[188] The principles include: accountability, purpose of collection (and use), consent, limiting collection, limiting use, disclosure and retention, accuracy, safeguards, openness, access and update, and the ability to challenge compliance.

Mexico

There is a newer federal data privacy law, the Federal Law Protecting Personal Data in Private Possession (LPPDPP).[189] It includes the principles of legality of collection and processing, consent, notice, data quality, purpose including deletion, fidelity, proportionality, and accountability,[190] plus the rights of access, rectification, deletion, and objection.[191] Consent must be express, especially for sensitive data, and is implicit if there is no objection

---

184. The Personal Health Information Protection Act S.O. 2004 (Ontario), The Health Information Act R.S.A. 2000 (Alberta), The Health Information Protection Act S.S. 1999 (Saskatchewan), The Personal Health Information Act C.S.M.1997 (Manitoba), E-Health (Personal Health Information Access and Protection of Privacy) Act S.B.C. 2008 (British Columbia), Personal Health Information Privacy and Access Act, S.N.B. 2009 (New Brunswick), Personal Health Information Act S.N.L. 2008 (Newfoundland and Labrador), An Act to amend the Act respecting health services and social services, the Health Insurance Act and the Act respecting the Régie de l'assurance maladie du Québec S.Q. 2008 (Quebec).
185. PIPEDA § 26(2)(b).
186. *Id.* § 6-9.
187. *Id.* § 5(1).
188. PIPEDA Schedule 1, CAN/CSA-Q830-96.
189. Mexico, Federal Law on the Protection of Personal Data Held by Private Parties, Ley Federal de Protección de Datos Personales en Posesión de los Particulares (2010).
190. *Id.* art. 6.
191. *Id.* art. 28

after notice is received.[192] The data controller is responsible for compliance with these principles and the privacy notice, even if the data is processed by a third party.[193]

Brazil

Brazil was the first country in the Americas to incorporate the *habeas data* principle into its constitution.[194] This provides for a right to annotate any disputed data (as opposed to updating the data or deleting it). There is also a *habeas data* statute that supplements these rights and provides procedural guidance.[195] In addition, there are also a number of other statutes providing for rights of privacy and various consumer-related protections of data, such as the General Telecommunications Law,[196] the Information Technology Law,[197] and provisions in the Civil Code[198] and the 1990 Consumer Protection Law.[199]

Argentina

The constitution of Argentina also has a guarantee of *habeas data* rights.[200] This has been supplemented by a data protection statute, the Law for the Protection of Personal Data (LPPD).[201] The LPPD includes among its rights and principles: data quality, consent, notice, confidentiality, request, access, information content, editing, and updating or deleting.[202] Sensitive data cannot be required to be given, and creating databases that disclose sensitive data is forbidden,[203] except by health care practitioners under an obligation of professional secrecy.[204] Databases intended for reporting must be registered.[205]

---

192. *Id.* art. 8-9.
193. *Id.* art. 14.
194. Brazil, Federal Constitution, art. 5.X.
195. Brazil, Habeas Data Act (1997).
196. Brazil, Federal Law No. 9472 (July 16, 1997).
197. Brazil, Federal Law No. 7232 (Oct. 29, 1984).
198. Brazil, Federal Law No. 10406 (Jan. 10, 2002).
199. Brazil, Federal Law No. 8078, art. 43 (Sept. 11, 1990).
200. Argentina, Constitution § 43.
201. Argentina, Ley No 25326 de Protección de Datos Personales, Law No. 25326 (2000).
202. *Id.* arts. 4-6, 10, 13-16.
203. *Id.* art. 7.
204. *Id.* art. 8.
205. *Id.* art. 21.

Personal data outsourced to a data processor must be done under contract and the data destroyed at termination.[206]

The Dirección Nacional de Protección de Datos Personales (DNPDP) has issued a regulation[207] on the type of security controls required, based on data sensitivity. All databases with personal data must have these safeguards: maintaining backup and security copies; implementing user identification and authentication procedures; applying preventative mechanisms against malicious software; and recording all security incidents. Financial institutions and public institutions are required to have periodic security audits; limit the number of unsuccessful attempts to access the database; identify any person who modifies or erases information; and prevent the recovery of information after it has been suppressed or deleted. Databases with sensitive data must use encryption when transmitting or transporting.

Cross-Border Data Transfers

Canada

PIPEDA does not contain any explicit restrictions on transfer of data outside Canada. Instead, organizations are "held accountable for the protection of personal information transfers under each individual outsourcing arrangement."[208] There are, however, limitations in provincial data protection statutes, such as Alberta's that requires notification before cross-border transfers are made,[209] and Nova Scotia has a separate statute addressing this same issue.[210]

Mexico

Data transfers to third parties, domestic and international, require the consent of the data owner, either express or implicit.[211] There are a number of

---

206. *Id.* art. 25.

207. DNPDP No. 11/2006, Security Measures for Maintenance of Personal Data.

208. Office of the Privacy Commissioner of Canada, Guidelines for Processing Personal Data Across Borders (2009).

209. Alberta Personal Information Protection Amendment Act (2009).

210. Personal Information International Disclosure Protection Act, S.N.S. 2006 (Nova Scotia).

211. LPPDPP, art. 36.

exceptions, such as execution of a contract, medical diagnosis, within a corporate group, in the public interest, or to exercise a legal right or defense.[212]

Brazil

There are no express restrictions under Brazilian law for transfer of personal information outside Brazil, beyond those protections listed above (e.g., the constitutional right to privacy).

Argentina

Without consent, international personal data transfers to any country or organization in a different country are forbidden "if adequate data protections are not provided."[213] There are exceptions for international treaties, terrorism, drug trafficking, organized crime, bank and stock exchange transfers, etc.

Information Security and Data Breach Notification

Canada

The safeguards in PIPEDA are required to be "appropriate to the sensitivity of the information."[214] The safeguards are to include physical, organizational, and technological measures.[215] Confidentiality should be maintained during the disposal or destruction of personal information.[216] If the information is provided to a third party for processing, the sending organization remains responsible and must utilize "contractual and other means" to ensure a comparable level of protection for the personal information under its control.[217] Although there are provincial data breach notification requirements,[218] the federal statute has not yet come into force.[219] It requires consent to send

---

212. *Id.* art. 37.
213. LPPD, art. 12.
214. PIPEDA § 5.4.7.
215. *Id.* § 5.4.7.3.
216. *Id.* § 5.4.7.5.
217. *Id.* § 5.4.1.3.
218. *See* Alberta's Personal Information Protection Amendment Act (2009).
219. Canada, An Act to promote the efficiency and adaptability of the Canadian economy by regulating certain activities that discourage reliance on electronic means of carrying out commercial activities, and to amend the Canadian Radio-television and Telecommunications Commission Act, the Competition Act, the Personal Information Protection and Electronic Documents Act and the Telecommunications Act (S.C. 2010, c. 23).

a commercial message, with certain exceptions, and requires valid sender and unsubscribe information.[220] It also prohibits nonconsensual software installations.[221]

Mexico

The requirement to establish and maintain physical, technical, and administrative controls applies to all parties that process personal data.[222] These safeguards must not be "inferior to those that they keep to manage their own information," taking into account risk, impacts, sensitivity of the data, and technology.[223] Material data breaches have to be reported immediately to the data owner.[224] Confidentiality must be maintained by all parties involved in personal data processing, even after the end of the respective relationships.[225]

Brazil

There are no express information security requirements under Brazilian law, although the unauthorized processing of personal information could violate the laws discussed above. There are also other industry rules, such as the self-regulatory regime set up by Internet service providers.[226]

Argentina

The person responsible for the personal data has to ensure its security and confidentiality by adopting all necessary "technical and organizational measures."[227] This is a requirement before personal data can be recorded. Personal data sent to third parties for processing must have the prior revocable consent of the data owner, with a number of exceptions, including if the data has been anonymized or if the data processor (the "assignee") is subject to the same "legal and regulatory obligations" as the data controller

---

220. *Id.* at § 6.
221. *Id.* at § 8.
222. LPPDPP, art. 19.
223. *Id.* art. 20.
224. *Id.* art. 21.
225. *Id.* art. 22.
226. Brazil Código De Auto-Regulamentação De Operadores De Rede E De Serviços Internet (2007).
227. LPPD, art. 9.

(the "assignor") and the data controller remains jointly and severally liable for compliance with this statute.[228] There is no data breach notification statute.

Blocking Statutes

Four countries in the Americas have joined the Hague Evidence Convention,[229] including Mexico and Argentina. Argentina has a reservation stating that it will not execute requests "issued for the purpose of obtaining pre-trial discovery of documents as known in the common law countries." Mexico's reservation allows only for requests "for the purpose of obtaining the production and transcription of documents." The Canadian federal Foreign Extraterritorial Measures Act gives the Attorney General of Canada the ability to block the production of records for use in foreign tribunals.[230] Canada also has certain provincial evidence laws that restrict transfer of documents.[231] Canada is not a party to the Hague Evidence Convention and thus letters of request must be sent to the Canadian court from the requesting country's court.

Cloud Computing Specific
Rules

In Canada, the Office of the Superintendent of Financial Institutions issued a memorandum[232] to federally regulated financial institutions, reminding them that cloud computing was subject to its revised (through March 2009) Guideline B-10, *Outsourcing of Business Activities, Functions and Processes.* This guideline includes accountability and control, a materiality assessment of the outsourcing arrangement, and a risk management program for the arrangement.

The Office of the Privacy Commissioner of Canada along with two of the provincial privacy offices has released cloud guidance for small- and

---

228. LPPD, art. 11.
229. Argentina, Barbados, Mexico, and Venezuela.
230. Canada, Foreign Extraterritorial Measures Act, chapter f-29, § 3.
231. *See e.g.,* Quebec's *Business Concerns Records Act* and Ontario's *Business Records Protection Act.*
232. Canada, Office of the Superintendent of Financial Institutions Canada, *New technology-based outsourcing arrangements* (Feb, 29, 2012).

medium-sized enterprises (SMEs).[233] It advises that "sensitivity of the information, the type of cloud, and the contractual arrangements should all play a key role" in deciding whether to move to the cloud or not and provides a series of questions to ask and recommendations. It reminds SMEs to consider whether they need to seek consent from their customers for potential new uses of their personal information.

Activities

In Canada, cloud computing has gotten a strong push from government[234] and industry[235] but there have been some privacy concerns about data being exported outside the country, especially to the United States. Data exports remain "stalled in Canada due to privacy concerns stemming from the US Patriot Act"[236] and "[f]ear of the U.S. Patriot Act and lack of familiarity are the final hurdles to clear before Canadian firms are ready to adopt cloud computing beyond the company firewall."[237] Admissions by large U.S. technology firms have continued to make users somewhat wary.[238] In addition, there are concerns about the limitations on data transfer volumes by broadband users as adverse to cloud computing growth[239] and the lack of firm direction from the national government on security.[240]

233. Office of the Privacy Commissioner of Canada, Office of the Information and Privacy Commissioner of Alberta, and Office of the Information and Privacy Commissioner of British Columbia, *Cloud Computing for Small and Medium-sized Enterprises: Privacy Responsibilities and Considerations* (June 2012).

234. *See e.g.* Canada CTO of Public Works Government Services, *Cloud Computing and the Canadian Environment* (2009).

235. *IBM Launches $42 Million Cloud Computing Centre in Canada*, IBM Press Release (Jan. 31, 2011).

236. Why is Canada reluctant to adopt cloud computing?, ZDNet (June 15, 2010).

237. *Canadian firms shy from cloud because of Patriot Act*, ITBusiness.ca (May 20, 2010).

238. *Cloud computing law puts Canadian users at risk of snooping by American spies*, Ottawa Citizen (Feb. 2, 2013).

239. *The Sorry State of Cloud Computing in Canada*, Forbes (Oct. 24, 2012).

240. *Why Canada lags in cloud computing*, The Globe and Mail (Feb. 9, 2012).

Chapter 4

INFORMATION SECURITY AND PRIVACY IN THE CLOUD: THE RISKS

When negotiating agreements with CSPs, lawyers must understand and attempt to control the risks involved in utilizing cloud computing services. Beyond purely legal risks are the information security and privacy risks that may arise when outsourcing an organization's data, systems, and processes. As discussed in Chapters 2 and 3, there are statutory obligations that specify certain information security and privacy policies and controls that organizations must implement. These include risk assessment programs to look for threats and vulnerabilities from both inside and outside the organization.

There are also contractual obligations to protect data contained in the organization's agreements with its customers, vendors, and business partners. And there is the obligation to protect the organization's own information, such as its intellectual property, its financial information, and its employee data. Each organization retains the responsibility to protect this data when outsourcing to a CSP, even though it may no longer be providing the IT personnel or infrastructure. It must ensure that the same safeguards it has implemented internally to protect these various types of data are also in place at the CSP.

This chapter first provides an overview of the protection of information, then discusses in order the information security, privacy (including big data), and virtualization-related risks of utilizing the cloud. To provide more in-depth practical analysis, it closes with a process used by the U.S. government to evaluate the privacy and information security risks when utilizing cloud computing. The risk treatments used to address these and other information-related risks are then fully discussed in Chapter 5.

Executive Takeaways

- High-level approach to protecting an organization's information
- Information security and privacy risks when using cloud computing
- Virtualization risks involved in cloud computing
- U.S. government's approach to information security and privacy risk in the cloud

4.1 Protecting Information

Many organizations are concerned that use of public cloud computing services will always mean that there is an increase in information security exposures.[1] But this view may be changing,[2] and the truth may actually be just the opposite: that cloud computing results in a stronger security profile for most organizations. The case can be made that cloud computing "provides

---

1. ITGI, *Global Status Report on the Governance of Enterprise IT* (Jan. 2011). Of the 40 percent of almost 1,000 executives and CIOs from 21 countries who did not have a current plan to utilize cloud computing, the chief reason cited was data privacy and security concerns; ISACA's 2012 IT Risk/Reward Barometer (Nov. 2012). While a majority of over 4,000 globally situated IT and business professionals felt the risks outweighed the benefits for use of the public cloud, a majority said the benefits outweighed the risks for use of private clouds.

2. *Why Cloud Computing is Slowly Winning the Trust War,* Forbes (Mar. 12, 2013).

opportunities for innovation in provisioning security services that hold the prospect of improving the overall security of some organizations."[3]

This derives from CSPs having more qualified staff, strengthened computing platforms, additional availability of resources, better backup capabilities, more rigorous security practices, a significant financial advantage in spreading security costs over a larger computing base, the concentration rather than spreading of data on untold devices, and the increased use of lightweight end-user devices that move processing and therefore primary risk exposures into centralized and protected host processors. The leading cyber organization in the U.S. military, U.S. Cyber Command, advocates migration to the cloud as a way to *improve* security.[4] It is important to see any migration of data and process to the cloud, when properly designed and implemented, as an opportunity to improve all information security and privacy practices, even for the largest organizations.

Objectives of Information Security

The three objectives of information security are confidentiality, integrity, and availability (CIA). These respectively mean to keep data from being disclosed or lost, to preserve it in the state it was provided with only approved modifications, and to ensure it is there to be accessed when needed. A more complete definition is provided under FISMA[5] as follows:[6]

Confidentiality

"Preserving authorized restrictions on information access and disclosure, including means for protecting personal privacy and proprietary information..." A loss of *confidentiality* is the unauthorized disclosure of information.

---

3. NIST, SP 800-144, *Guidelines on Security and Privacy in Public Cloud Computing* (Dec. 2011).

4. Cyber Command Chief: DoD Moving to the Cloud, NextGov (Mar. 16, 2011).

5. Federal Information Security Management Act (FISMA), Pub L. No. 107-347 (2002).

6. FIPS, Publ. 199, *Standards for Security Categorization of Federal Information and Information Systems* (2004).

Integrity

"Guarding against improper information modification or destruction, and includes ensuring information non-repudiation and authenticity…" A loss of *integrity* is the unauthorized modification or destruction of information.

Availability

"Ensuring timely and reliable access to and use of information…" A loss of *availability* is the disruption of access to or use of information or an information system.

To implement these three objectives, organizations set up information risk management programs. These programs involve a lifecycle approach in a variety of phases and disciplines revolving around information risk. This includes first broadly understanding the data that the organization both owns and is responsible for (custodial data), the value of that data, its criticality, and its sensitivity. With this foundation, the risk assessment process can be initiated. Risk assessment involves understanding the external and internal threats to the organization's information assets and the vulnerabilities of the systems hosting, and people, facilities, and processes protecting these assets. From there, the impact and the likelihood of the threats materializing to take advantage of any vulnerability are determined and the resultant risks ranked in priority order.

Risk treatment is what an organization does to respond to these risks. There are basically four approaches: to avoid the behavior causing the risk, to share via insurance or outsource the risk, to do nothing and so retain the risk, or to attempt to mitigate the risk by implementing some form of information security or privacy controls. After designing and implementing the controls, there is an ongoing risk monitoring process, a remediation process for new threats, vulnerabilities, or ineffective controls, internal and management reviews of the effectiveness of the risk management process, and hopefully independent third-party reviews of the process.

Components of Reasonable and Defensible Information Security

Organizations need to create an information security and privacy program that is both "defensible" against any legal claims and "reasonable" to comply with statutory and regulatory requirements. What makes up defensible and reasonable information security and privacy practice is not defined anywhere but consists of a collection of policies, procedure, actions and awareness that cumulatively provides protection against claims and non-compliance. The best approach to accomplish many of these requirements is to comply with best practices vis-à-vis global standards. For those involved with electronic payment cards, PCI DSS[7] can be used as a foundation standard but for these and all other businesses, the security guidance provided by the International Organization for Standardization[8] (ISO) is sufficiently comprehensive as a foundation standard. For those organizations in highly-regulated industries such as banking and those under specific local consumer protection mandates, the ISO standard is a necessary prerequisite. Several cloud-specific standards are beginning to emerge (covered in Chapter 5) that build on these existing standards. While individual organizations must address their own unique security situations, implementing all three of the following high-level steps should provide a solid foundation for what is arguably a "reasonable" and "defensible" information security and privacy program.

The first step is the information security and privacy policy. In this document (or multiple documents, as necessary), the organization lays out its direction for information security and privacy, and importantly, management's commitment to information security and privacy within the organization. It also specifies the roles of the key security and privacy players and delineates the organization's acceptable use policy, defining and signaling to all employees what security-related behavior is proper and what is not in dealing with the organization's information assets, including those of customers. It also defines restrictions on external information assets, such as those available on the Internet (e.g., blogs, personal email accounts, social networks). Finally, it sets the direction on high-level standards, protocols, and procedures to guide the design, implementation, and review of the necessary controls. Documentation of this policy and its wide dissemination is essential. When assessing the risk of using a certain CSP, the organization

---

7. Payment Card Industry (PCI) Data Security Standard (DSS) Requirements and Security Assessment Procedures, ver. 2.0 (2010).

8. ISO/IEC 27001, Information technology - Security techniques - Information security management systems – Requirements (2005) and ISO/IEC 27002, Information technology — Security techniques — Code of practice for information security management (2005).

needs to ensure that the CSP can fulfill all of the requirements in the organization's own information security and privacy policy and provide the evidence to prove such compliance.

The second step is the risk assessment process. An organization must clearly understand the information security and privacy risks it is faced with, made up of external (and internal) threats and vulnerabilities that may be exploited. External threats come from sources such as malware and hackers. Internal threats come from insiders acting against the objectives of the organization. Vulnerabilities come from poor software coding practices or a lack of rigor in system maintenance procedures or network design. Together, the external and internal threats may create an exploit by attacking a vulnerability. The risks are ranked by the amount of damage that each exploit may cause, such as exposing sensitive data or taking offline critical resources. After the risks are understood, a decision is made as to how to treat them by mapping the risks to the control objective and then the control procedure to achieve that objective. Because threats and vulnerabilities are constantly changing, the risk assessment process must be regularly repeated and all documents revised accordingly. This risk assessment process must be expanded to the CSP, to include new risks, both from the CSP's services and from the interactions between the CSP and the organization. Some of the risks specific to the cloud are presented below.

The third step is to design, implement, monitor, review, remediate, and audit the risk treatments that are acceptable to the risk profile of the organization. For each individual risk, there must be a decision whether to retain a risk, avoid it, outsource it, share it via insurance, or to try to reduce it through information security and privacy controls. These controls are collected into frameworks by a number of standards bodies and organizations. These control frameworks are discussed in Chapter 5. In the cloud environment, the same controls that are essential in the non-cloud environment, such as those involved with network and system security, physical data center and office security, access, and human resources remain vital and serve as a base to add the cloud-specific controls.

There are additional factors in creating the defensibility of information security and privacy controls, including understanding local court cases and procedural rules in the applicable jurisdictions and litigation techniques that are not discussed here. Suffice it to say that strict adherence to well-recognized international standards and all applicable statutes and regulations is the safest way to make an information security and privacy program legally defensible and statutorily reasonable.

Key Cloud Controls: Encryption and Identity Management

Three categories of information security and privacy controls take on a bigger focus in the cloud. Two (encryption and identity management) are discussed in this section and the third (isolation) in the section on privacy in the cloud.

Encryption

Cryptographic controls contribute to confidentiality and integrity of data hosted outside of the organization's custody. In the open environment, it is safest if information security controls are "data-centric" instead of "location-centric" or "perimeter-based." This is possible when using encryption, which does not primarily depend on the rigor of third-party control implementations. Encryption has at least three different uses: when data is at rest (i.e., being stored), in transit, and in use. When utilizing an IaaS service model, the organization should have almost complete control over encrypting its data at rest and in transit. Encrypting data in use is more complicated, due to the fact that data in use must be decrypted to be used and the different locations to which data may be copied when decrypted (e.g., main memory, paged memory, swap memory, both physical and virtual, plus communications conduits between these). Utilizing a PaaS service model may mean the loss of some ability to encrypt data at rest (if using a CSP's data storage service) and data in transit (for certain execution environments and inter-process calls and data passing). In the SaaS service model, data encryption will be under the control of the CSP, except for data in transit on import and export into the CSP's application system.

In addition, cryptographic controls are also used in the authentication of cloud providers, network users, and trusted intermediaries. This encompasses the creation, management, and deletion of cryptographic keys. Symmetric and asymmetric key methodologies will both likely be used in the data encryption, identity management, and authentication functions by the organization and the CSP. The asymmetric keys are typically part of a public-private key pair used in a public key infrastructure (PKI) that provides for third party verification of identity and authentication credentials. Symmetric or private keys may be session-specific or long-lived. Organizations need to determine which types of encryption systems are used by CSPs and try to integrate a system with the one currently used by the organization, while retaining as much control as possible of the keys themselves. CSPs now offer cloud consumers of CSP-hosted private clouds the ability to completely control the creation and management of cryptographic keys, with only single-tenant access to the security module that hosts the keys.

Identity Management

The second important set of controls in the cloud consists of those involved with identity management and authentication. These include the ability to initially identify new users or programs, to authenticate them on login/API calls to various services, and to provide the proper access to authenticated users, programs and devices. In the cloud, users may be unknown to the CSPs, so it is vital that the cloud users be pre-identified for later authentication and access so that CSPs are able to rapidly provision cloud services. But with so many websites to access, the vast number of user identities and passwords that users must remember has become excessive. As a White House report stated, "In the current online environment, individuals are asked to maintain dozens of different usernames and passwords, one for each website with which they interact."[9] As such, the objective of the organization would be for its users to be able to utilize cloud services under its existing identity and authentication systems, without adding new user IDs, passwords, or other identity tokens.

The solution may involve federated identity management, in which a trusted third-party credential provider can authenticate the identity of cloud users to the CSP. To communicate among themselves and establish the necessary trust, these entities will require a common protocol. The leading

---

9. Obama Administration, *National Strategy for Trusted Identities in Cyberspace - Enhancing Online Choice, Efficiency, Security, and Privacy* (Apr. 2011).

protocols are currently SAML,[10] OpenID,[11] and WS-Federation.[12] They also utilize the PKI public and private key pairs and standards-based (e.g., ITU-T X.509)[13] digital certificates to authenticate users and websites on the Internet between otherwise unknown entities. Organizations will need to understand what type of identity management scheme is being used by the CSP, what security tokens or other authentication devices are required for the organization's users to access the cloud, and whether federation of identity and authentication management is possible between the CSP and the organization. Given that credential providers will be tempting targets for hackers,[14] it is important to also understand the strength of the security controls implemented by such providers.

4.2 Information Security Risks in the Cloud

The cloud poses a number of information-related risks that are common to all outsourced computing environments. But it also has risks that are unique to the cloud architecture, based primarily on its sharing of a number of open resources. For example, the access point into the public cloud is by definition a shared resource and is thus more easily exposed to attack. The network used to reach the access point is also a shared network, likely the Internet. Also, the physical hardware in a virtualized environment (explained below) is by definition a shared resource, with only layers of software protecting the data of one organization from access by a totally separate organization, whose data may or may not be physically nearby. The following sections will describe information security risks unique to the cloud.

The cloud's architecture provides for a number of immediate issues for information security. These risks may be present (or not) based on which

---

10. OASIS Security Services Technical Committee, Security Access Markup Language, v2.0 (2005).

11. OpenID Foundation, OpenID, v2.0 (2007).

12. Web Services Federation Language, v1.1 (2006).

13. ITU-T, Recommendation X.509, Information technology – Open Systems Interconnection – The Directory: Public-key and attribute certificate frameworks (2005).

14. LastPass Security Notification (May 4, 2011).

cloud service model and cloud deployment model is being utilized. These possible risks include:[15]

- *Exposure of authentication interface*: The entry point into the public cloud must be publicly available and so is more exposed to possible attack and subsequent compromise from any number of sources.
- *Unclear trust boundaries*: No longer are the shape and boundaries of the components of the organization's network clear, nor the lines where trusted entities might begin or end. There will be a variety of players in the cloud who may stand in the middle between the organization and the CSP.
- *Data segregation*: Data that was formerly physically segregated from other organizations (and locked behind physical and network barriers) is now only logically segregated on common devices. Co-located tenants could include competitors.
- *Data mobility*: The cloud model means that data may be physically moved without advance notice to different hosts that have the necessary capacity or services that could reside in different countries, which will potentially implicate other rules of law and possibly increase risk of exposure during governmental investigations.
- *Isolation failures*: The use of virtualization and multi-tenant architectures implies the possibility that the isolation safeguards between these tenants using the same physical resources may be breached. This is further discussed in the virtualization section below.
- *Exposure of virtual environment management interface*: Part of the virtualized environment includes interfaces that allow the hypervisor to control the various virtual machines and in turn to provide operational data back to the virtual management system. Access to this interface could cause security issues for co-tenants.
- *Lack of secure transmission/storage*: While the use of encryption in protecting confidentiality and integrity and in authentication is widespread,

---

15. Some of these risks were identified In Cloud Computing – Benefits, Risks and Recommendations for Information Security, European Network and information Security Agency (2009).

encryption may not be in use in all cases of data transmission and storage by the CSP and its subcontractors.

- *Shared use or poor management of encryption keys*: Encryption capabilities provided by the CSP may isolate the guests but may not do the same for the encryption keys used by customers or for VMs, which may be shared. Loss or disclosure of encryption keys with so many shared participants is also a risk.

- *Lack of portability*: This may be due to specific non-standard applications, data formatting, custom APIs, or other features of a CSP's service offerings, or because of confidentiality concerns (e.g., inability to export system logs that contain data about many users), all of which may limit the rigor of the organization's security regime.

- *Loss of governance*: The inability to get certain monitoring information means that the organization cannot easily verify the performance of the CSP or perform certain other procedures that it needs in order to respond to security incidents in a timely manner. Users may also contract for cloud services directly with a CSP without informing the IT department, thereby exposing corporate information.

- *Loss of assurance*: Typical assurance activities such as internal and independent operational audits, vulnerability assessments, and penetration testing may not be easily available, if at all. Organizations may be forced to rely on audits and assessments done by auditors hired by the CSP, which may not have the same security concerns.

- *Increased resource exposure*: All resources, including the networks and applications, are outside the organization's security perimeter and thus more exposed to attacks. Data that was previously behind the corporate firewall now must be stored on a publicly available resource more accessible to malefactors.

- *Increased consolidation*: The fact that more data is aggregated in a single location makes it a more tempting target for both external and internal bad actors. Much as a bank is a more tempting target for robbers than an individual house, so now is the CSP a target and may not be the subject of traditional frontal attack but perhaps a social engineering attack (e.g., phishing) against its employees. It is not just the content information the CSP has but also the profiles of website usage that may be of interest to bad actors.

- *Data copies proliferation*: Besides backup/mirror copies of data made for business continuity purposes out of primary datacenters, copies may now exist in any number of data centers and also in virtual machine images. While it is better to have more rather than fewer copies, accounting for and controlling these copies and their implications for data theft may prove difficult.

- *Data deletion difficulties*: With all of the extra copies of data residing in different locations, assurance of deletion of all copies upon service termination may be extremely complex. This can potentially cause problems in meeting records retention requirements and in leaving data that may become available in litigation.

- *Evidence gathering for compliance*: Evidence may be required for any number of compliance reasons, such as legal compliance with information security statutes, industry security regulations, contract security provisions, and international security standards. The ability to gather that information may be limited by the CSP's physical and system controls and rules about access to certain log information.

- *Evidence gathering for litigation/investigation*: Evidence may be required for civil litigation, criminal cases, or governmental regulatory investigations, including not only the data itself but perhaps forensic images of the hardware. Obtaining such information and implementing "legal hold" (preservation of potential evidence) procedures may be much harder from a CSP, requiring the use of a less secure CSP or third-party resources.

- *Subcontractor issues*: While this is possible in any outsourcing situation, CSP subcontractors may be used only during times of requiring additional resource and so may be harder to locate later if there are issues related to their services, and it may be difficult to ensure that all data is secured and access authentic.

- *Resource availability*: CSP resources that are being relied upon may not be available as needed. This can range from actual service problems emanating from the CSP or the connecting network to a sudden lack of the required processing or data storage or network resources, due to simultaneous common needs from many cloud customers. Security controls then may not be available as needed.

- *Lowest common denominator*: Security settings may be set at the least restrictive for those security controls not controlled by the virtualized environment or they may use a moderate to lower setting that satisfies a security profile different from the one needed by the organization.

- *Use of BYOD/mobile devices*: The use of a web browser to access cloud resources from tablets and mobile phones may imply a lower security profile, given the lower penetration of rigorous security controls on these devices. This is compounded by the personal sourcing of BYOD usage, in which the organization may have no control over the device's security profile, encryption techniques, or the apps and plug-ins used for cloud access. The users of these devices cannot be consistently assured, given their mixed business/personal use and mobility. In addition, these devices tend to be always on and connected to their networks, allowing an exploit to be repeatedly taken advantage of. And authentication credentials may be saved in or originate from these devices, allowing access to cloud data by unauthorized users.

- *Principal-agent problem*: This occurs if the CSP resources and energies are not aligned with the priorities of the organization.[16] This can occur in large public cloud environments when it is more expeditious for the CSP to take a less time-consuming path (e.g., responding positively to requests for voluntary disclosures of information).

- *Attenuation of expertise*: As time goes on, the organization may no longer have people on staff who can properly evaluate the security controls needed at the CSP.[17] As in any outsourcing situation, as resources are redeployed, the specific information security expertise may shift to the service provider.

In addition, all organizations today face not only potential digital threats from entities like hackers and malware writers that have long been on the scene but also face more complex threats from sophisticated criminal organizations

---

16. NIST, SP 800-144, *Guidelines on Security and Privacy in Public Cloud Computing* (Dec. 2011).

17. *Id.*

and state-backed actors. Often with objectives beyond just short-term financial gain, these malefactors are more patient and well-funded and can afford to wait for the right time to strike, in pursuit of objectives such as theft of intellectual property or certain data for political reasons.[18] These entities are behind a newly realized type of threat hitting organizations called an Advanced Persistent Threat (APT).[19]

The characteristics of APTs are that they use randomized techniques that are hard to compare to established threats, lie low until triggered, attack from multiple vectors at once, are tailor-made for specific targets, and have redundant nodes that can continue an attack if eradicated elsewhere.[20] The impact to organizations was made clear by an APT attack that impacted over 200 companies, many very high profile firms.[21] These characteristics make them very difficult to deal with but the virtualized environment in the cloud may be of benefit in responding to APTs by allowing the creation of virtualized quarantine areas (sandbox VMs) for these threats and the ability to re-direct traffic there over the virtualized networks.

4.3 Security Risks with Virtualization

One of the key technologies identified with cloud computing is virtualization. Although not unique to cloud computing and by no means a new technology, virtualization in essence allows multiple "guest" operating systems belonging to many different organizations to have access to all of the resources of a computing resource such as a physical server. In simplified terms, these are "virtual" machines (VMs), virtual in that each operating system and its applications and data are abstracted from the underlying physical machine but still operate as if they control all of the hardware. A "hypervisor" controls all of these virtual machines, controlling the memory, CPU, disks, network and other devices. The advantage of such an architecture is much higher utilization of the same physical resources. But this efficiency also introduces a

---

18. *What you can do about Chinese APT attacks*, InfoWorld (Feb. 26, 2013).
19. *NYT, WSJ Hacks Scrutinized by Security Community*, Information Week (Feb. 1, 2013).
20. *Mobilizing Intelligent Security Operations for Advanced Persistent Threats*, RSA and VMware (Feb. 2011).
21. eWeek.com (Mar. 11, 2011) names many well-known alleged victims of the Operation Aurora attacks.

number of security concerns, which must be understood when negotiating an agreement with a CSP.

Virtualization does bring a number of security benefits, such as the ability to isolate VMs that contain a security or application problem (better incident handling), the ability to create new VMs from a single secured baseline copy (higher security and easier maintenance), easy capture of discrete images (for forensic analysis purposes), isolation of high risk or high value applications and data, separate VMs for each application development environment (ease of development and testing), and migration of VMs to other physical hosts (ease of maintaining the physical machines and load balancing).

The security issues arise due to the use of the additional layer of abstraction. Because there are multiple tenants running in the same physical space, it is possible for leakage to occur and one tenant to be able to access the data or process of another tenant. Although perhaps over-emphasized in terms of the number of occurrences, this issue has been proven to exist and must be accounted for.[22] The new security issues from this architecture include:

- Compromise of a hypervisor/virtual system access interface or management interface from inside the virtual environment by escaping from a guest VM
- Inserting a rogue hypervisor into the virtualized environment
- Lack of visibility to virtualized network between related VMs and attacks on virtual networks interfaces
- Use of a single physical disk mapping to multiple virtual disks available to the VMs
- Guest hopping between the multi-tenant guest images within a hypervisor
- Differing security profiles between co-tenants on the same physical host
- Lack of timely images (full copies) and snapshots (incremental copies) of the guest OSs
- Planting malware into VMs, just as in a non-virtualized environment
- Compromise of the data contained inside images and snapshots
- Lack of portability of the metadata associated with each VM's image

---

22. Kostya Kortchinsky, *CLOUDBURST: A VMware Guest to Host Escape Story*, presentation to BlackHat USA 2009.

A minimum set of controls for cloud computing virtualization services includes at least these:

- Firewall-like protection between interfaces to virtual resources such as disk and memory and the actual physical devices
- Up-to-date patch management and the use of security-baselined template VMs
- Minimal access to the hypervisor/virtual environment administrative functions and logging of all such use
- Hardening through closure of all unused services and devices, and unneeded remote management interfaces
- Monitoring and logging of activity from the hypervisor down to each guest OS
- Controlling the launch of the hypervisor[23]
- Non-sharing of authentication credentials/encryption keys between guest OSs
- Granting virtual resource access to only the specific guest OSs that will be using them
- Grouping of VMs with similar data sensitivity profiles (e.g., high, medium, low) together on a physical host

Just like an operating system (OS) utilizing a non-virtual environment, an OS in a VM needs the same kind of protection. This includes malware protection, firewall, and intrusion detection/prevention system (IDS/IPS) functions. These functions may be carried out by modules located inside each VM, outside VMs but within virtual network segments or from a single location attached to the virtualization management system or individual hypervisors, with various trade-offs involved. In any case, VMs should be created from secure templates. In addition, up-to-date patch management and hardening techniques such as turning off unneeded services and devices, clearly still apply. This must also be applied to template and dormant VMs, as well as those used to support business continuity exclusively. And as with all

---

23. *See e.g.*, the Trusted Boot process of the Trusted Computing Group, to perform a "measured and verified launch" of a virtualization management system.

systems, control of superuser passwords, closing down of all but essential remote access, proper configuration and change management (including accounting for and minimizing VM copies), logging of all key events across the entire virtual infrastructure, and monitoring of access to and modifications of important accounts and files are essential.

In addition to virtualization of the server, the end-user access device can be and increasingly is run in a virtualized manner. For example, in a laptop or desktop PC environment, the various components including the display, the OS, the software applications, the user's profile and settings, and some part of the user's data would be stored on the physical PC. In a virtualized environment, these components may reside in a number of different combinations utilizing virtual resources on the PC and various servers (e.g., each desktop OS may be a different VM on a server). The centralization and standardization of these components should generally reduce security and privacy risk (plus increase user accessibility and decrease system maintenance), because the various components will inherit the safeguards set up either in the more secure datacenter where the servers are located or the more standardized end-user access device. Personal, confidential, or secret information would then never need to be stored on end-user devices, and thus theft or loss of such devices would not compromise the organization. Desktop instances running as VMs can also more easily be imaged for business continuity.

It is important to understand that multi-tenancy does not always use virtualization in all cloud service models. For example, while VMs would be used in an IaaS model, in an SaaS model, the CSP may utilize only a single VM to handle each (and possibly all) discrete function for all customers who are using a single application. This is dependent on the application architecture. For a more detailed understanding of cloud virtualization, NIST provides a useful publication.[24] In addition, besides vendor-specific guidelines for hardening a virtualized environment, there are general benchmarks that provide useful guidance from the Center for Internet Security (CIS)[25] and the Defense Information Security Agency[26] and CIS provide guidance

---

24. NIST, SP 800-125, *Guide to Security for Full Virtualization Technologies* (Jan. 2011).
25. Center for Internet Security, *Virtual Machine Security Guidelines, v 1.0* (2007).
26. Defense Information Security Agency, *ESX Server Security Technical Information Guide, ver. 1 r.1* (2008).

for specific vendor OSs.[27] The Payment Card Industry Security Standards Council has released its own virtualization guidelines.[28]

4.4 Privacy in the Cloud

Cloud's Potential Impacts on Privacy

The privacy of consumers is protected by consumer protection statutes, invasion of privacy statutes, and constitutional privacy provisions in jurisdictions across the globe, while the privacy of organizations is protected by trade secrets laws and by the terms of contracts that they enter. There are a number of areas where use of cloud computing services potentially impacts the privacy of the data owner. These include:[29]

- *Legally privileged information*: It is not yet clear whether the use of a CSP lets a third person into the privileged conversation and so reduces or eliminates the legal privilege that requires confidentiality (e.g., doctor-patient privilege).
- *Professional confidentiality requirements*: Professionals such as lawyers typically must keep their communications with clients confidential but the use of the cloud may interfere with this confidentiality (e.g., CSP operators can perhaps read such messages). The relationship between lawyers and clients is discussed further in Chapter 9.
- *CSP bankruptcy/sale*: In the bankruptcy of a CSP, private data may be sold to satisfy creditors' debt reduction demands, as almost occurred in the sale of a bankrupt website.[30] Sales may require disclosure of all relevant information for due diligence reasons in potential mergers and acquisitions.
- *Legal seizures:* Either CSPs that are involved in litigation or government investigations, or their customers who are, may have their computing

---

27. CIS VMware ESX Server 4 Security Configuration Benchmark, v.1.1.0 (2012) and CIS Xen 3.2 Benchmark, v.1.0.0 (2008).

28. PCI Security Standards Council, *Information Supplement: PCI DSS Virtualization Guidelines* (June 2011).

29. Some of these privacy risks were identified in World Privacy Forum, *Privacy in the Clouds: Risks to Privacy and Confidentiality from Cloud Computing* (2009).

30. Letter from FTC's Bureau of Consumer Protection (July 1, 2010).

assets and therefore private information seized, which may also include the private information of co-tenants.

- *Temporary seizures:* As discussed in Chapter 2, using surveillance statutes, governments review data flowing through the cloud. Certain software relies on deep packet inspection (DPI) to perform security functions such as malware protection. A new confidential standard[31] for DPI highlights the potential impacts on privacy of cloud data, beyond its illicit use in outright spying on citizens, as occurred in Libya under Gaddafi.[32]

- *Compelled disclosures:* CSPs may be required to disclose information based on civil litigation-related requests, cases, or governmental investigations. These can include the requirements to monitor and report child pornography, terrorism, legal fugitives, missing children, money laundering, and violations of intellectual property law.

- *Voluntary disclosures:* CSPs may voluntarily disclose information that is not protected or information that was voluntarily disclosed to them. Certain statutes allow disclosure to third parties who request information, especially in the absence of rigorous data protection laws, such as those covering sensitive or personal information.

- *Trade secrets statutes:* The Uniform Trade Secrets Act,[33] the model for U.S. trade secrets laws, requires reasonable efforts to protect the trade secret. It is not clear if storing a trade secret in a cloud, especially a public cloud, would be deemed a reasonable effort, with or without encryption.

- *Consumer privacy:* The statutes discussed in Chapters 2 and 3 exist to a large extent to protect the privacy of health, financial, credit reporting, and other personal information of consumers. Using the cloud may impact the privacy of all these protected data types.

- *Organizational privacy:* Not only do businesses protect trade secrets, but also safeguard the privacy of their confidential corporate information, their employees' personal information, and the custodial data from

---

31. ITU-T, Y.2770, *Requirements for deep packet inspection in Next Generation Networks* (Nov. 2012).

32. CNET, *U.N. summit votes to support Internet eavesdropping* (Dec. 5, 2012).

33. Uniform Trade Secrets Act, National Conference of Commissioners on Uniform State Laws (1985 as amended).

customers, vendors, and partners, based on law, regulations, contracts, and the need for business competitiveness and reputation.

- *Governmental privacy*: Governments have various types of information that require varying degrees of privacy, including diplomatic, defense, and critical infrastructure data, and are subject to a plethora of statutes regarding how they must protect such information.

- *Selected industries privacy*: Highly regulated industries are required to safeguard the privacy of their customers, including the telecom industry, utilities, financial industry, medical industry, and Internet service providers, in manners comporting with their access to certain kinds of sensitive and personal information.

- *CSP's policies*: The CSP's privacy policies and its cloud services terms of use (standardized contract) will implicate privacy considerations. These includes the availability of common record stores such as log data, backups, and mirror sites and policies on the secondary use of customer personal information.

- *Data versioning/mobility*: The fact that data may exist in multiple locations, that there may be multiple copies of the data (either backup or in databases or in VMs) and that there can be multiple versions of the data provide multiple opportunities to impact the privacy of the data owner.

Big Data and Privacy

A newly emerging risk to the privacy of personal information in the cloud comes from "Big Data." In one sense, this is a euphemistic name for large collections of data that may have been sourced from individuals with their consent, may have been collected without explicit consent online (e.g., tracking data or online purchase data), collected by wireless devices, GPS systems, sensors, cameras, and microphones in public places, or possibly extracted by spotting relationships in various kinds of data mining techniques. Now this data is available in extremely large data stores for analysis to further understand the needs of consumers, for big and small scientific purposes, and for societal benefit. There are two major areas where this impacts cloud computing: one is processing capability and the other is privacy.

For processing capability, because of the extremely large size of the datasets involved, extremely scalable processing powers are required, running parallel processing software on a large number of servers. This is ideal for the cloud computing environment and vendors offer services addressing this need. For example, Google's BigQuery, advertised as being "Reliable & Secure, Scale Infinitely, Blazing Fast," allows directing "massive computing power" at datasets in the hundreds of terabytes with billions of rows with relational database SQL queries. As discussed in Chapter 2, the U.S. government started a big data initiative,[34] which was subsequently expressed as focusing on national priorities including health, the environment, manufacturing, securing cyberspace, transportation, and education.[35] Reportedly, the CIA has decided to use an AWS-built private cloud to perform big data analytics.[36]

For privacy, the relationships that can be derived among these large datasets, only some of which were collected with consent, would go beyond the purposes for which the data was collected. Other data was collected without consent. In a recent report from the World Economic Forum on personal data,[37] ensuring the accountability of stakeholders (data custodians and processors) is much more difficult now as it is not clear who has a data subject's personal data. The report noted that consumers are no longer just data subjects but are data producers (e.g., data collected about their own health by personal devices) and that traditional data protection approaches were based on "1970's computing architectures." It recommends focusing less on the data and its collection and more on the usage, if "data that impacts an individual directly…would require different levels of governance" than data which is used in an aggregated or anonymized manner. These principles would help to alleviate some of the privacy concerns for big data as it is used in the cloud.

---

34. Office of Science and Technology Policy, Executive Office of the President, *Obama Administration Unveils "Big Data" Initiative: Announces $200 Million in New R&D Investments* (Mar. 29, 2012).

35. National Science Foundation, *Big Data R&D Initiative presentation at NIST Big Data Meeting* (June 2012).

36. *Sources: Amazon and CIA ink cloud deal*, FCW (Mar. 18, 2013).

37. World Economic Forum, *Unlocking the Value of Personal Data: From Collection to Usage* (Feb. 2013).

The EU's Article 29 Working Party recently elaborated on some privacy risks of big data.[38] These include:

- Sheer scale of data collection, tracking and profiling, the variety and detail of data collected and the fact that data are often combined from many different sources
- Security of data, with levels of protection shown to be lagging behind the expansion in volume
- Transparency: unless they are provided with sufficient information, individuals will be subject to decisions that they do not understand and have no control over
- Inaccuracy, discrimination, exclusion and economic imbalance
- Increased possibilities of government surveillance
- Type of analytics application used can lead to results that are inaccurate, discriminatory or otherwise illegitimate
- Highly intrusive, disruptive, and personalized targeted advertisements and offers

4.5 U.S. Government's Approach to Privacy/Infosec Risk in the Cloud

The U.S. government has created a process to enhance the use of cloud computing on federal department and agency systems through a series of steps that evaluates the privacy impact of new or revised systems, assesses the information security risks involved when the system is being authorized, proposes a set of controls for such systems and after authorization and implementation, continuously monitors these safeguards. These are addressed through a variety of processes, including those for Privacy Impact Assessments and security guidelines from ISIMC, which are discussed below, and FedRAMP, which is discussed in Chapter 5.

Privacy Impact Assessments

As discussed in Chapter 2, the U.S. government and its agencies are bound by the Privacy Act of 1974,[39] regardless of whether data is stored and processed

---

38. Article 29 Data Protection Working Party, *Opinion 3/2013 on purpose limitation*, Annex 2 (Apr. 2013).

39. 5 U.S.C. § 552a.

on servers owned or controlled by the government or by third-party CSPs. As such, new or modified federal systems processing personally identifiable information must first go through a Privacy Impact Assessment (PIA) as dictated by the E-Government Act of 2002.[40] This is preceded by a Privacy Threshold Analysis (PTA) to determine if a PIA is required. The PTA would ask questions such as who data is collected from, what types of personal data is collected, how such data is shared, if the data is merged, and if any determinations have been made as to the CIA aspects of the system.[41]

The Privacy Act requirements include the rights to receive timely notice of location, routine use, storage, retrievability, access controls, retention, and disposal, rights of access and change to personal information, consent to disclosure, and maintenance of accurate, relevant, timely, and complete records.[42] As such, the PIA will describe in detail the information collected or maintained, the sources of that information, the uses and possible disclosures, and potential threats to the information. The uses that the information is put to by the system are described next, including the legal authority for collecting the data, the retention periods and eventual destruction, and any potential threats based on its use. Also included are any information dissemination and the controls used, the rights listed above, the information security program used, and compliance with the Privacy Act.[43]

The U.S. federal government's view, as espoused by the Federal CIO Council, has delineated an additional set of cloud-related privacy risks that need to be considered in negotiations:[44]

- The permitted uses of collected information may not be clearly defined in the agreement (either the terms of service or contract), enabling the CSP to analyze or search the data for its own purposes or to sell to third parties.

---

40. 44 U.S.C 3501 and OMB Memorandum 03-22.

41. *See e.g., Privacy Threshold Analysis*, The Privacy Office, U.S. Department of Homeland Security.

42. 5 U.S.C. § 552a(d)-(e).

43. *See e.g.*, U.S. Department of Homeland Security, *Privacy Impact Assessment for ECS* (Jan. 2013).

44. CIO Council Privacy Committee, *Privacy Recommendations for the Use of Cloud Computing by Federal Departments and Agencies* (2010).

- The data could be become an asset available for sale to discharge debts in bankruptcy, particularly if the agreement does not include retention limits.
- If the data mobility moves it overseas, the CSP might allow or be required to permit certain local or foreign law enforcement authorities to search its data pursuant to a court order, subpoena, or informal request that would not meet the standards of the Privacy Act.
- The individual providing the information has no notice that his/her information is being stored on a server not owned or controlled by the government. This may impact the rights of redress and other rights described in the Privacy Act above.
- If the data stored with the CSP is breached but the CSP does not inform the government or any of the individuals affected by the incident.
- The CSP improperly implements federal security requirements (i.e., finds them cost-prohibitive or cumbersome) and thus inadvertently allows the data it is storing in the cloud to be viewed by unauthorized parties.
- The CSP fails to keep access records that allow agencies to conduct audits to determine who has accessed the data.
- The federal government cannot access the data to perform necessary audits.
- The data has been moved to a different country and a different server and the government suffers a loss in reputation and trust.
- The federal government fails to keep an up-to-date copy of its data.
- The CSP accidentally loses all of the government's data and does not have a backup.

What this means is that, in addition to the existing PIA requirements, a PIA for cloud computing should assess a series of additional points, as follows:[45]

- What information the agency will collect and put into the cloud (e.g., nature and source)
- Why the agency is collecting the information (e.g., to determine eligibility for a benefit or service)

---

45. *Id.*

- Intended use of the information (e.g., to verify existing data)
- With whom the agency will share the information (e.g., another agency for a specified programmatic purpose)
- What opportunities individuals have to decline to provide information (i.e., where providing information is voluntary) or to consent to particular uses of the information (other than required or authorized uses), and how individuals can grant consent
- How the agency and CSP will secure information in the cloud (e.g., administrative and technological controls)
- Whether the agency is creating a system of records under the Privacy Act and if so, drafting the mandated notice for publication in the *Federal Register.*
- Where the server on which the data will be stored is physically located.

The Federal CIO Council had previously issued a document with the elements of a privacy program to help implementations.[46] In addition, as part of the new version of NIST SP 800-53, a catalog of privacy controls has been issued to help protect personally identifiable information.[47] These can be selected along with the information security controls as part of risk management, to help "organizations enforce requirements derived from federal privacy legislation, policies, regulations, directives, standards, and guidance." There are eight control families with the following controls:

- *AP Authority and Purpose* (AP-1 Authority to Collect, AP-2 Purpose Specification)
- *AR Accountability, Audit, and Risk Management* (AR-1 Governance and Privacy Program, AR-2 Privacy Impact and Risk Assessment, AR-3 Privacy Requirements for Contractors and Service Providers, AR-4 Privacy Monitoring and Auditing, AR-5 Privacy Awareness and Training, AR-6 Privacy Reporting, AR-7 Privacy-Enhanced System Design and Development, AR-8 Accounting of Disclosures)

---

46. Federal CIO Council, *Best Practices: Elements of a Federal Privacy Program*, ver. 1.0 (2010).

47. NIST, SP 800-53, Rev. 4, *Recommended Security and Privacy Controls for Federal Information Systems and Organizations*, Appendix J (Feb. 2013).

- *DI Data Quality and Integrity* (DI-1 Data Quality, DI-2 Data Integrity and Data Integrity Board)
- *DM Data Minimization and Retention* (DM-1 Minimization of Personally Identifiable Information, DM-2 Data Retention and Disposal, DM-3 Minimization of PII Used in Testing, Training, and Research)
- *IP Individual Participation and Redress* (IP-1 Consent, IP-2 Individual Access, IP-3 Redress, IP-4 Complaint Management)
- *SE Security* (SE-1 Inventory of Personally Identifiable Information, SE-2 Privacy Incident Response)
- *TR Transparency* (TR-1 Privacy Notice, TR-2 System of Records Notices and Privacy Act Statements, TR-3 Dissemination of Privacy Program Information)
- *UL Use Limitation* (UL-1 Internal Use, UL-2 Information Sharing with Third Parties)

Information Security Guidelines

Overview

The Information Security and Identity Management Committee (ISIMC) is responsible for the recommendation of IT security and identity management initiatives to the Federal CIO Council. It has created a series of security guidelines for federal agencies using the cloud.[48] The purpose of these guidelines is to:

- Provide a framework to help federal departments and agencies make sound, risk-based security decisions about how to securely embrace cloud computing.
- Assist program managers in deciding what type of cloud model to use for their system from a risk-based security perspective.
- Support the initiatives identified in FedRAMP efforts for cloud authorization.

---

48. Federal CIO Council Information Security and Identity Management Committee, *Federal Guidelines for Secure Use of Cloud Computing by Federal Departments and* Agencies, ver. 0.41 (July 2011), ver. 010 (Aug. 2010).

Although intended to be complementary efforts, the ISIMC security guidelines' scope is different from FedRAMP security controls (described in Chapter 5) in at least two respects. The ISIMC guidelines address the high-, moderate-, and low-impact systems, while the FedRAMP program addresses only low- and moderate-impact systems under the FIPS 199 categories. Also, while FedRAMP is used to authorize CSPs for use by any appropriate government agency, the ISIMC guidelines should be used to determine which cloud model to use for individual systems and can apply to public or private deployment models.

The guidelines use the following sixteen domains that map to the NIST SP 800-53, CSA, and FedRAMP domains (see Chapter 5). Each of these ISIMC domains looks at a variety of use cases, starting with the six basic variants based on the deployment of either private or public clouds over the three service models (IaaS, PaaS, SaaS). It also investigates the key issues inherent in each domain. The following discussion highlights the risk management considerations within each domain, asking questions to identify areas of risk.

ISIMC Risk Management Considerations (modified)

Within these considerations, risk is evaluated with a score of 5 being high risk and 1 being low risk. From this list of considerations, those selected below have been modified to be applicable to any organization and explanations have been added as necessary. While very detailed, these questions would be appropriate to use in most any scenario of evaluation of cloud computing use by private and public organizations, so they are presented here so that organizations may more fully understand the nature of inquiries to make when considering outsourcing to CSPs.

As always when performing these assessments, it is appropriate to first ask these questions of the organization itself, even if it has already started the virtualization process or implemented a private cloud for at least certain workloads. The key terms in the edited list are underlined for easier reading and explanations are in parentheses. The questions from the following domains are not included here, as they are covered extensively elsewhere: Contingency Planning; Data Center Operations, Maintenance, Configuration, Physical, and Personnel Security; Privacy, Electronic Discovery and

Other Legal Issues; Compliance, Audit, and Accountability; Cloud Lifecycle Management; Awareness and Training; and System and Information Integrity.

Architectural Framework for Cloud Computing
- Does the data need to be *accessed* by a single service (1) or a variety of services (5)?
- Is the *availability* of the data to its users Low (1), Moderate (3), or High (5)?
- Is the granularity of *audit requirements* for data and system access minimal (1) or detailed (5)?
- Does the *interconnectivity* of the system with other systems require minimal services (1 PaaS) or extensible, flexible service offerings (5 IaaS)?
- Is maintaining the *patch level* for vendor products currently in use a priority (5 IaaS) or not (1 PaaS)?
- Does the system have flexibility to *interoperate* with many different service offerings (5 IaaS) or do you have to build this capability into your system manually (1 PaaS)?
- Is the function of the system highly *specialized* (5 IaaS) or generalized (1 PaaS)?

Encryption, Key Management, and Media Protection
- Does the organization have control of data inspection software to *identify data changes* (5) or does the CSP notify the organization prior to restoring data (3) or does the CSP identify data changes (1)?
- Does the CSP allow the *organization control of keys*, from generation to destruction (5), using an external third party (3), or is the CSP controlling and tracking key generation and destruction (1)?
- Does the organization retain a *copy of all keys* for encryption/decryption (5) to a copy being kept by a third party at an alternate location (3) to the CSP keeping all copies of the keys (1)?
- Does the CSP allow organization to have control of the *logical boundary* around the cloud infrastructure (5) to the CSP ensuring logical boundaries around the logical infrastructure (1)?

- Does the need exist for using full time *encryption* of all data (5) encryption for storage and offsite processing (3) or can the data be kept in plain text formats (1)?

Identification, Authentication, and Access Control Management

- Has the organization assessed the *potential impact categories* for E-Authentication into the cloud as per OMB Memorandum 04-04[49] (5) or has the organization and CSP agreed upon impact categories in the cloud (3) or has the CSP assessed impact in the cloud (1)?
(The categories of potential impact are: Inconvenience, distress, or damage to standing or reputation; Financial loss or agency liability; Harm to agency programs or public interests; Unauthorized release of sensitive information; Personal safety; Civil or criminal violations.)

- Does the CSP support *Assurance Level* 4 access into the cloud (5), the CSP support Assurance Levels 1, 2, and non-PKI 3 (3), or the CSP support Assurance Level 1 and 2 (1)?
(The four assurance levels described are: Level 1: Little or no confidence in the asserted identity's validity; Level 2: Some confidence in the asserted identity's validity; Level 3: High confidence in the asserted identity's validity; Level 4: Very high confidence in the asserted identity's validity.)

- Does the CSP recognize *identity credentials* from multiple sources (e.g., Fed PKI, OpenID, SAML) (5), the CSP recognize identity credentials from organization supplied sources (3), or the CSP provides institutes recognition through self-generated sources (1)?
- Does the CSP allow the organization to *collect logging information* on all systems setup for the organization (5), the CSP collect logging information for specified systems upon request or an agreed upon schedule for collection (3), or the CSP collect logging information and provides only requested, specific incidences (1)?

---

49. OMB M-04-04, *E-Authentication Guidance for Federal Agencies* (Dec. 16, 2003).

Virtualization and Resource Abstraction

- Is there assurance that network, systems, and storage *controls are well defined* and understood (5)?
- Is there the ability to provide *continuous compliance* and assurance visibility to organizations (5)?
- Are there well defined standard operating procedures for *provisioning*, disaster recovery, *backups/recovery*, and *separation of duties* (either through controls in automation tools or manual inspection) that are visible and auditable (1)?
- Is the visibility into *intra-system communication* critical (5) or not (1)?

Portability and Interoperability

- Does the process to get *data out*: incur a high *cost* (5) or low cost (1)? and require extensive *planning* and time delay (5) or a simple process based on standards (1)?
- Are *interfaces compatible* with another CSP (1) or proprietary to a cloud CSP (5)?
- Is the *data* required to be *controlled* or vetted by the organization (5) or CSPs (1)?
- Will there be a challenge *moving from private cloud* to public cloud and vice versa (5) or will exchange be relatively easy (1)?
- Are there *legal restrictions* with the type of data housed (5) or are there no restrictions (1)?

Application Security

- Does the environment require adequate controls testing, review and analysis of *application code vulnerabilities* including session hijacking, stealth eavesdropping and application data access (1) or are prevention controls are major concerns (5)?
- What access controls are established in the cloud computing site for *monitoring and watching the CSPs* and all their key personnel involved in handling critical and sensitive government information for effective application security (5)?

- What are the deterrence *controls against astute hackers*, including effective monitoring, log aggregation, correlation and analysis of application-specific events (5)?

Security Risk Assessment, Authorization, and Management

- Is there clear documentation on how the CSP will meet facility and services for risk and audit of *control weaknesses*, the frequency of assessments, and how mitigation is performed in a timely manner (5) or does it not exist (1)?
- Are the definitions of *critical service and information security success factors*, key performance indicators, and measurements relative to IT Service and Information Security Management identified and agreed upon (5) or left to basic service definitions (1)?
- Have *upgrades, patches and fixes* been tested in a full simulated network environment to include legacy applications (5), in a simulated network environment with key applications loaded (3), or in a generic test lab (1)?
- When would updates, patches, and fixes be applied: deployed upon the *schedule the organization specifies* (5), as a result of organization and CSP compromise (3), or when the CSP deems it necessary (1)?
- When should *scans be conducted* on cloud infrastructure: The organization decides the schedule to conduct scans (5), the organization and the CSP negotiate the schedule when a scan is conducted (3), or the CSP conducts scans when deemed necessary (1)?
- Do CSP scans perform *reliable scans* (NIST 800-40v2[50] and NIST 800-23[51]) (5), perform minimum scans (3), or do not scan installed equipment (1)?
- Does the cloud CSP report *OS vulnerabilities* of their own (5), inform clients when there is a problem (3), or not inform clients of a compromise (1)?

Incident Response

- Is physical access to the equipment for *imaging and chain of custody* (5) required or does the data not warrant possible legal investigation and reporting requirements (1)?

---

50. NIST, SP 800-40 ver. 2.0 *Creating a Patch and Vulnerability Management Program* (2006).

51. NIST, SP 800-23 *Guidelines to Federal Organizations on Security Assurance and Acquisition/Use of Tested/Evaluated Products* (2000).

- Are dedicated *incident response specialists* with appropriate background and credentials required (5) or are commercially provided, shared incident response teams within a public cloud incident response environment sufficient (1)?
- Is the CSP able to provide *PII incident response* and reporting capabilities as mandated (5) or not (1)?
- Is there a possibility that a *breach of secret/classified data or PII data* in a cloud environment (5) or does the organization not process classified (3) or PII (1) data?
- Does the organization able to provide *forensically sound data images* for investigations (5) or will it rely on the CSP to provide copies of forensically sound data images (1)?
- Does the organization incident response program require *thorough logging and a full packet capture* to conduct network forensics (5) or will it rely on built-in public cloud logging and commercial SOC data capture capabilities (1)?

System and Communication Protection
- Are there detailed (5) requirements for the control of ingress/egress communications outside the system boundary or not (1)?
- Are there detailed (5) requirements for the control of ingress/egress and intra-system communications or not (1)?
- Can the CSP provide perimeter and intra-system controls or does the organization need to provide these controls and are these controls auditable or can the organization provide reports/status on these controls (5)?
- Do security requirements call for full packet capture, enhanced security monitoring (5) or are commercial monitoring capabilities sufficient (1)?
- Does the CSP have sufficient security experience and robust capability to meet security controls or the assessment of security control effectiveness (1) or does the organization have specific reason to believe that the external system has a substantially reduced set of security controls or an increased threat posture relative to the internal system (1)?

Chapter 5

INFORMATION SECURITY AND PRIVACY IN THE CLOUD: RISK RESPONSE

After understanding the information security and privacy risks involved in outsourcing to the cloud, an appropriate set of responses must be created to address the identified risks. There are several mechanisms for doing so, which depend on where in the organization's outsourcing lifecycle the risk arises. These responses are all part of a continuum that concerns assessing, treating, monitoring, remediating, and auditing the information security and privacy risks of cloud computing. When assessing a CSP and negotiating a CSP agreement, the organization must understand not only how the CSP will assess, treat, monitor, remediate, and audit information security and privacy risk but how it does so for its own risks. Rigorous attention to a risk response approach by the CSP gives the organization not only the confidence in the CSP but also the metrics upon which to measure the CSP and so incorporate into them any agreement.

This chapter first looks in much greater detail at how risks that were described in Chapter 4 are addressed through control and assessment frameworks, both general frameworks usable for all situations and those specific to the cloud. It discusses in detail an approach, applicable to all organizations, that the U.S. government has used to enhance its set of controls for the cloud. The various security, portability, and interoperability standards needed for utilizing the cloud are discussed next, followed by a set of approaches that can be used in both assessing and auditing CSPs. The impact of business continuity in the cloud is then discussed and the chapter closes with a discussion of the major steps to address information security and privacy risk in the cloud.

Executive Takeaways

- Cloud-risk-specific modifications in information control frameworks
- Emerging cloud standards and their supporting organizations
- Audit and assessment criteria for cloud providers
- An approach to managing risk in the cloud

5.1 Cloud Assurance and Control Frameworks

There are many assurance and control frameworks that facilitate the assessment and treatment of information risk. These include the following:

- ISO 27002[1]
- NIST SP 800-53[2]
- COBIT[3]
- FFIEC IT Handbook[4]
- PCI DSS[5]

---

1. ISO/IEC 27002, *Information technology - Security techniques - Code of practice for information security management* (2005).
2. NIST, SP 800-53, Rev. 4, *Recommended Security and Privacy Controls for Federal Information Systems and Organizations* (Feb. 2013).
3. ISACA, *Control Objectives for Information and Related Technology 5* (June 2012).
4. FFIEC, *Information Technology Examination Handbook, Information Security* (2006).
5. PCI Security Standards Council, *PCI - Data Security Standard*, ver. 2.0 (2010).

The ISO 27002 set of controls is used in conjunction with obtaining information security certification under ISO 27001. It has been supplemented by security and privacy controls aimed specifically at cloud computing services[6] (but not a new certification). The NIST set of controls is used as part of the certification and authorization process in the U.S. federal government, including for cloud computing services. The COBIT set of controls is part of a larger IT framework, which has been supplemented for the cloud.[7] The FFIEC IT Handbook is for controls at financial institutions in the United States used as part of regulatory audits, with additional guidance in the cloud.[8] The PCI DSS controls are part of a certification for the security controls surrounding electronic card payment processing, which has been supplemented for cloud specifics.[9]

What they all have in common is a foundation based on information security and privacy policies, ongoing risk assessments, and risk treatment approaches that encompass controls necessary for the business model that they represent. While none has every possible control that an organization should use in treating its information risks, they provide a reasonable basis from which to then implement the specific controls unique to the organization's industry and business scenario. To understand the types of coverage in these frameworks, for example, ISO 27002 is organized in the following twelve categories: Risk Assessment and Treatment; Security Policy; Organizing Information Security; Asset Management; Human Resources Security; Physical and Environmental Security; Communications and Operations Management; Access Control; Information Systems Acquisition, Development, and Maintenance; Information Security Incident Management; Business Continuity Management; and Compliance.

---

6. ISO/IEC 27017, *Information technology - Security techniques - Information security management - Guidelines on information security controls for the use of cloud computing services based on ISO/IEC 27002*
(in development); ISO/IEC 27018, *Information technology - Security techniques - Code of practice for data protection controls for public cloud computing services* (in development).
7. ISACA, *IT Control Objectives for Cloud Computing: Controls and Assurance in the Cloud* (July 2011).
8. FFIEC, *Outsourced Cloud Computing* (July 10, 2012).
9. PCI Security Standards Council, *PCI DSS Cloud Computing Guidelines Information Supplement* (Feb. 2013).

The following control frameworks were all created or supplemented specifically for the cloud computing model and complement these existing information security frameworks.

ENISA

European Network and Information Security Agency (ENISA), a European agency that advises EU Member States and is a center of excellence in network and information security, has created a list of questions for risk assurance and a list of controls to utilize in the cloud environment. The assurance document, *Cloud Computing Information Assurance Framework*,[10] considers the division of responsibility across all three service models and the division of liability between the CSP and the organization. It presents questions to consider in the following ten information assurance requirement categories. One key example is listed in each of the categories.

- *Personnel Security* — Are there different policies depending on where the data is stored?
- *Supply-Chain Assurance* — Are there any SLA provisions guaranteed by outsourcers lower than the SLAs you offer to your customers?
- *Operational Security* — Are there any SLA provisions guaranteed by outsourcers lower than the SLAs you offer to your customers?
  - *Software Assurance* — Is a software release penetration tested to ensure it does not contain vulnerabilities?
  - *Patch Management* — Does the patch management process cover all layers of the cloud delivery technologies?
  - *Network Architecture Controls* — What controls are used to mitigate DDoS (distributed denial of service) attacks?
  - *Host Architecture* — Does the CSP provide hardened virtualized images that do not contain the authentication credentials?
  - *PaaS — Application Security* — Does the provider ensure that the PaaS platform sandbox is monitored for new bugs and vulnerabilities?
  - *SaaS — Application Security* — Is the SaaS access control fine-grained and can it be customized to your organization's policy?

---

10. ENISA, *Cloud Computing Information Assurance Framework* (2009).

- *Resource Provisioning*—In the event of resource overload (processing, memory, storage, network), what information is given about the relative priority assigned to a customer's request in the event of a failure in provisioning?

- *Identity and Access Management*
  - *Authorization*—Are any high-privilege roles allocated to the same person? Does this allocation break the segregation of duties or least privilege rules?
  - *Identity Provisioning*—What checks are made on the identity of user accounts at registration? Are any standards followed?
  - *Management of Personal Data*—What data storage and protection controls apply to the user directory (e.g., AD, Lightweight Directory Access Protocol (LDAP)) and access to it?
  - *Key Management*—Are procedures such as key revocation lists in place in the event of a key compromise?
  - *Encryption*—Can encryption be used in multiple places, including data in transit, data at rest, and data in processor or memory?
  - *Authentication*—Is two-factor authentication used to manage critical components within the infrastructure, such as firewalls, etc.?
  - *Credential Compromise or Theft*—What provisions exist in the event of the theft of a customer's credentials (detection, revocation, evidence for actions)?
  - *Identity and Access Management Systems Offered to the Cloud Customer*—How does the cloud provider identify itself to the customer (i.e., is there mutual authentication)?

- *Asset Management*—Are assets classified in terms of sensitivity and criticality and does the CSP employ appropriate segregation between systems with different classifications and for a single customer who has systems with different security classifications?

- *Data and Services Portability*—Does the CSP provide interoperable export formats for all data stored within the cloud?

- *Business Continuity Management*—Has the CSP categorized the priority for recovery and what is the organization's relative priority to be restored?

- *Incident Management and Response*—Is it possible for the customer to build intrusion detection in the VM image?
- *Physical Security*—Do your personnel use portable equipment (e.g., laptops, smart phones) that can give access to the data center and if so, how are these protected?
- *Environmental Controls*—What procedures or policies are in place to ensure that environmental issues do not cause an interruption to service?
- *Legal Requirements*—How will the data provided by the organization and its customers be collected, processed and transferred?

In addition, ENISA has issued a second document that addresses a cloud computing risk assessment.[11] *Cloud Computing Benefits, Risks and Recommendations for Information Security* presents a series of cloud-specific risks and vulnerabilities and the assets they affect. From this list and based on the experience and expertise of ENISA, the report targeted small and medium enterprises (SMEs), and considered the likely probability of occurrence and the impact level of the risk materializing and causing some kind of loss. Although obviously different for each organization, this typical level of risk and impact is important in determining possible use of cloud computing for the SMEs that make up most all European businesses. In addition, it has recently issued the *Security & Resilience in Governmental Clouds* document discussed in Chapter 3.

ENISA has now introduced a new document on critical infrastructure and the cloud.[12] Starting from a European Commission report on critical information infrastructure protection (CIIP),[13] the report notes the importance of cloud computing, especially IaaS and PaaS services (as other cloud services are founded upon them). Cloud computing is becoming part of the critical infrastructure for two reasons. One is the significant growth in cloud computing service usage "on a day to day basis." The second is that cloud

---

11. ENISA, *Cloud Computing Benefits, Risks and Recommendations for Information Security* (2009).
12. ENISA, *Critical Cloud Computing: A CIIP perspective on cloud computing services*, ver. 1.0 (Feb. 2013).
13. EC, Communication on Critical Information Infrastructure Protection – Protecting Europe from large scale cyber-attacks and disruptions: enhancing preparedness, security and resilience (Mar. 30, 2009).

computing is being used in critical sectors (finance, energy, transport, and government). The report looked at key threats to cloud computing services that can have large scale impacts, including natural disasters, power outages, hardware failures, resource exhaustion due to DDoS attacks, cyber attacks due to software flaws, and administrative or legal issues (e.g., Megaupload). It recommends that national governance of critical cloud computing services include risk assessments (including identifying the critical assets in scope and their logical and physical dependencies), appropriate security measures (including logical redundancies, standardization, and audits, monitoring, and testing), and incident reporting thresholds within defined services with incentives to CSPs to report (e.g., immunity for self-reporting security incidents). It also noted the benefits of cloud computing in dealing with natural disasters and DDoS attacks (due to elasticity).

CAMM

The Common Assurance Maturity Model (CAMM) is based on existing frameworks including ISO/IEC 27001, PCI DSS, COBIT, ENISA Information Assurance Framework, and the CSA Controls Matrix. This means that organizations already implementing these frameworks will be able to leverage their existing investments into creating policies and procedures under any of these frameworks. It is backed by ENISA, CSA and private and public organizations.

Based on its initial document,[14] CAMM provides a set of core controls based on existing standards essential to all solutions irrespective of size, geography, or industry, allowing efficient risk assessment. The risk assessment provides a score representing the information risk management maturity (and thus trustworthiness in information transactions) of the service based on the core controls. The core controls can then be supplemented by additional modules (e.g., specific country or industry requirements).

CSA

The Cloud Security Alliance (CSA) promulgates best practices about cloud security. It has created a set of recommendations to utilize in the cloud

---

14. CAMM, *Common Assurance Maturity Model Guiding Principles,* ver. 1.1 (2010).

environment, broken down into the following fourteen categories, with a key example recommendation selected from each category as an illustration.[15]

Section I. Cloud Architecture

Domain 1: *Cloud Computing Architectural Framework* — The prospective cloud service model must be gap analyzed against the applicable information security control (e.g., NIST SP 800-53) model and an applicable compliance (e.g., regulatory, standards) model to understand the general security posture of a cloud service.

Section II. Governing in the Cloud

Domain 2: *Governance and Enterprise Risk Management* — Organizations should look at the security of the CSP's entire supply chain and risk management.

Domain 3: *Legal Issues: Contracts and Electronic Discovery* — The CSP and organization should have a unified process for responding to subpoenas, service of process, and other legal requests, including preservation orders, and should deal with data collection and production.

Domain 4: *Compliance and Audit Management* — CSPs should have processes to collect and store compliance evidence including audit logs and activity reports, copies of system configurations, change management reports, and other test procedure output.

Domain 5: *Information Management and Data Security* — It is important to use the lifecycle of data (create, store, use, share, archive, and destroy) to identify security exposures.

Domain 6: *Interoperability and Portability* — Portability issues between CSPs differ by the cloud service model used (e.g., VM portability is important to IaaS customers but not to SaaS customers), so look to open and published APIs.

---

15. CSA, *Security Guidance for Critical Areas of Focus in Cloud Computing*, ver.3.0 (Nov. 2011).

Section III. Operating in the Cloud

Domain 7: *Traditional Security, Business Continuity, and Disaster Recovery* — The increased centralization of data means that the risk of insider abuse is heightened in the cloud environment.

Domain 8: *Data Center Operations* — Cloud customers should understand the CSP's patch management policies and procedures and how these may impact their environments.

Domain 9: *Incident Response* — To facilitate detailed offline analyses, look for CSPs with the ability to deliver snapshots of the customer's entire virtual environment — firewalls, network (switches), systems, applications, and data.

Domain 10: *Application Security* — Securing inter-host communications must be the rule; there can be no assumption of a secure channel between hosts, whether in a common data center or even on the same hardware device.

Domain 11: *Encryption and Key Management* — It is important to remember to encrypt data on backup media and to secure all key stores.

Domain 12: *Identity, Entitlement, and Access Management* — Customers should leverage standard identity management connectors provided by CSPs to the extent practical, preferably built on Service Provisioning Markup Language (SPML) schema.

Domain 13: *Virtualization* — VM-specific security mechanisms embedded in hypervisor APIs must be utilized to provide granular monitoring of traffic crossing VM backplanes, which will be opaque to traditional network security controls.

Domain 14: *Security as a Service* — This provides for the outsourcing of the functions of detection, remediation, and governance of security to a trusted third-party.

CSA has other projects, such as the Trusted Cloud Initiative, which is intended to help cloud providers develop industry-recommended, secure and interoperable identity, access and compliance management configurations, and practices through reference models, education, certification criteria and a cloud provider self-certification toolset.[16] CSA has also produced the CSA Control Matrix,[17] with the following control categories: compliance, data

---

16. CSA, *TCI Reference Architecture Model* (Feb. 2013).
17. CSA, *Cloud Controls Matrix, ver. 1.4* (Sept. 2012).

governance, facility security, information security, legal, operations, risk management, release management, resiliency, and security architecture. There is a cross-reference to the applicable cloud service model and to the major statutes and standards, such as COBIT, HIPAA/HITECH, ISO 27002, BITS AUP, NIST SP 800-53, FedRAMP, (Generally Accepted Privacy Principles) GAPP, and PCI DSS. To more easily facilitate the use of its documents, the Consensus Assessments Initiative was created to provide more transparency in cloud service offerings. It has created a deliverable in the form of questionnaire with yes/no questions to be to be answered by CSPs.[18]

BITS AUP

BITS is a consortium that has created a set of agreed-upon procedures (AUP) for evaluating vendors providing services to financial companies and a Standardized Information Gathering (SIG) Questionnaire for gathering the information.[19] It has expanded the AUP for the cloud with *Evaluating Cloud Risk for the Enterprise*.[20] Beyond looking at the "common" controls that should be present in all IT systems including cloud systems, there is a new set of "delta" controls, specific to cloud computing, that may be considered higher risk, including:

- *Multi-Tenant Platforms*: These controls look to the separation in networks, storage and computer platform
- *Multi-Client Prioritization*: For the timing and type of requested changes
- *Agile Delivery:* Can CSP processes handle the risk assessment and treatment needed for a continuous stream of rapid changes in short timeframes?
- *Virtualization*: A detailed understanding of hypervisor controls is needed
- *Data Location, Cloud Layers and Cloud Providers*: Control and reporting on data locations
- *Cloud Management: Roles and Division of Responsibilities*: Vendor management controls

---

18. CSA, *Consensus Assessments Initiative Questionnaire, ver. 1.1* (Sept. 2011).
19. BITS AUP 2013 and SIG 2013.
20. BITS, *Evaluating Cloud Risk for the Enterprise: A Shared Assessments Guide* (2010).

- *Contracts, Data Privacy and Jurisdictional Issues:* Including whose privacy policy will control, the organization's or the CSP's
- *Identity and Log Management:* Controls for cooperatively managing identities.
- *Web Application Security:* The controls must be able to sufficiently protect APIs exposed on the cloud, including during all (System Development Life Cycle) SDLC phases
- *Cloud Vendor Interdependence and Governance:* For dealing with multiple CSPs
- *Data Retention, Management, Recovery and Destruction Cycles*: Data lifecycle controls
- *E-Discovery and Forensics*: To match with potential litigation needs

5.2 FedRAMP

With the goal of "deploying secure cloud computing services to improve performance and lower the cost of government operations," the Federal CIO Council in conjunction with a number of other agencies and organizations has rolled out the Federal Risk and Authorization Management Program (FedRAMP).[21] FedRAMP is designed to solve the information security assessment and authorization problems related to use of cloud computing by U.S. government systems and infrastructure. The stated objectives of FedRAMP are:

- Ensure that information systems/services used government-wide have adequate information security
- Eliminate duplication of effort and reduce risk management costs
- Enable rapid and cost-effective procurement of information systems/ services for Federal agencies

FedRAMP's first of three principle phases is the selection of appropriate security baseline controls for low- and moderate-impact cloud systems. Phase two involves the continuous monitoring of these controls and CSP compliance

---

21. Federal CIO Council, *Proposed Security Assessment & Authorization for U.S. Government Cloud Computing*, ver. 0.96 (2010).

with the Federal Information Security Management Act (FISMA).[22] Phase three concerns the assessment and authorization process, including the CSP's responsibility to hire an independent third party assessor to perform initial system assessment and on-going monitoring of controls and to provide continuous monitoring reports and updates to FedRAMP.

The security baseline controls include those from NIST SP 800-53[23] for systems defined under the FIPS 199[24] classification as low or moderate risk. Low-impact systems in FIPS 199 are those whose potential impact is such that the "loss of confidentiality, integrity, or availability could be expected to have a limited adverse effect on organizational operations, organizational assets, or individuals." Medium impact systems have a "serious" adverse effect, while high impact systems, not covered under this FedRAMP process, have a "severe or catastrophic" adverse effect. Cloud-based threats are classified as high, medium and low based on the following characteristics of each type of threat. Low risk threats are those typical technical threats on the Internet, medium risk threats are those from cybercriminal groups and high risk threats are those advanced persistent threats (APT) originating from state-sponsored groups.[25]

Beyond those controls and control enhancements listed in SP 800-53 for low and medium impact systems are FedRAMP specifically-selected cloud controls and control enhancements, as follows. These are the same processes organizations will have to consider as they outsource to the cloud and consider implementing additional controls and control enhancements specifically for the cloud.

22. U.S., Federal Information Security Management Act of 2002, Pub. L. No. 107-347, Title III (2002).

23. NIST, SP 800-53 rev. 4, *Security and Privacy Controls for Federal Information Systems and Organizations* (Feb. 2013).

24. FIPS, Pub. 199, *Standards for Security Categorization of Federal Information and Information Systems* (2004).

25. Federal CIO Council Information Security and Identity Management Committee, *Federal Guidelines for Secure Use of Cloud Computing by Federal Departments and Agencies*, v 0.10 (2010).

Cloud-Specific Controls Added

Within these seventeen control categories,[26] it is useful to look in some depth at these cloud-specific controls and control enhancements. The additions that the government has made to its standard information security and privacy controls are ones that organizations themselves should consider. In addition to adding new controls, specific values are now being required that were previously left to local definition and the role of the government is shifting from operations to oversight of the CSP. This need to pre-set certain parameters and to move from an operational to an oversight function is what organizations must do in outsourcing to the CSP. The key points in each cloud-specific change have been italicized for easier reading, with each section summarized before the edited details are presented. Those categories that do not have additional controls selected may have control enhancements or special requirements not shown here.

1. Access Control (AC)

The changes focus on ensuring that all access controls will be based on roles, that there are defined limits to the sessions, the wireless access is scrutinized and where the CSP will be creating certain processes, the organization retains oversight control.

- Account Management: AC-2 (7). The organization: (a) Establishes and administers *privileged user accounts* in accordance with a role-based access scheme that organizes information system and network privileges into roles; and (b) *tracks and monitors* privileged role assignments.
- Access Enforcement: AC-3 (3). The information system *enforces role-based access control* over *all users and resources* where the policy rule set for each policy specifies: (a) Access control information (i.e., attributes) employed by the policy rule set (e.g., position, nationality, age, project, time of day); and (b) Required relationships among the access control information to permit access. The CSP: (a) Assigns user accounts and authenticators in accordance with CSP's role-based access control policies; (b) Configures the information system to request user ID

---

26. FedRAMP Security Controls Baseline, ver. 1.0 (Jan. 2012).

and authenticator prior to system access; and (c) Configures the databases containing federal information in accordance with CSP's security administration guidelines to provide role-based access controls enforcing assigned privileges and permissions at the file, table, row, column, or cell level, as appropriate.

- Concurrent Session Control: AC-10. The information system *limits* the number of concurrent sessions for each system account to *one session*.
- Session Lock: AC-11. The information system: (a) Prevents further access to the system by *initiating* a session lock after *fifteen minutes* of inactivity or upon receiving a request from a user.
- Security Attribute: AC-16. The CSP defines the security attributes. The security attributes need to be *approved* and accepted by the Joint Authorization Board (JAB).
- Wireless Access: AC-18(2). The organization *monitors* for unauthorized wireless connections to the information system, including scanning for unauthorized wireless access points *at least quarterly*, and takes appropriate action if an unauthorized connection is discovered.

2. Awareness and Training (AT)

This enhancement requires the organization to stay focused on security, even though it may no longer be operationally carrying out the security functions. This ensures that the organization is aware of the risks to its information.

3. Audit and Accountability (AU)

With the information being processed by a third-party organization, the audit function becomes critical to stay informed as to the effectiveness of controls regarding unusual activity.

- Audit, Review, Analysis and Reporting: AU-6(a). The organization: Reviews and analyzes information system audit records *at least weekly* for indications of *inappropriate or unusual activity*, and reports findings to designated organizational officials.
- Audit, Review, Analysis and Reporting: AU-6(1). The information system integrates audit review, analysis, and reporting processes to support

organizational processes for *investigation and response* to suspicious activities.

- Audit, Review, Analysis and Reporting: AU-6(3). The organization analyzes and correlates *audit across different repositories* to gain organization-wide situational awareness.
- Protection of Audit Information: AU-9(2). The information system *backs up audit records at least weekly* onto a different system or media than the system being audited.
- Nonrepudiation: AU-10. The CSP protects against an individual *falsely denying* having performed whatever they were doing that required authentication.
- Nonrepudiation: AU-10(5). The CSP implements FIPS-140-2 validated *cryptography* (e.g., DOD PKI Class 3 or 4 tokens) for service offerings that include SaaS with email.

4. Assessment and Authorization (CA)

With the information no longer under the direct custody of the organization, the independent assessment of the CSP's security controls is critical.

- Security Assessments: CA-2(b). The organization *assesses the security controls* in the information system *at least annually* to determine the extent to which the controls are implemented correctly, operating as intended, and producing the desired outcome with respect to meeting the security requirements for the system.
- Security Assessments: CA-2(1). The organization employs an *independent assessor* or assessment team to conduct an assessment of the security controls in the information system.
- Continuous Monitoring: CA-7(2). The organization plans, schedules, and conducts *assessments annually, unannounced penetration testing and in-depth monitoring,* to ensure compliance with all *vulnerability* mitigation procedures.

5. Configuration Management (CM)

The organization must stay in control of the baseline configuration of the system and only allow changes through approved procedures. Automated mechanisms should enforce access restrictions, auditing and configuration changes and monitor for unauthorized devices.

- Baseline Configuration: CM-2 (5) (a). The CSP defines and maintains a list of software programs *authorized to execute* on the information system. The list of authorized programs is approved and accepted by the JAB.
- Access Restrictions for Change: CM-5 (1). The organization employs *automated mechanisms* to enforce access restrictions and support auditing of the enforcement actions.
- Access Restrictions for Change: CM-5 (5). The organization: (a) *Limits* information system developer/integrator privileges to change hardware, software, and firmware components and system information directly within a production environment; and (b) Reviews and *reevaluates* information system developer/integrator privileges *at least quarterly*.
- Configuration Settings: CM-6 (1). The organization employs automated mechanisms to *centrally manage*, apply, and verify configuration settings.
- Information System Component Inventory: CM-8 (3). The organization: (a) Employs automated mechanisms *continuously, using automated mechanisms with a maximum five-minute delay in detection* to detect the addition of *unauthorized components/devices* into the information system; and (b) *Disables* network access by such components/devices or notifies designated organizational officials.

6. Contingency Planning (CP)
The backups should occur and the contingency plan review should occur in any scenario but
  when a CSP is used, the organization must insist on these controls.

- Contingency Plan: CP-2 (b). The CSP defines a list of *key contingency personnel* (identified by name and/or by role) and organizational elements.
- Contingency Plan: CP-2 (d). The organization *reviews* the contingency plan for the information system *at least annually*.

- Information System Backup: CP-9 (a). The organization *conducts backups* of user-level information contained in the information system *daily incremental and weekly full*.
- Information System Backup: CP-9 (3). The organization stores backup copies of the operating system and other critical information system software, as well as copies of the information system inventory (including hardware, software, and firmware components) *in a separate facility* or in a fire-rated container that is not co-located with the operational system.

7. Identification and Authentication (IA)

The authentication techniques are essential when a CSP is used and these controls describe the need to protect the authentication and identification regime.

- Identifier Management: IA-4 (d). The organization manages information system identifiers for users and devices by *preventing reuse* of user or device identifiers for *at least two years*.
- Identifier Management: IA-4 (4). The organization manages user identifiers by *uniquely identifying* the user as by uniquely identifying the user as a contractor or foreign national.
- Authenticator Management: IA-5 (6). The organization *protects authenticators* commensurate with the classification or sensitivity of the information accessed.
- Authenticator Management: IA-5 (7). The organization ensures that *unencrypted* static authenticators are *not embedded* in applications or access scripts or stored on function keys.

8. Incident Response (IR)

This is a typical outsourcing requirement, to ensure that incident response functions are integrated as appropriate.

- Incident Response Assistance: IR-7 (2). The organization: (a) Establishes a *direct, cooperative* relationship between its incident response capability and external providers of information system protection capability; and (b) Identifies organizational incident response team members to the external providers.

9. Maintenance (MA)

This ensures that no data is disclosed on maintenance tools.

- Maintenance Tools: MA-3 (3). The organization prevents the unauthorized removal of maintenance equipment by one of the following: (a) verifying that there is *no organizational information contained* on the equipment; (b) sanitizing or destroying the equipment; (c) retaining the equipment within the facility; or (d) obtaining an exemption from a designated organization official explicitly authorizing removal of the equipment from the facility.

10. Media Protection (MP)

Encryption of information is required for any digital media leaving the area under the control of the CSP or the organization.

- Media Sanitization: MP-6 (4). The organization *employs cryptographic mechanisms* to protect the confidentiality and integrity of information stored on digital media during transport outside of controlled areas.

11. Physical and Environmental Protection (PE)

This requires the CSP to ensure that appropriate controls over physical access exist within the environment of the facility.

12. Planning (PL)

The organization is required to document its plans for security.

13. Personnel Security (PS)

The organization oversees the transfer of key personnel.

14. Risk Assessment (RA)

Continuous vulnerability scanning is required.

- Vulnerability Scanning: RA-5 (2). The organization *updates* the list of information system vulnerabilities scanned *continuously, before each scan* or when new vulnerabilities are identified and reported.

- Vulnerability Scanning: RA-5 (3). The organization employs *vulnerability scanning procedures* that can demonstrate the breadth and depth of coverage (i.e., information system components scanned and vulnerabilities checked).

- Vulnerability Scanning: RA-5 (5). The organization includes *privileged access authorization* to *operating systems/infrastructure, databases, web applications* to facilitate more thorough scanning.

- Vulnerability Scanning: RA-5 (6). The organization employs *automated mechanisms* to compare the results of vulnerability scans over time to determine trends in information system vulnerabilities.

- Vulnerability Scanning: RA-5 (9). The organization employs an independent penetration agent or penetration team to: (a) Conduct a *vulnerability analysis* on the information system; and (b) Perform *penetration testing* on the information system based on the vulnerability analysis to determine the exploitability of identified vulnerabilities.

15. System and Services Acquisition (SA)

Security assessments are required before outsourcing security services, during software development and for the supply chain.

- Acquisitions: SA-4 (7). The organization limits the use of commercially provided information technology products to those products that have been *successfully evaluated* against a validated U.S. Government Protection Profile for a specific technology type.

- External Information System Services: SA-9 (1). The organization: (a) Conducts an organizational *assessment of risk prior* to the acquisition or outsourcing of dedicated information security services. The CSP documents all existing outsourced security services and *conducts a risk assessment* of future outsourced security services.

- Developer Security Testing: SA-11 (1). The organization requires that information system developers/integrators *employ code analysis tools* to examine software for common flaws and document the results of the analysis. The CSP submits a *code analysis report* as part of the authorization package and updates the report in any reauthorization actions.

The CSP documents in the Continuous Monitoring Plan how newly developed code for the information system is reviewed.

- Supply Chain Protection: SA-12(1). The organization protects against supply chain threats by employing: as part of a *comprehensive, defense-in-breadth* information security strategy. The CSP defines a *list of measures to protect* against supply chain threats. The list of protective measures is approved and accepted by JAB.

16. System and Communications Protection (SC)

A variety of controls address the servers, workstations and the network, the use of encryption, protection of mobile code, virtualization, and preparing for transmission.

- Resource Priority: SC-6. The information system *limits* the use of resources by priority.
- Boundary Protection: SC-7(8). The CSP defines the *internal* communications traffic to be routed by the information system *through authenticated proxy servers* and the external networks that are the prospective destination of such traffic routing. The internal communications traffic and external networks are approved and accepted by JAB.
- Boundary Protection: SC-7(12). The information system implements host-based boundary protection mechanisms for *servers, workstations, and mobile devices.*
- Boundary Protection: SC-7(13). The CSP defines key information security tools, mechanisms, and support components associated with system and security administration and *isolates* those tools, mechanisms, and support components from other internal information system components via physically or logically separate subnets.
- Boundary Protection: SC-7(18). The information system *fails securely* in the event of an operational failure of a boundary protection device.
- Trusted Path: SC-11. The CSP defines the security *functions* that require a trusted path, including but not limited to system *authentication*, re-authentication, and *provisioning* or de-provisioning of services (i.e., allocating additional bandwidth to a cloud user). The list of security functions requiring a trusted path is approved and accepted by JAB.

- Cryptographic Key Establishment and Management: SC-12(2). The organization produces, controls, and distributes symmetric cryptographic keys using *NIST-approved key management technology* and processes.
- Cryptographic Key Establishment and Management: SC-12(5). The organization produces, controls, and distributes asymmetric cryptographic keys using approved PKI Class 3 or Class 4 *certificates* and hardware security *tokens* that protect the user's private key.
- Use of Cryptography: SC-13(1). The organization employs, at a minimum, *FIPS-validated cryptography* to protect unclassified information.
- Secure Name/ Address Resolution Service (Recursive or Caching Resolver): SC-21. The information system performs *data origin authentication and data integrity verification* on the name/address resolution responses the system receives from authoritative sources when requested by client systems.
- Protection of Information at Rest: SC-28(1). The organization *employs cryptographic* mechanisms to prevent unauthorized disclosure and modification of information at rest unless otherwise protected by alternative physical measures.
- Virtualization Techniques: SC-30. The organization *employs virtualization* techniques to present information system components as other types of components, or components with differing configurations.

17. System and Information Integrity (SI)
Security functions must be regularly checked.

- Security Functionality Verification: SI-6. The information system verifies the *correct operation of security functions upon system startup and/or restart and periodically every ninety days* and *notifies the system administrator* when anomalies are discovered.

Lessons from New Cloud Controls

The addition of these controls to the already rigorous control listing used in SP 800-53 illustrates the additional controls that even the most well run information security and privacy programs should consider. At a minimum, organizations should take away the importance of the following ten key points:

- Staying abreast of information security threats and emerging protection technologies
- Continuous monitoring of the CSP's system for identifying and addressing vulnerabilities
- Knowing and protecting the boundaries of the cloud system, including all attempts at intrusion
- Utilizing independent third-party auditing and assessment of the information security controls
- Utilizing automated continuous monitoring tools and protecting audit logs
- Properly implementing and staying in control of identity management and authorization
- Basing access controls on roles, not people, and requiring that changes be approved by the organization
- Fully utilizing encryption and rigorously protecting the key management functions
- Pre-approving the basic security configuration and approving any changes to it
- Integrating all required functions, such as incident response and business continuity

5.3 Cloud Standards

As with any technology initiative, there is a need for standardization to allow disparate users to seamlessly utilize all the resources of the new technology. With cloud computing, given the layers of abstractions, the use of unseen and perhaps unknown service providers, and the intent to make these services work on the utility model, international standardization efforts take on an even greater level of importance. As such, there have been a variety of organizations formed to address the varying aspects of cloud computing needing standardization. These standards efforts and the CSPs compliance therein represent another area that must be evaluated during the assessment process.

While these standards groups are, with the exceptions of standard setting organizations representing governments like ISO, ITU, and IEEE comprised mainly of various vendors or similar groupings, the vendor names will not be mentioned here but can be found on the groups' respective websites. There are also user groups to feed requirements into the standardization process. Because these remain early days in cloud standardization, expect to have to check for the current status of these initiatives when negotiating an agreement with a CSP and to also have to check for new organizations or standards that may arise. With all standards efforts in the early going, there is likely to be overlap that will eventually be resolved, but multiple standards may be implicated in a number of areas of cloud computing for the foreseeable future. Only groups with significant active national or international exposure and membership are discussed.[27] CSA and ENISA were previously introduced in the cloud control frameworks section discussed previously.

The areas of possible standardization in cloud computing include:

- Governance
- Information Security/Privacy
- Exchanges of Data/Metadata
- Interoperability of Applications
- APIs and Protocols
- Provisioning
- Quality of Service
- Monitoring/Metering
- Billing
- Auditing/Certification
- Agreements/SLAs
- Definitions/Classifications

While information security and privacy are the focus of this chapter, the other areas of standards may impact it, such as governance, data exchanges, monitoring and auditing. As such, most major standards groups Standards

---

27. There are many groups in varying stages of activity not discussed here. A complete list is shown in the Appendix. Due to the rapidly evolving nature of cloud standards, this list will need verification when used.

Developing Organizations, industry alliances, end-user forums) that have arisen to date in the cloud computing area will be discussed, to provide an initial context of the types of standards that need to be analyzed when negotiating with the CSP.

ISO/IEC JTC 1

The two standards bodies behind this standards group are the International Organization for Standardization (ISO), the world's largest developer and publisher of international standards from the national standards bodies of 160 countries and the International Electrotechnical Commission (IEC), responsible for preparing and publishing international standards for all electrical, electronic, and related technologies. The Joint Technical Committee (JTC) is focused on information technology. Within this committee are at least three sub-committees working on standards related to the cloud. Sub-committee (SC) 38 is responsible for Distributed Application Platforms and Services, including Web Services, Service Oriented Architecture (SOA), and Cloud Computing. The sub-group on cloud computing (SGCC) has produced a final document, which looked at the standards for interoperability between different cloud service models and portability for data and workloads.[28]

SC 7 is responsible for software and system engineering. It has produced the ISO/IEC 20000 standard for IT service management.[29] SC 7 is developing a new standard of service management for cloud computing.[30] There are other efforts in this sub-committee for software architecture and development environments in the cloud. As mentioned above SC 27 is working on the information security and privacy standards 27017/27018[31] and on 27036-4,

---

28. ISO/IEC, JTC 1 SC38 SGCC, *Study Group Report on Cloud Computing* (Sept. 2011).

29. ISO/IEC, 20000-1, *Information technology – Security Techniques – Part 1: Service management system requirements* (May, 2011).

30. ISO/IEC, 20000-7, *Information technology – Security Techniques – Part 7: Application of ISO/IEC 20000-1 to the cloud* (in development).

31. ISO/IEC, 27017, *Information technology - Security techniques - Information security management - Guidelines on information security controls for the use of cloud computing services based on ISO/IEC 27002* (in development); ISO/IEC 27018, *Information technology - Security techniques - Code of practice for data protection controls for public cloud computing services* (in development).

involving security in supplier relationships for cloud outsourcing services.[32] And ISO has published the standard for managing cloud data, CDMI (see below), as ISO/IEC 17826.[33]

ITU-T

The International Telecommunications Union—Telecommunications Standardization Sector (ITU-T) is the UN agency that produces the "world's most universally-recognized infocommunications standards." In addition to working with ISO and other Standards Developing Organizations (SDOs), the ITU-T Focus Group (FG) on Cloud Computing was formed to collect and document information and concepts that would be helpful for developing recommendations to support cloud computing services/applications from a telecommunication/ICT perspective. It wound up its work at the end of 2011 by producing a seven-part technical report.[34] The parts covered are:

- Introduction to the cloud ecosystem: definitions, taxonomies, use cases and high-level requirements
- Functional requirements and reference architecture
- Requirements and framework architecture of cloud infrastructure
- Cloud resource management gap analysis
- Cloud security
- Overview of SDOs involved in cloud computing
- Cloud computing benefits from telecommunication and ICT perspective

In January 2012, the ITU-T started the ITU Joint Coordination Activity on Cloud Computing (JCA-Cloud). Various ITU-T groups are involved in cloud computing questions, including ITU-T Study Group 13 (Future Networks including cloud computing, mobile and Next Generation Network (NGN), which hosts Working Party 6/13: Cloud Computing. This group was given the responsibility for going forward with developing ITU-T

---

32. ISO/IEC, 27036-4, *Information technology – Security Techniques – Information security for supplier relationships - Part 4: Guidelines for security of outsourcing* (in development).

33. ISO/IEC, 17826, *Information technology – Cloud Data Management Interface* (Nov. 2012).

34. ITU-T, Focus Group on Cloud Computing Technical Report (Feb. 2012).

recommendations based on the technical reports from FG Cloud. It has rolled out three standards related to cloud computing on networks.[35] Separately, ITU-T Study Group 17 on security is working on three recommendations related to cloud security.[36]

IEEE

The Institute of Electrical and Electronics Engineers (IEEE), which promulgated the Ethernet and related wireless transmission standards, has formed two working groups to deal with cloud computing and address the specific issues of portability and interoperability. The first group, P2301, will address portability and interoperability between CSPs. It is developing a guide of cloud interfaces for portability, interoperability, applications, and management.[37] The second group, P2302, will focus on interoperability between CSPs. It is developing a standard for inter-cloud interoperability and federation.[38]

ETSI

The goal of ETSI (European Telecommunications Standards Institute) TC (Technical Committee) GRID is to address issues associated with the convergence between IT and telecommunications for not only grid computing but also cloud computing. This convergence leads to an emphasis on the IaaS delivery model. TC GRID focuses on interoperable applications and services based on global standards and the validation tools to support these standards, with the goal of a coherent and consistent general purpose infrastructure.

ETSI TR 102 997 is the standardization requirement for cloud services.[39] It defines these requirements as: portability; interoperability of clouds; closer

---

35. ITU-T, Y.3501, *Cloud computing framework and high-level requirements* (Mar. 2013); *Cloud computing Infrastructure Requirements* (Mar. 2013); *Cloud computing framework for end-to-end resource management* (Mar. 2013).

36. ITU-T, X.sfcse, *Security functional requirement for SaaS application environment* (in development); ITU-T, X.srfcts, *Security requirements and framework of cloud-based service environment* (in development); ITU-T, X.ccsec, *High-level security framework for cloud computing* (in development).

37. IEEE, P2301, *Guide for Cloud Portability and Interoperability Profiles* (in development).

38. IEEE, P2302, *Standard for Intercloud Interoperability and Federation* (in development).

39. ETSI, TR 102 997, *Initial analysis of standardization requirements for Cloud services*, ver.1.1.1 (2010).

integration of IT and network resources; APIs to networking/data movement functionality; support for building, modeling, testing and deploying applications; support for optimization of distributed applications; clearly defined SLAs fit for business use; Data protection, privacy, and security in clouds; near real time cloud (e.g., media transformation (rendering/transcoding)); and software licensing. ETSI has also delivered ETSI TR 103 125, which covers SLAs for cloud services[40] and ETSI TR 103 126, providing cloud private sector user recommendations.[41] From the push by the European Commission (see Chapter 3), ETSI started a Cloud Standards Coordination initiative in December 2012 to identify a detailed set of cloud standards on security, interoperability, data portability, and reversibility.

Open Cloud Consortium

The Open Cloud Consortium (OCC) is a member-driven organization that develops reference implementations, benchmarks, and standards for cloud computing. Though not technically a standards organization, the OCC operates cloud testbeds, such as the Open Cloud Testbed (which currently consists of four geographically distributed data centers connected by high-speed connections) and the OCC Virtual Network Testbed plus the new High Performance Computing (HPC) applications in the cloud workgroup. The OCC also manages cloud computing infrastructure to support scientific research, such as the Open Science Data Cloud, which allows for the management and sharing of larger scientific datasets.

Distributed Management Task Force

The Distributed Management Task Force (DMTF) is dedicated to enterprise and systems management and interoperability. One definition provided is the lifecycle of a cloud service, involving these six phases: description of the cloud service in a template, deployment of the cloud service into a cloud, offering of the service to consumers, consumer entrance into contracts for the offering, provider operation and management of instances of the service,

---

40. ETSI, TR 103 125, CLOUD: *SLA for Cloud services*, ver.1.1.1 (Nov. 2012).

41. ETSI, TR 103 126, CLOUD: *Cloud private-sector user recommendations*, ver.1.1.1 (Nov. 2012).

and removal of the service offering. There are four working groups focused on the cloud.

The Cloud Management Working Group is focused on creating standards for interoperable cloud management between CSPs and their consumers and developers. Specifications include the Open Virtualization Format (OVF), a standard format for packaging and describing virtual machines and applications for deployment across heterogeneous virtualization platforms.[42] It has been designated as an international[43] and American National Standards Institute (ANSI) standard.[44] Other specifications include those for interfaces for managing cloud infrastructure.[45]

The Cloud Auditing Data Federation Working Group focuses on standards for CSP audit data and has created a specification.[46] The Software Entitlement Working Group focuses on software license management in cloud environments and has developed appropriate metrics.[47] The System Virtualization, Partitioning, and Clustering Working Group has taken over the OVF standard and released a new specification.[48]

Open Grid Forum

The Open Grid Forum (OGF) is committed to driving the rapid evolution and adoption of applied distributed computing, to develop new, innovative and scalable enterprise applications and infrastructures within the scientific community. Standards that OGF has consolidated from best practices into standards are categorized as belonging to: data, computing, security, architecture, and management. The Open Cloud Computing Interface (OCCI) is a set of specifications that is delivered through OGF. OCCI is a protocol and

---

42. DMTF, DSP0243, *Open Virtualization Format Specification*, ver. 1.1 (2010).

43. ISO/IEC, 17203:2011, *Information technology - Open Virtualization Format (OVF) specification*.

44. ANSI, INCITS 469-2010, Information Technology – Open Virtualization Format (OVF) Specification.

45. DMTF, DSP0263, *Cloud Infrastructure Management Interface (CIMI) Model and RESTful HTTP-based Protocol*, ver. 1.0.1 (Sept. 2012); DMTF, DSP0264, *Cloud Infrastructure Management Interface – Common Information Model (CIMI-CIM)*, ver. 1.0.0 (Jan. 2013).

46. DMTF, DSP0262, *Cloud Auditing Data Federation (CADF) – Data Format and Interface Definitions Specification, ver. 1.0.0a* (Oct. 2012).

47. DMTF, DSP-IS0301, *Software Identification and Entitlement Usage Metrics*, ver. 1.0.0 (June 2012);

48. DMTF, DSP0243, *Open Virtualization Format Specification*, ver. 2.0 (Jan. 2013).

API for management tasks that grew out of a remote management API for IaaS, allowing for the development of interoperable tools for common tasks, including deployment, autonomic scaling, and monitoring. Its specification is made up of three documents, addressing all the cloud service models.[49]

Organization for the Advancement of Structured Information Standards

The Organization for the Advancement of Structured Information Standards (OASIS) consortium produces more Web services standards than any other organization as well as standards for security, e-business, and standardization efforts in the public sector and for application-specific markets. It also developed the Security Assertion Markup Language (SAML) used in authentication between different domains in the cloud. It has many technical committees involved with the cloud, including OASIS Identity in the Cloud (which has produced use cases[50]), Cloud Application Management for Platforms, Cloud Authorization, and Topology and Orchestration Specification for Cloud Applications (which has produced a specification[51]).

Object Management Group

The Object Management Group (OMG) is an open international industry consortium to develop integration standards. The Cloud Standards Customer Council is an advocacy group for end users set up by OMG, focusing on complementing cloud standards with additional end-user requirements. It intends to drive client requirements into SDOs and provide best practices and use cases back to cloud clients.

Storage Networking Industry Association

The Storage Networking Industry Association (SNIA) has developed the Cloud Data Management Interface (CDMI)[52] that is used by applications to create, retrieve, update and delete data elements from the cloud. This allows clients to discover the capabilities of the cloud storage offering and use this

---

49. OGF, GFD 183 – OCCI Core, ver. 1.1; GFD 184 – OCCI Infrastructure, ver. 1.1; GFD 185 – OCCI HTTP Rendering, ver. 1.1 (June 2011).

50. OASIS, *Identity in the Cloud Use Cases*, ver. 1.0 (May 2012).

51. OASIS, *Topology and Orchestration Specification for Cloud Applications*, ver. 1.0 (Nov. 2012).

52. SNIA, Cloud Data Management Interface (CDMI), ver. 1.0.2 (June 2012).

interface to manage containers and the data that is placed in them and the set on the containers. It also can be used to manage containers, accounts, security access and monitoring/billing information, across storage protocols. As described above, it has been accepted as an ISO standard.

Trusted Computing Group

The Trusted Computing Group is a not for profit industry consortium that promotes open, vendor neutral standards for trusted computing. It includes some of the largest names in chip manufacturing, PCs makers and over 100 other companies. Some of the areas of its focus include trusted multitenant infrastructure, trusted network connect, trusted platform module, metadata access protocols, and secure self-encrypting storage drives.

Association for Retail Technology Standards

The Association for Retail Technology Standards (ARTS) is an international membership organization dedicated to "reducing the costs of technology through standards" and has created several standards, such as the standard relational data model and RFP for retail vendors. It has created a Request for Proposal (RFP) for cloud computing solutions and also written a white-paper on cloud computing for retailers.

TM Forum

The TM Forum is a buyer-based consortium that has established the Enterprise Cloud Buyers Council Goals. Its goals are to:

- Foster an effective and efficient marketplace for cloud computing infrastructure and services across all industry verticals and global geographies
- Accelerate standardization and commoditization of cloud services and identify common commodity processes best consumed as a service
- Solicit definitions for standardized core and industry-specific SLAs for cloud services
- Achieve transparency of cost, service levels and reporting across the ecosystem
- Enable benchmarking of services across service providers and geographies

- Enable vendor measurement against normalized and agreed service level metrics
- Radically reduce cost of acquisition and operations for commodity computing and services

Cloud Industry Forum

This is a group that provides a self-certification process for CSPs, based on a code of practice, which covers the three areas of transparency, capability, and accountability. It aims to educate, inform, and represent users, CSPs, resellers, system integrators, and SDOs.

Open Data Center Alliance

The Open Data Center Alliance (ODCA) is trying to ensure interoperable standards. It has produced a number of usage models focused on the cloud. Examples of these usage models and other standards include those that deal with federation,[53] automation,[54] common management and policy,[55] transparency,[56] and master usage models (computer infrastructure as a service).[57] The documents are available in several languages, including Chinese.

---

53. ODCA, *Data Security Framework*, ver. 1.0, *Security Provider Assurance*, ver. 1.1, *Security Monitoring*, ver. 1.1, *Identity Management Interoperability Guide*, ver. 1.0, *Cloud Based identity Governance and Auditing*, ver. 1.0, *Cloud Based Identity Provisioning*, ver. 1.0, *Single Sign On Authentication*, ver. 1.0 (2011-2012).

54. ODCA, *IO Control*, ver. 1.1, *VM Interoperability in a Hybrid Cloud Environment*, ver. 1.2, *Long Distance Workload Migration*, ver. 1.0 (2011-2013).

55. ODCA, *Software Entitlement Management Framework*, ver. 1.0, *Regulatory Framework*, ver. 1.0 (2011-2013).

56. ODCA, *PaaS Interoperability*, ver. 1.0, *SaaS Interoperability*, ver. 1.0, *Interoperability Across Clouds*, ver. 1.0 (2011-2013).

57. ODCA, *Master Usage Model: Computer Infrastructure as a Service*, ver. 1.0 (2012).

Open Cloud Manifesto

Less a standards organization than a plea for the proper direction, the Open Cloud Manifesto, which attracted many adherents after its publication, sets out the following principles related to standards in the cloud:

- Cloud providers must work together to ensure that the challenges to cloud adoption are addressed through open collaboration and the appropriate use of standards.
- Cloud providers must use and adopt existing standards wherever appropriate. The IT industry has invested heavily in existing standards and standards organizations; there is no need to duplicate or reinvent them.
- When new standards (or adjustments to existing standards) are needed, we must be judicious and pragmatic to avoid creating too many standards. We must ensure that standards promote innovation and do not inhibit it.
- Any community effort around the open cloud should be driven by customer needs, not merely the technical needs of cloud providers, and should be tested or verified against real customer requirements.
- Cloud computing standards organizations, advocacy groups, and communities should work together and stay coordinated, making sure that efforts do not conflict or overlap.
- Cloud providers must not use their market position to lock customers into their particular platforms and limit their choice of providers.

NIST Summary of Standardization Efforts

NIST's Cloud Computing Standards Roadmap Working Group has produced a rather detailed list of standardization efforts.[58] Its website lists the universal standards that power Internet usage (TCP/IP, DNS, HTML, HTTP, SOAP, XML, etc.), the cloud-related standards discussed above (OVF, OCCI, CDMI, OpenID, SAML, etc.) and cloud standards still in progress (ID Cloud, etc.). It also contains a much more detailed taxonomy of cloud computing standards in the four general constituencies and sub-categories of cloud service customer (SaaS, PaaS, IaaS), cloud service provider (service model,

---

58. NIST, Inventory of Standards Relevant to Cloud Computing (Oct. 2012).

deployment model, provisioning/configuration, portability/interoperability, business support, service creation, security), and cloud carriers (distribution, access devices) and cloud brokers (service customization, service aggregation). Given the fractured and extremely dynamic nature of cloud computing standardization, it is recommended that the reader revisit this site regularly for the foreseeable future as standards evolve. NIST has also created a portal, the Standards Acceleration to Jumpstart Adoption of Cloud Computing (SAJACC) to help facilitate more rapid standardization in the cloud space.

5.4 Assessing and Auditing CSPs

Organizations will need to assess CSPs before selecting the appropriate cloud partner and to audit the CSP after commencement of the service to ascertain compliance with statutes, standards, and contractual commitments. As explained in Chapter 8, the assessment of the CSP follows an internal assessment of the organization itself and can include any of the methodologies described above, based on the type of organization and its needs. In addition to the methodologies described above (ISIMC, FedRAMP, ENISA, CSA CAI, BITS AUP) additional risk assessment guidance is available for the PCI DSS standard,[59] ISO 27002,[60] ISACA,[61] (COSO's) Committee of Sponsoring Organizations of the Treadway Commision *Enterprise Risk Management—Integrated Framework*,[62] and the federal government.[63] It is very likely an organization will utilize a combination of assessment methodologies to try to uncover all the risks that it will be subject to.

This section focuses on auditing the CSP at some point after service commencement, but no later than one year, and regularly thereafter. It does not include the regular monitoring and reporting activities, the periodic risk assessment and remediation processes, or the vendor governance functions that should all be occurring on their own schedules. Audits and assessment should and do use much of the same criteria, although for different sets of

---

59. PCI Security Standards Council, *PCI DSS Risk Assessment Guidelines* (Nov. 2012).
60. ISO/IEC, 27005, *Information Technology—Security Techniques—Information Security Risk Management*
(2008).
61. ISACA, *Security Considerations for Cloud Computing* (2012).
62. COSO, *Enterprise Risk Management for Cloud Computing* (June 2012).
63. NIST, SP 800-30 Rev. 1, *Guide for Conducting Risk Assessments* (Sept. 2012).

data at different periods of time. As such, several of the following audit programs can also be used as part of the pre-engagement assessment process.

ISAE 3402/SSAE 16

The international standard for auditing the internal controls of third party service provider organizations such as CSPs is the International Standard on Attestation Engagements (ISAE) 3402 from the International Auditing and Assurance Standards Board (IAASB). In the United States, this was called the *Statement on Auditing Standards* (SAS) 70, *Service Organizations*[64] but is now being replaced by the attestation standard AT 101, *Attestation Engagements* and Statement on Standards for Attestation Engagement (SSAE) 16, *Reporting on Controls at a Service Organization.* SSAE 16 is based on the IAASB's ISAE 3402. The requirements for auditing the financial statements of the entities that use service organizations will remain an auditing standard, *Audit Considerations Relating to an Entity Using a Service Organization.*

Although commonly used in Sarbanes-Oxley (SOX) audits for assessing information security and privacy controls that are relevant and material to outsourcing entities' financial reporting, the purpose is often broader. CSP customers want assurance about the design and operational effectiveness of these controls, but CSPs do not have the resources to be audited by every customer's auditor. To deal with actual use and needs of these reports, a new set of reports have been created by the AICPA (American Institute of Certified Public Accountants). These are the Service Organization Control (SOC) 1, 2 and 3 reports.

SOC-1 will operate under SSAE 16 using the AICPA Guide *Applying SSAE No. 16, Reporting on Controls at a Service Organization,* which will look at those controls relevant to financial reporting, as used in SOX audits and will be for a restricted use and audience.[65] SOC-2 will operate under AT 101 using the AICPA Guide *Reporting on Controls at a Service Organization Relevant to Security, Availability, Processing Integrity, Confidentiality or Privacy* and will provide some of the assurance sought by CSP customers.

---

64. Local standards based primarily on SAS 70 in other countries, such as The United Kingdom, Japan, and Canada.
65. AICPA, Service Organization Controls Managing Risks by Obtaining a Service Auditor's Report (2010).

These will generally also be restricted use reports in that they will contain detailed descriptions of the auditor's test of controls and the results therein. They will also include the auditor's opinion of management's description of the service organization's system (SOC-1 also includes both of these). Security, availability, processing integrity, confidentiality, and privacy are the principles used in the AICPA's Trust Services.[66]

SOC-3 will operate under AT 101 using the AICPA Technical Practice Aid *Trust Services Principles, Criteria and Illustrations,* which is based on the existing SysTrust audits. While SOC-3 reports will cover the same Trust Services areas as SOC-2 reports, they will not include information about the control system and the audit tests, only whether the controls comply with the Trust Services criteria. A SOC-3 report does not have a restricted use and so can be posted on the service organization's website. The SOC-1 and SOC-2 reports have two types, just as did the SAS 70 report, a Type I (reporting on only the control design) and Type II (reporting on control design and operating effectiveness of the controls).

In these audits, unlike other control audits, there is no prescribed list of controls to check the CSP's controls against. Rather, it is up to the service auditor's judgment. Management of the service organization creates a description of the system and outsourcing services provided to users and how the services are performed, including the controls utilized. The result of the attestation engagement is based on the judgment of the auditor about the design and effectiveness of the controls in scope (management determines which controls or organizational groups are in scope). The ISAE 3402 standard requires that management of the service organization provide a written assertion of the fairness of their description of their system and control design and (if in scope) control effectiveness.

ISACA

ISACA has developed an audit program that extends its current audit programs into the cloud. The Cloud Computing Management Audit/Assurance Program[67] was created to align with ISACA's COBIT 4.1. It is cross-referenced

---

66. AICPA/Canadian Institute of Chartered Accountants (CICA), *Trust Services, Principles and Criteria* (2009).

67. ISACA, *Cloud Computing Management Audit/Assurance Program* (2010).

also with the COSO controls. With a scope of governance, and contractual and cloud-specific controls, the objectives of this review are to:

- Provide stakeholders with an assessment of the effectiveness of the cloud computing service provider's internal controls and security
- Identify internal control deficiencies within the customer organization and its interface with the service provider
- Provide audit stakeholders with an assessment of the quality of and their ability to rely on the service provider's attestations regarding internal controls

Under the broad categories of Governing the Cloud and Operating in the Cloud, some of the specific controls that deal with cloud computing are:

- Governance and Enterprise Risk Management
- Legal and E-Discovery
- Compliance and Audit
- Portability and Interoperability
- Incident Response, Notification and Remediation
- Application Security
- Data Security and Integrity
- Identification and Access Management
- Virtualization

CloudAudit

This organization was originally called A6 (Automated Audit Assertion Assessment and Assurance API). As its name suggests, its mission is focused on the differences in auditing entities involved in cloud computing. Given the levels of abstraction involved in virtualization, new questions need to be asked that were previously more easily understood when there was a one-to-one relationship between hosts and users. The objective is to provide security assertions and audit information in an automated manner through a standardized but strongly authenticated interface that ultimately could be used by consumers to determine which CSP matches their requirements in this functional area. Because auditors do not have to spend so much time in data collection, they can perform more frequent compliance audits.

The first repositories in the current namespace are for common compliance areas: HIPAA, COBIT, ISO 27001, PCI DSS, BITS, GAPP and NIST SP 800-53.[68] The control categories are compliance, data governance, facility security, HR, information security program, legal, operations, risk management, release management, resiliency, and security architecture, the same used by CSA, which is not surprising given their relationship.

ISO 27007/27008

ISO has rolled out one standard and one technical recommendation on security auditing. The first is for auditing information security management systems (ISMS) against the ISO 27001 standard.[69] The second is a technical report with guidelines for auditors of ISO 27002 security controls.[70] A few points to note: the former is for those entities such as external auditors, internal auditors, or management who are auditing the ISMS (but not certifiers of the ISMS), while the latter is for those checking the controls instead of the ISMS. The 27008 standard is somewhat less than a full international standard.

5.5 Business Continuity in the Cloud

The role of the cloud in providing business continuity during disasters has already been demonstrated. The earthquake/tsunami/nuclear disaster in Japan in 2011 "showed how resilient cloud computing can be in the face of disaster and in the aftermath. Cloud services survived power outages by using emergency fuel and data connections over mobile networks and fixed networks held up. Traditional IT deployments in the disaster area on the other hand went offline. In the aftermath of the disaster, cloud service providers provided support for emergency services, and in the recovery phase cloud computing was used by organizations to quickly get services up and running."[71]

---

68. CloudAudit, *Namespaces v 1.1* (2010).

69. ISO/IEC, 27007, Information technology – Security techniques – Guidelines for information security management systems auditing (2011).

70. ISO/IEC, TR 27008, Information technology – Security techniques – Guidelines for auditors on information security controls (Oct. 2011).

71. ENISA, *Critical Cloud Computing: A CIIP perspective on cloud computing services*, ver. 1.0 (Feb. 2013).

There are many approaches to keeping a business running after a disaster occurs. A business continuity plan (BCP) is essential to deal with IT outages of all varieties that minimize the impact on organizations and their customers and other stakeholders. There are a number of considerations when creating and testing a BCP, such as determining how much data must be recovered, and setting appropriate numbers for the recovery time objective (RTO) and recovery point objective (RPO). RTO is the maximum amount of time after a disaster that a system and its data must be available to users, while RPO is the point of data and system consistency to which the recovery should occur (i.e., the maximum amount of allowable data loss). It also requires not only having backup specialized facilities ready when disaster strikes but determining if these are hot, warm or cold sites (varying degrees of hardware, software, and network readiness).

In the cloud, the need to create specialized backup facilities should no longer be a major concern, as the ability to expand resources rapidly means that sufficient facilities should always be available. Of course, if a disaster affects a large number of organizations in a geographic area or with a certain CSP, there could be bottlenecks somewhere along the path of getting all of that workload moved rapidly. Organizations must ensure what the limits are. The ubiquitous network access should allow access even in the loss of an office, so the focus would be to ensure that secure access devices are available. In general, the organizational focus should shift from needing backup processing facilities and disaster recovery of data centers to data-specific parameters, to ensure that if processing must be moved elsewhere in a disaster, minimal data loss occurs and data integrity, availability, and confidentiality are preserved.

There are some technical considerations that must be weighed in any BCP. With the availability of ubiquitous network access, employees, customers, and vendors should still be able to get to the applications and data in the cloud. But there must be the same authentication credentials to access the resources in its new location. The encryption key management process must likewise be redundant and current. And if the organization wants to avoid a user-aware recovery process, it can mirror its data and programs to another site. This includes technical considerations of transaction mirroring, data mirroring, virtual machine images, and snapshots. Whichever technology is utilized, considerations have to be made for in-flight sessions, transactions, log data, and security controls.

One study lent credence to utilizing the cloud for business continuity purposes.[72] The survey of more than 100 companies with formal BCPs made the following findings concerning organizations that used the cloud at least partly for BCP and those who did not.

- Organizations using the cloud recovered four times faster than those who did not
- Organizations using the cloud met their RTOs more often
- The number of downtime events was larger among non-cloud users
- Best practices include having a secure connection to the cloud and using server failover

When looking at the BCPs for CSPs, organizations should keep in mind that there are appropriate international standards that can be utilized by the CSP to address its own commitment to ensuring that RTOs and RPOs are met. There is a relatively new international standard[73] and each country may have its own standards,[74] but so far the leading standard has been the British Standard (BS) 25999[75] (which will be gradually withdrawn to let the ISO 22301 standard take precedence). Made up of parts 1 and 2, the respective code of practice and specification provide a process for certification and the appropriate controls for business continuity of business processes, much in the same way that the aforementioned ISO 27001 and 27002 work together to provide an information security certification capability. In addition, there is

---

72. The Aberdeen Group, Small and Mid-Sized Organizations Gain Disaster Recovery Advantages Using Cloud Storage (Oct. 2010).

73. ISO/PAS, 22399: 2007, Societal security—Guideline for incident preparedness and operational continuity management; ISO/DIS, 22301: 2012, Societal security—Business continuity management systems—Requirements; ISO/DIS, 22313: 2012, Societal security—Business continuity management systems—Guidance.

74. See e.g. in the United States, NFPA, 1600: Standard on Disaster/Emergency Management and Business Continuity Programs (2013).

75. British Standards Institution, BS 25999-1: 2006, Code of Practice for Business Continuity Management; BS 25999-2: 2007, Specification for Business Continuity Management.

the standard BS 25777[76] that addresses business continuity for information and continuity technology (ICT) and serves as a code of practice working within the BS 25999 framework. The narrower ICT approach focuses on the ability to protect, detect, react, recover, operate, and return the ICT. The RTOs of the ICT should be relatively less than the business processes they support. Although certification under these business continuity standards will not be as widespread as with information security standards, CSPs that have them have shown a commitment to availability of customer information in all circumstances.

The service model used clearly has implications for the depth of the BCP designed by organizations. With a SaaS model, the expectation is that the CSP will handle all aspects of the restoration of service. The organization may only need to primarily plan for loss of its own facilities, equipment, or connectivity. With that said, the wiser course would be to find out not only as many details as possible about the CSP's BCP (since the organization is in essence integrating their plan with the CSP) but also to plan for the scenario of extended downtime. In that case, an organization should be taking regular extracts of their data, and perhaps logs and VMs, so that it can port them to a new CSP if the need arises in a disaster that severely impacts the CSP's ability to return to normal service levels. PaaS and IaaS models will increasingly move more of the BCP responsibilities over to the organization. For organizations using private or hybrid clouds, a BCP on-demand service from a CSP can be utilized.

5.6 An Approach to Managing Risk in the Cloud

To fully assess and manage the information security and privacy risk in the cloud, there are a number of steps that all organizations, both in government and the private sector, must take. These include identifying the proper risk management program to utilize, performing the risk assessment of both the cloud and non-cloud factors, and understanding the specific controls to be applied to the prioritized risks. The cloud-specific controls may now be split into the operational, technical, and administrative controls carried out

---

76. British Standards Institution, BS 25777: 2008, *Information and Communications Technology Continuity Management: Code of Practice.*

by the CSP and the oversight controls that remain in the organization. In addition, there will be multiple interface points between the cloud system and the organization's systems that remain outside the cloud.

Organizations must clearly identify who in the organization is responsible for cloud security. With the ability of business divisions to acquire cloud computing services themselves and with the explosion in BYOD, the division of responsibility for ensuring security over these services is not as clear as when all IT capability was procured through the IT organization. A recent survey of experienced IT and IT security practitioners[77] showed that the respondents felt that end-users had the responsibility for cloud security when SaaS applications were involved and 21 percent when IaaS was involved, while only 8 percent felt the IT security team had this responsibility for SaaS and 10 percent for IaaS. The responsibility for cloud security must be included not only in organizational policies and procedures but in awareness training for all parties. The high-level recommendations to address the information security and privacy risk in the cloud for organizations are as follows:

- Do not consider the cloud until there is a rigorous information security and privacy program implemented in the organization
- Create a baseline assessment of the organization's current information security and privacy program, including known risks
- Understand the organization's abilities to oversee and manage outsourced risks
- Determine any incremental risks for systems, data and/or infrastructure that will be placed into the cloud and their interfaces back to systems that will not be placed into the cloud
- Determine appropriate risk treatments for these incremental risks and the impact on overall residual risk
- Perform a risk assessment of the prospective CSPs utilizing a methodology such as those introduced in this chapter
- Discuss a risk treatment plan with the prospective CSPs, utilizing a methodology such as those introduced in this chapter

---

77. Ponemon Institute, *Security of Cloud Computing Users Study* (Mar. 2013).

- Incorporate the risk treatment plan and the monitoring, measuring, and reporting capabilities into the SLA with the selected CSP
- Incorporate the periodic auditing and certification requirements into the CSP contractual agreement, utilizing a methodology such as those introduced in this chapter
- Request access to appropriate security monitoring tools and reports
- Follow up on all security incidents, both to understand the immediate fixes and the more systematic remediations necessary
- Review all internal and independent audit reports and certifications
- Independently research new information security and privacy risks and new technologies and discuss as appropriate with the CSP

Chapter 6

DATA PRESERVATION AND BREACH IN THE CLOUD

There are many reasons that organizations and government agencies must properly record, preserve, and disclose information. Organizations have a duty to record information under a variety of statutes and regulations, including those discussed in Chapters 2 and 3. But the ability to record information in an environment under the control of third parties requires new processes and controls. Organizations and CSPs must be ready and able to respond to requests for information, including those related to civil or criminal litigation, for audit and regulatory compliance, and for government agencies, under public disclosure laws. The requested information may be contained on paper or electronic documents, audio or visual recordings, email messages, websites, mobile devices, or social networks. It may be just for the content, in its original format or may also include the metadata that supports all of these forms of communication. The first section in this chapter discusses the preservation and authorized disclosure of information in the cloud to third parties via the discovery process.

When the data is improperly disclosed via a data breach, organizations must know how to respond. This topic is never far from the headlines.[1] While

---

1. Thousands have data exposed in Microsoft security breach, ITProPortal (Mar. 20, 2013); Central Hudson Gas & Electric Cyberattack, Privacyrights.org (Feb. 20, 2013); Yahoo Passwords Stolen in Latest Data Breach, Wall Street Journal (Jul. 12, 2012); LinkedIn Suffers Data

the previous chapters discussed how to keep data safeguarded, the second section will discuss how organizations can first clarify what qualifies as a data breach with their CSP and then plan for and respond to a data breach in the cloud if and when a breach occurs. Part of the planning and response to a data breach involves the use of cyber insurance, which is discussed in the third section. Common to both the discovery process and data breach response process is the need to sometimes capture different types of electronic data from certain locations, some of which may be in the cloud, and from devices connected to the cloud, to help provide evidence for litigation or investigations or to help track the cause of a break-in that led to the data breach. The final section covers forensic data capture and how it changes in the cloud environment.

Executive Takeaways

- Understanding U.S. and international e-discovery rules applicable to the cloud
- Steps in preparing for and responding to a data breach in the cloud
- How cyber insurance can be used as part of risk response
- Forensic data capture techniques used in the cloud

6.1 E-Discovery in the Cloud

The storage of data in the cloud has implications for both litigation and government investigations involving organizations. While the ability to request access to data in the custody and control of an organization involved in litigation (including data that is stored with their CSP) varies with the discovery and evidence rules across countries, organizations in all countries are subject

Breach, Reuters (Jun. 6, 2012); Global Payments Data Breach Exposes Card Payments Vulnerability, Forbes (Apr. 3, 2012); Zappos Hack Exposes Passwords, InformationWeek (Jan. 17, 2012); Data breach hits 70m Sony customers, Financial Times (Apr. 26, 2011).

to government investigations. As such, all organizations have the need to be able to address requests for compelled disclosure. Although the source of the request may be from parties in civil or criminal litigation or government initiated, the duties to preserve and produce the requested data will be similar. Because the rules for civil discovery in the U.S. are well developed and the most liberal, the discussion will center on those rules, with an explanation of how civil litigation discovery rules differ across the world. Given data mobility, organizations should be familiar with these various rules that may impact their discovery obligations.

As discussed in Chapters 2 and 3, there are other sources of requests for data, such as government requests for records related to potential terrorism, requests from the general public under the various freedom of information acts,[2] and requests based on the rights of data subjects to access and revise their personal information held by data controllers under data protection laws. Although at least one case suggests that these requests may have some of the requirements of civil discovery requests (such as whether metadata should be produced with an FOIA requested document),[3] it is the U.S. e-discovery rules that may place the most significant potential burdens on CSPs and cloud consumers. This section does not address the use of the cloud to perform e-discovery service processing or data hosting.

U.S. Federal Rules of Civil Procedure

Under the changes to the Federal Rules of Civil Procedure (FRCP) that became effective in late 2006, a party in civil litigation in U.S. federal courts is allowed to request that the other party[4] or a non-party[5] produce data. This data can involve "any nonprivileged matter that is relevant to any party's claim or defense."[6] The responding party may voluntarily reply to these requests, but if it does not, the initiating party may request a court order

---

2. Besides the U.S. FOIA referenced in Chapter 2, *See e.g.* Australia's Freedom of Information Act (1982), Canada's Access to Information Act (1983), and the U.K.'s Freedom of Information Act (2000).

3. National Day Laborer Organizing Network, et al., v. United States Immigration and Customs Enforcement Agency, et al., Case No. 10 Civ. 3488 (SAS) (S.D.N.Y. 2011).

4. Fed. R. Civ. P. 34(a).

5. Fed. R. Civ. P. 45(a)(1).

6. Fed. R. Civ. P. 26(b)(1).

compelling discovery.[7] To issue such an order, the court must have personal jurisdiction over the party who will be compelled and that party must have control of the documents.[8] For responding parties located outside the U.S. that control data that is the subject of a discovery production request, the court may have to consider a second set of procedural rules available from the Hague Conference on Private International Law, as discussed briefly in Chapter 2, if the country has not made a reservation against discovery (most have).

For purposes of this discussion, it will be assumed that organizations will always negotiate appropriate provisions to retain "possession, custody or control"[9] of their own information stored with CSPs. In the absence of such agreements or for organizations that have to operate under standard terms of service, it is not assured that a CSP would be required or even likely to preserve information required by a litigant. And further, a CSP may not be required, under provisions of the Stored Communications Act (discussed in Chapter 2) to even produce such information. As such, negotiation with the CSP for the rights of preservation and production, along with retention schedules, is essential. Also, the role of a CSP custodian of the data must be clearly identified, as this person may be required to testify in court or otherwise authenticate the requested data that is in possession of the CSP.

The parties have an obligation to preserve relevant electronically stored information (ESI), including the cessation of records destruction processes, when they become aware of potential or actual litigation. Failure to do so can result in significant sanctions against the offending party for spoliation.[10] Records retention policies and backup procedures both play a significant role in how well an organization and its CSP are able to avoid spoliation sanctions. CSP agreements must address who (organization, CSP, subcontractors) has the duty to preserve each type of ESI. Data that must be preserved must be first located, and with the data mobility principle, this may not be simple to accomplish.

---

7. Fed. R. Civ. P. 37(a).
8. In re Uranium, 480 F. Supp 1138, 1144 (N.D. Ill. 1979).
9. Fed. R. Civ. P. 34(a)(1).
10. Fed. R. Civ. P. 37(b).

It is important to understand all of the possible sources of ESI, to understand how each of these types can be preserved, and also the impact of these sources on the scope of records retention obligations, deriving from statutory, regulatory and contractual mandates. Courts have found many different sources to be considered to be ESI, as the following partial list shows:[11]

Metadata	Websites, blogs, social networks
Removable media	Collaboration tools
Backup tapes	Image and sound files
Archives	Home computers (business use)
Email (corporate & personal) + attachments	RFID info
Calendars	System and phone usage logs
Voice mail	Internet and network access usage logs
Enterprise systems (active and legacy)	Superseded correspondence
Local databases	Deleted files
Spreadsheets/word processor documents	Caches
Instant messages/tweets	Cookies
Mobile phones	Fragments
IPods/PDAs/iPads	Random Access Memory (RAM)

The FRCP states that "[a]bsent exceptional circumstances, a court may not impose sanctions under these rules on a party for failing to provide electronically stored information lost as a result of the routine, good faith operation of an electronic information system."[12] Data may be deleted, according to a regular program (which of course is suspended when a litigation hold is implemented). The organization must ensure that the CSP actually and permanently deletes such information, otherwise it may become discoverable. This includes data in any mirror locations or any backup data copies, including those stored offsite for business continuity.

---

11. Thomas Shaw, *E-Discovery in Asia/Pacific: Litigation Readiness for Asian Companies*, The Privacy Advisor (Nov. 2009).

12. Fed. R. Civ. P. 37(e).

Under U.S. law,[13] parties involved in foreign (non-U.S.) litigation can seek discovery from parties or non-parties over whom a U.S. court has jurisdiction (e.g., an American office). These section 1782 requests allow access to documents (and testimony) through subsidiaries that might not otherwise be available through discovery rules in the foreign jurisdiction. The statute's purpose is to assist foreign tribunals or those appearing before them. The district court's order can be made pursuant to an "application of any interested person." Documents are to be produced in accordance with the FRCP. One case involved a German manufacturer and an international firm and a lawsuit in Germany where there was a "demonstrated need for extensive discovery for aid in that foreign lawsuit where…manufacturer could not obtain even remotely comparable discovery by utilizing German procedures…a party to litigation in a foreign country…can obtain as much discovery as it could if the lawsuit had been brought in that court rather than abroad."[14] This can also be used for litigation in other common law countries for parties or non-parties in the United States.[15]

International Discovery Rules

In other countries around the world, discovery or its equivalent may be allowed, based very broadly on whether the country has a civil law or common law heritage. Common law countries typically inherited their legal systems from the United Kingdom and may require discovery in some form. These countries include not only the United States, but Canada, Australia, India, Hong Kong, and Singapore. Civil law countries include not only those countries that are continental members of the EU like Germany and France, but other countries that modeled their civil codes after EU countries, including Japan, China, South Korea, and those in Latin America. As mentioned previously, the Hague Evidence Convention may control how evidence is discovered between member states that have acceded to this treaty. Within the EU (except Denmark), there is a regulation that countries follow for

---

13. 28 U.S.C. § 1782, Assistance to foreign and international tribunals and to litigants before such tribunals.
14. Heraeus Kulzer GMBH v. Biomet Inc., Case Nos. 09-2858, 10-2639 (7th Cir. 2011).
15. Texas Keystone, Inc. v. Prime Natural Resources, Inc., Case No. 12-20515 (5th Cir. 2012).

obtaining evidence from other EU members.[16] Within the Americas, there is also an agreement between the major members of the Organization of American States[17] (except Canada) that addresses the "obtaining of information abroad." [18]

In the United Kingdom, the Revised Code of Civil Procedure states that a party is required to disclose (state that the document exists/existed) and then allow inspection for those documents in the party's control upon which the party relies, those which may adversely affect the case or which the party is required to disclose by relevant practice directives.[19] In addition to readily accessible documents, it includes documents on "servers and back-up systems and electronic documents that have been 'deleted'. It also extends to additional information stored and associated with electronic documents known as metadata."[20] It is intended that the parties can perform this in a "proportionate and cost-effective manner."[21] In Germany, under the Code of Civil Procedure, litigants only have to produce documents that support their case but the court can summon parties or third parties to disclose documents in their possession.[22] In France, under the new Code of Civil Procedure, parties can disclose certain documents through the judge.[23] Judges also determine the relevance of any requests for discovery outside the country, perhaps supported by an analysis from the French data protection authority.[24]

In Australia, under "Fast Track" litigation, parties must provide those documents "on which a party intends to rely and documents that have significant probative value adverse to a party's case."[25] Under normal litigation, parties are encouraged to agree upon the scope and timetables for discovery and strategies for preservation, reasonable searches (including information not

16. Council Regulation (EC) No. 1206/2001 of 28 May 2001 on cooperation between the courts of the Member States in the taking of evidence in civil or commercial matters.

17. Thirty five members, including Argentina, Brazil, Canada, Mexico, and the United States.

18. Inter-American Convention on Letters Rogatory (1975).

19. U.K. Rev. Civ. Proc. Rules 31.2-31.8.

20. U.K. Practice Directive 31A 2.A1 under CPR Part 31.

21. U.K. Practice Directive 31B under CPR Part 31.

22. German Code of Civil Procedure (Zivilprozessordnung, ZPO) §142.

23. France, New Code of Civil Procedure) §138-142.

24. Délibération n° 2009-474 du 23 juillet 2009 portant recommandation en matière de transfert de données à caractère personnel dans le cadre de procédures judiciaires américaines dite de « Discovery ».

25. Federal Court of Australia, Practice Notes CM 8 Part 7.1.

reasonably accessible) and the management of ESI and the related document management protocols.[26] In Singapore, an opt-in framework has been established to include discovery and inspection of electronically stored documents, computer databases, and electronic media or recording devices.[27] Parties are encouraged to agree on discovery protocols and utilize reasonable searches. Provisions also cover metadata, forensic discovery, and factors to consider if needed to order discovery. In Hong Kong, the practice direction instructs parties to exchange documents without having to prepare lists of documents.[28] In Taiwan, parties are required to produce documents that the party is using or that the opposing party may require.[29] Japan allows for the application for discovery of documents held by the other party or third parties.[30]

Just like the U.S., Canada has federal and provincial rules of procedure. At the federal level, the Federal Court Rules state that the court can order a party to produce "all relevant documents that are in the possession, power or control."[31] Relevant are those documents that one party intends to rely on or that "tends to adversely affect the party's case or to support another party's case."[32] Because most litigation will originate in the provinces, the provincial rules of civil procedure will govern discovery. For example, in British Columbia discovery is required of any documents that relate to a matter in "question."[33] In Ontario the rules require that "Every document relevant to any matter in issue in an action that is or has been in the possession, control or power of a party to the action shall be disclosed,"[34] while containing many e-discovery-specific provisions, such as for discovery plans and proportionality.[35] In Quebec, with its dual legal heritage, parties and third parties still can be ordered to produce documents "relating to the issues."[36]

---

26. Federal Court of Australia, Practice Note CM 6.
27. Supreme Court of Singapore, Practice Direction 3 of 2009.
28. Practice Direction 5.2 of the Government of Hong Kong.
29. Taiwan Code of Civ. Procedure, art. 344.
30. Japan Code of Civ. Procedure, art. 221.
31. The Rules for Regulating the Practice and Procedure in the Federal Court of Appeal and the Federal Court (SOR/98-106), art. 225.
32. *Id*. art. 222.
33. British Columbia Rules of Court, B.C. Reg. 221/90 R. 26.
34. Ontario Rules of Civ. Procedure Rule 30.02(1).
35. Ontario Rules of Civ. Procedure Rule 29.
36. Quebec Code of Civ. Procedure, art. 402.

Mexico is a civil law country and so discovery is much more limited. A kind of discovery can occur in the context of commercial issues, where merchants may be required to produce information, if a judge so orders.[37]

E-Discovery Issues with Cloud Computing

To understand the issues that cloud computing raises in e-discovery, it is perhaps easiest to frame these issues within the well-known Electronic Discovery Reference Model (EDRM). This nine-phase model starts with the data and its related processes from information management done by the organization and continues through its presentation in a court during the litigation.

Information Management

The organization needs to at least perform a complete inventory of data, document the life cycle of records, create a records management policy for dealing with duplicates, metadata, retention and disposition, archiving, and backups, and ensure that there is a regular records destruction program that complies with all contractual and statutory obligations. When utilizing a CSP, the organization needs to determine how a complete and current inventory of its data can be maintained. The records life cycle must remain the same and retention/destruction policies must be enforced in the same manner. Failure to carry out timely and comprehensive records destruction activities could make additional information subject to discovery by potential adversaries. The issue of determining which version of a document to consider a record and the procedures for deleting prior draft versions needs to be shared between the organization and the CSP, depending on the service model used (e.g., CSPs will increasingly control more document versions, deleted files, and backup copies as the service model moves from IaaS to SaaS). And the amount and types of related metadata that the CSPs can make available in the different service models should be determined in advance of commencing service.

---

37. Mexico Federal Commercial Code, arts. 49-50.

Identification

After a lawsuit is initiated or anticipated or when discovery requests, retention letters or orders are received, the scope of the requested data, its sources and locations, and the identity of custodians can be determined. The relevant data needs to be categorized by degree of accessibility (e.g., live, archived, backup tape). "Meet and confer" sessions[38] with the other party are required in order to reach agreement on identification, preservation, collection, processing and production procedures, including formats for production,[39] any not reasonably accessible data,[40] and confidentiality and clawback agreements.[41] Even though the data is located in the cloud, the company is still responsible for knowing where its data is,[42] as previous outsourcing cases have held.[43] In the cloud, the sources and locations of data will require the CSP to take part in identifying these areas. The data custodian will now likely be an employee of the CSP and may need to testify,[44] so this should be agreed to up front in the CSP agreement. Assuming that the collected data will be moved to a separate system outside control of this CSP (perhaps with another CSP providing specialized discovery search and analysis services), the original CSP will need to be part of the sessions to discuss the preservation and collection procedures. These procedures should have been agreed to during the original contract discussions between the organization and the CSP.

Preservation

The organization must ensure that relevant ESI is preserved and protected against destruction and alteration, by preparing and circulating litigation hold communications. Although there are no sanctions for ESI deleted due to "routine, good-faith operation" of a system,[45] backup tape deletions and other automatic deletion programs under the records retention program must be halted. Also, preservation may require forensics imaging techniques to

---

38. Fed. R. Civ. P. 26(f).
39. Fed. R. Civ. P. 34(b).
40. Fed. R. Civ. P. 26(b)(2).
41. *See* Fed. R. Evid. 502(b) and Fed. R. Civ. P. 26(b)(5)(B).
42. Fed. R. Civ. P. 26(a)(1)(A).
43. *See e.g.,* In re NTL Inc. Sec. Litig., 244 F.R.D. 179 (S.D.N.Y. 2007).
44. Fed. R. Civ. P. 30(b)(6).
45. Fed. R. Civ. P. 37(e).

copy information of key players or devices or for deleted or hidden data. In the cloud, the litigation hold procedures must now include both the organization and the CSP. Preservation in the multi-tenant environment of a CSP may be especially complex, given all the possible types of ESI described above. Virtual data stores (i.e., shared physical storage), virtual memory, and shared backup tapes make preservation complicated and implicate data privacy concerns. Perhaps even more complicated are deleted files, file versions, and shared system and other logs. This becomes more problematic as the service model moves from IaaS to SaaS. With IaaS, the ability to image VMs may actually make the preservation process easier than it would be normally. It is essential to stop routine deletion of data and backup tape cycling at the CSP. This may be more difficult in a SaaS environment, where the organization has little leverage over the CSP or where the shared resources are system-wide, such as RAM and logs of various kinds. Preservation techniques in implementing, maintaining and updating a legal hold process and forensic capabilities should be part of the CSP agreement, as should any considerations of who bears the costs related to any liability for spoliation sanctions based on lost or deleted ESI.

Collection

The preserved information must be narrowed down, based on search results, reasonable accessibility, removal of duplicates (de-duplication) and relevance (e.g., system files may be irrelevant). Data collection requires a valid chain of custody and authenticity protocols, including preserving metadata, hashes, labeling and identification. In the cloud, the data must be collected from the CSP based at least on a narrowing by search criteria, elimination of duplicates and perhaps near duplicates, and irrelevant data. The in-scope data may itself remain in the cloud and be searched by various tools using APIs provided by the CSP (e.g., SaaS email systems). With procedures agreed to in advance, the CSP needs to work with the organization's internal and external counsel and e-discovery teams, following the proper protocols. Collection of the applicable metadata on transfer from the CSP is critical. The organization must understand, especially in some PaaS environments (e.g., shared databases) and in most all SaaS environments what restrictions (e.g., search response times, locations, time of day/day of week/month) there will be on collection activities. Collection procedures and related costs should be part of the CSP agreement.

Processing, Review, Analysis, and Production

For purposes of this discussion, it is assumed that these steps happen outside the control of the organization's CSP, so the cloud would implicate no new issues here. In case the data remains in the cloud with the same CSP during these phases, the CSP may have to provide additional storage space, new VMs, and additional user provisioning with specialized access (for both the producing party and potentially the other party), in addition to having to continue its preservation and chain of custody responsibilities. When the data is finally then transferred from the cloud, the production may need to occur in either the original or a format specified by the requesting party.[46] The procedures and costs of doing so should be agreed upon in advance.

Presentation

Introducing the data in court involves a number of litigation issues involving the use of the cloud. The issues with the authentication and admissibility of electronic evidence are further discussed below. Issues with privilege and confidentiality are discussed in Chapter 9. One of the most significant issues is whether the data held by the CSP on behalf of the organization is within the "possession, custody or control"[47] of the organization. While the analysis can be complex, control by the organization over its service providers is typically found, especially given their contractual relationship.[48] It is likely that all organizations will establish via agreements that they own all data that is transferred to or created in the cloud. But is metadata and log data, which are generated during the use of the data and the systems and not transferred to the cloud, in the control of the organization? The scope of the CSP agreement must include all data potentially needed during discovery, including such secondary data as this.

---

46. Fed. R. Civ. P. 34 (b)(2)(E).
47. Fed. R. Civ. P. 26(a)(1)(A)(ii) for initial disclosures and Fed. R. Civ. P. 34(a)(1) for document production.
48. *See* Flagg v. City of Detroit, 252 F.R.D. 346, 352-64 (E.D. Mich. 2008).

A second issue is whether the CSP can be compelled to produce the organization's data without the organization's consent when the CSP is served with a non-party subpoena.[49] As discussed in Chapter 2, the content of communications that is stored on the service provider's servers should not be disclosed to third parties in the United States under the Stored Communications Act[50] (although customer records could be).[51] So a CSP is likely not bound to answer a discovery request from a party to litigation with which it has no relationship.[52] In any situation, in the CSP agreement the organization will want to specify exactly how the CSP will respond to any requests for the organization's information, including the notification that will be provided to the organization upon receipt of any such request. It is important that the CSP comply with the organization's needs in litigation and investigation, including advance notice of all actions.

A third issue is whether the principle of data mobility could perhaps change the argument about whether data is reasonably accessible (e.g., if it is moved to a country with more, or less, stringent data protection laws). Under U.S. federal rules, data may not be reasonably accessible based on undue burden or cost.[53] This burden or cost is undue when it "outweighs its likely benefit, taking into account the needs of the case, the amount in controversy, the parties' resources, the importance of the issues at stake in the litigation, and the importance of the proposed discovery in resolving the issues."[54] The Sedona Conference listed twelve possible factors to determine the accessibility of data, based on the type of media used to store data and the relative complexity, of which several (e.g., transient complexity and dispersion complexity) may apply to the cloud.[55] Based on the analysis done by courts on the issue of reasonable accessibility, cloud data transferred overseas

---

49. Fed. R. Civ. P. 45.

50. 18 U.S.C. §§ 2701-2712.

51. 18 U.S.C. § 2702(c)(6).

52. *See Crispin v. Christian Audigier, Inc.*, Case No. CV 09-09509 MMM-JEMx (C.D. Cal. 2010); *In re Subpoena Duces Tecum to AOL LLC*, 550 F. Supp. 2d. 606 (E.D. Va. 2008).

53. Fed. R. Civ. P. 26(b)(2)(B).

54. Fed. R. Civ. P. 26(b)(2)(C). as quoted in Barrera v. Boughton, 2010 WL 3926070 (D. Conn. 2010).

55. *Preservation, Management and Identification of Sources of Information that are Not Reasonably Accessible*, The Sedona Conference Working Group 1 (July, 2008).

may also be one of the factors considered.[56] The CSP agreement should provide that organization data transferred to the cloud should always be made reasonably accessible.

A fourth issue has involved e-discovery requests for data posted to third party cloud sites, and whether in such cases organizations retain their rights to privacy. In a series of cases,[57] courts have answered across the spectrum but the overarching theme appears to be that privacy rights are not assured (and e-discovery requests will be ordered) when the purpose of the site is for sharing, such as in social network sites. When the data is posted to the cloud with no expectation for sharing, as organization data should be, then privacy rights should remain inviolate. But in at least one of these cases, the court held that because the operations personnel of the cloud site could access the information, there was no reasonable expectation of privacy and so the discovery order could proceed.[58] The CSP agreement should state clearly that it is the intention of the organization that all data it provides or creates in the cloud is intended to always be considered private.

A fifth issue is related to privacy rights but this involves privacy rights as protected by data protection laws and blocking statutes. These laws were discussed in Chapters 2 and 3, but one additional consideration is whether privacy laws have any impact on discovery requests. In the view of U.S. courts, the answer is most likely not, and motions for discovery requests will be granted for data that is located outside the U.S.[59]

6.2 Data Breach in the Cloud

Before considering outsourcing, organizations need to plan for and respond, both proactively and reactively, to any breach of their employee, customer, or corporate data, for statutory, regulatory, business competitive, reputational, and litigation reasons. Organizations that outsource remain responsible for

---

56. See Thomas Shaw, *e-Discovery in Asia/Pacific: Litigation Readiness for Asian Companies*, The Privacy Advisor (Nov. 2009).

57. See e.g. Romano v. Steelcase, Inc., 907 N.Y.S.2d 650 (N.Y. Sup. 2010); E.E.O.C. v. Simply Storage Management, LLC, 2010 WL 3446105, 1 (S.D. Ind. 2010); Crispin v. Christian Audigier, Inc. et. al., Case No. CV 09-09509 MMM-JEMx (C.D. Cal. 2010); McMillen v. Hummingbird Speedway, Inc., No. 113—2010 CD (Jefferson County, Pa. 2010).

58. McMillen v. Hummingbird Speedway, Inc., No. 113-2010 CD (Jefferson County, Pa. 2010).

59. See AccessData Corp. v. ALSTE Technologies GMBH, 2010 WL 318477 (D. Utah 2010).

data breaches after transferring data to a CSP,[60] both in responding and in the potential exposures to a data breach. In some ways, the potential for a data breach may increase, due to the CSP being a more inviting target for hackers, criminals and state actors. Several breaches in recent years of some of the largest players in cloud computing have demonstrated the need for organizations to be prepared for responding when a breach occurs at a CSP or major cloud organization.

For example, a breach of data stored in Microsoft's cloud-based Office Suite was caused by an "unspecified 'configuration issue' in Microsoft's data centers in the United States, Europe and Asia."[61] The source code used by Internet security firm Symantec was accessed and published by hackers.[62] RSA, a provider of data protection solutions for CSPs and their customers (e.g., SecurID), was breached, with unknown impacts on those utilizing RSA security solutions to protect their own data.[63] The personal and financial information of over 20 million customers was accessed in a breach of an Amazon.com-owned company.[64] Hackers were able to gain access to cloud storage firm Dropbox.[65] Cloud OS firm VMware had part of its software exposed after a breach.[66] As such, an organization must not only risk assess CSPs and integrate its data breach handling procedures with those of the CSP, but also should do the same with any of its business partners with whom it shares its confidential data, and then regularly update these risk assessments to ensure that its security safeguards and those of its partners continue to be rigorous and that the likelihood of a breach is minimized to the extent possible.

Indicia of a Data Breach

While the concept of a breach of an organization's data seems an easy one, it is not always easy to agree on just what qualifies as a data breach. Is it only

---

60. See e.g. U.K., Data Protection Act (1998).

61. Microsoft cloud data breach heralds shape of things to come, Computerworld UK (Dec. 24, 2010).

62. *Symantec confirms source code leak in two enterprise security products*, Computerworld (Jan. 6, 2012).

63. Art Coviello, Executive Chairman, RSA, *Open Letter to RSA Customers* (Mar. 2011).

64. *Zappos customer data access in security breach*, CNET (Jan. 15, 2012).

65. *Dropbox confirms it was hacked, offers users help*, CNET (July 31, 2012).

66. *Hacker leaks VMware ESX kernel source code online*, ZDNet (Nov. 4, 2012).

an attempt at unauthorized access to a system or is it only the successful use of data acquired in an authorized manner to enrich the taker or harm the data subject? In Europe, ENISA (discussed in Chapter 5) has documented the differences of belief among EU data protection regulators about just what constitutes a data breach, while at the same time listing some types of breaches that organizations can refer to:[67]

- Loss of IT equipment—misplaced or stolen equipment—laptops, USB sticks, etc.
- Mailing—distribution of a letter in the mail or an email to an incorrect address that includes personal data
- Improper disposal of documents—leaving personal data in documents deposited in a garbage bin that can be accessed by the public
- Hacking—malicious attacks on computer networks
- Technical error—unforeseen complication in an IT system exposing data to outside parties
- Theft—data in the form of documents, electronically stored data, etc., that is stolen
- Unauthorized access—employees taking advantage of vulnerabilities to access personal data of customers stored in files or electronically
- Unauthorized distribution—distributing personal data on P2P (Peer 2 Peer) networks

The Ponemon Institute's benchmark study[68] of U.S. data breaches has again found that certain costs of data breaches are increasing. These costs include detection, escalation, notification, and after-the-fact response, including engaging forensic experts, in-house investigations and communication, outsourced hotline support, free credit monitoring subscriptions, and discounts for future products and services. It also looks at the economic impact of lost or diminished customer trust and confidence as measured by customer

67. ENISA, *Data breach notifications in the EU* (Jan. 2011).
68. Ponemon Institute, *2011 Cost of Data Breach Study: United States* (Mar. 2012).

turnover (churn) rates. This report made the following significant points for the cloud computing environment:

- Customer turnover in direct response to breaches remains a significant driver of data breach costs
- The number of breaches attributed to negligence is the most common threat
- Breaches by third-party outsourcers account for 41 percent of the total surveyed
- Breaches caused by lost or stolen devices was 39 percent of the total surveyed
- Organizations with better security postures have much lower data breach costs
- Average cost of a data breach in the U.S. was $194 per record, compared to €146 for Germany, [69] €122 for France,[70] £79 for the United Kingdom,[71] €78 for Italy,[72] ¥11,011 for Japan, [73] AUD 138 for Australia, [74] and INR 2,105 for India[75]
- The cost of malicious data breaches, as opposed to non-malicious (negligence-based) data breaches, is significantly higher[76]
- Endpoints and databases were most often involved in the non-malicious data breach and applications and user accounts for malicious data breach incidents[77]
- The most serious consequence of a non-malicious breach is lost reputation, brand value and market place image while for a malicious breach it is lost time and productivity and loss of reputation[78]

---

69. Ponemon Institute, *2011 Cost of Data Breach Study: Germany* (Mar. 2012).

70. Ponemon Institute, *2011 Cost of Data Breach Study: France* (Mar. 2012).

71. Ponemon Institute, *2011 Cost of Data Breach Study: United Kingdom* (Mar. 2012).

72. Ponemon Institute, *2011 Cost of Data Breach Study: Italy* (Mar. 2012).

73. Ponemon Institute, *2011 Cost of Data Breach Study: Japan* (Mar. 2012).

74. Ponemon Institute, *2011 Cost of Data Breach Study: Australia* (Mar. 2012).

75. Ponemon Institute, *2011 Cost of Data Breach Study: India* (Mar. 2012).

76. Ponemon Institute, *The Post Breach Boom* (Mar. 2013), survey of more than 3500 IT and IT security practitioners in the United States, Canada, The United Kingdom, Australia, Brazil, Japan, Singapore and the United Arab Emirates.

77. *Id.*

78. *Id.*

At the same time, it is important to have a firm understanding of the constantly changing profile of data breaches. In a recent survey of thirty-six countries by Verizon and its partners,[79] the reported data breaches in the survey in 2012 showed the following characteristics. The majority of the attacks (and 80-90 percent of breached records) involved some type of hacking or malware. Ninety-eight percent of the data breaches (and 99 percent of breached records) were from external agents. Ninety-two percent of breaches are discovered by third parties. Ninety-four percent of the data breaches were avoidable through simple or intermediate controls.

The report tried to identify the link between cloud computing and data breaches by looking for certain characteristics of the cloud within data breaches. Defining a cloud-based asset as one "that you do not own, is hosted in an external facility, and is managed or administered by a third party (or some combination of these)," the percent of breaches that occurred at externally or co-located facilities was 29 percent, of externally managed or co-managed assets was 52 percent, and on partner-owned assets was percent.

Responding to a Data Breach

In the non-outsourced environment, the organization has to undertake a number of steps to prepare for and respond to data breaches. This assumes the implementation of a rigorous information security and privacy program, as explained in Chapters 4 and 5. The steps that focus just on the data breach program include:

- Define exactly what is and what is not considered a data breach (e.g., is any unauthorized access a data breach?)
- Determine which specific information is considered to be in-scope personal information and understand whether it is encrypted and when (at rest, in transit, in use)
- Have a complete map to where all data is currently located and how each is classified
- Understand the exact triggers that start the data breach process

---

79. *2012 Data Breach Investigations Report*, Verizon Risk Team, Australian Federal Police, Dutch National High Tech Crime Unit, Irish Reporting and Information Security Service, Police Central e-Crime Unit, and United States Secret Service.

- Create an incident response team, with members from all applicable disciplines including information security, legal, data owners, public relations and top executives
- Make a breach response contact list and an escalation personnel list
- Define the breach response steps (e.g., quarantine, gather evidence, investigate) and prioritize the steps, including what causes escalation to each succeeding level
- Understand which breach notification statutes apply and the organization's responsibilities under each
- Determine the role that law enforcement will play and the applicable law enforcement agencies
- Determine if there are contractual requirements with the organization's customers or vendors to notify them in case of a data breach
- Understand the notification process involving applicable regulatory officials
- Prepare the respective breach response roles for public relations (for business reputation and brand impacts), customer relationship management, and help desk support (to deal with consumer calls)
- Train on, monitor, and keep up to date the intrusion detection and prevention tools and processes
- Create a process for legal review after a breach to determine potential legal liabilities and litigation strategies
- Prepare for the possibilities of implementing cloud consumer credit monitoring and identify theft prevention efforts
- Understand potential costs of data breaches and which are covered by insurance
- Regularly review all security and intrusion incidents, even if they do not lead to a breach, and document and implement all remediation actions
- Test run a practice intrusion leading to breach with the appropriate members of the incident response team

How Breach Response Differs in the Cloud

In the cloud environment, planning for and responding to data breaches has several new aspects.[80] Each of these new aspects introduces a potential risk and as such, the organization needs to adapt an appropriate risk treatment for each. All coordination activities will need to occur between the organization and the primary CSP (if several are involved) and the primary CSP needs to ensure that the secondary CSPs have synchronized their data breach response procedures appropriately.

- *The CSP will now be the first to know when a breach occurs.* The CSP, through its own monitoring and incident detection capabilities, will likely be the first to know that a breach has occurred. This means that the incident response procedures of the CSP will be invoked, including the determination of whether there has been a breach. But as the organization retains the legal obligations and exposures after a breach, it must be fully involved in these determinations. As such, the incident response procedures including the determination of whether a breach has occurred must fully involve the organization. It must not only integrate its procedures for incident response and escalation with the CSP's procedures but must ensure that it maintains an accurate and up-to-date contact list with the CSP, including holiday contact information.
- *The multitenant environment may make it more difficult to determine who is affected.* The rigorous isolation controls in the multitenant environment ensure that the co-tenants are always kept virtually segregated. But as attacks may be against physical and not logical devices and environments, it may not be easy to tell which tenants are affected by a breach. This complexity in the multitenant environment can be addressed by having monitoring tools imbedded inside the virtualization system, to help identify unauthorized activity and the affected areas and tenants. There may be monitoring and investigation tools that can be extended from the CSP to the customer to assist with the organization's own breach response activities.

---

80. *See* Thomas Shaw, *Legal Response to Data Breaches in the Cloud,* The Privacy Advisor (Oct. 2012).

- *The definition of a breach may be different.* The various CSPs will have differing definitions of what they consider a data breach. Some may consider a breach to occur only if there is a violation of the local applicable laws, while others may require proof that data has been removed and utilized in a manner harmful to the data subjects. An organization would most likely want to know of any unauthorized access to their systems and data and then be able to determine how to comply with its applicable statutory, regulatory and contractual obligations. The organization and the CSP need to ensure that they have come to a complete agreement about this definition.

- *The conflicting breach notification statutes.* The proliferating number of such statutes and regulatory rules may make it extremely complex for a CSP to respond completely to all of these requirements. Besides, it may not be clear whether the CSP or the organization is always primarily responsible for responding to the breach notification requirements. The organization must clarify the respective roles of the organization and the CSP in the case of a breach in each applicable jurisdiction. Sending breach notification notices may be something that is more logical for the CSP to do but it may want to be compensated accordingly if it is not at fault for the breach.

- *Whether and to which law enforcement body to report.* If the data breach impacts more than a single state or country, there will be differing law enforcement agencies to report to and that get involved. Again, the CSP and the organization need to determine the roles of each in reporting to the appropriate law enforcement agencies and under which circumstances a report should be made. For their own differing business reasons, the organization and the CSP may or may not want to report a breach to law enforcement.

- *The differing RPOs and RTOs of customers may complicate a breach-related recovery.* As discussed in Chapter 5, the organization will have a specific minimum amount of data loss (RPO—Recovery Point Objective) and maximum recovery time (RTO—Recovery Time Objective) that it will accept if the breach affects data such that it requires a recovery. Multiple tenant environments will likely have to move to both the minimum RTO and maximum RPO to satisfy all of the tenants. Organizations

199

will want to find a way to have their business continuity requirements appropriately addressed.

- *The impacts of different cloud service models.* SaaS customers have the least control and so may have to rely totally on the breach response processes and capabilities of the CSP. PaaS customers may have additional visibility and control and IaaS even more so over the breach response, recovery, and investigation procedures. Therefore organizations will need to consider the multiple cloud service models that they use and have multiple breach response procedures utilizing the tools that are available with each. This will also likely impact the RTOs and RPOs that are obtainable.

- *Differing rules of escalation, quarantine, and remediation.* The CSP and the organization will have different rules for when to escalate the data breach, quarantine the source of the data breach, and remediate the problem. When the organization has less leverage with the CSP, it may need to use its own procedures to create a superset of beach response procedures. When it has more leverage, it will need to integrate each of these areas to the fullest extent possible, but even then, there will be some differences, as the CSP has a wider audience it has to address, so the organization should also maintain a superset of rules for breach response.

- *Reduced visibility to problem.* The tools that organizations use to understand breaches, such as intrusion detection alerts and system and transaction logs, may not be available. Physical access to servers for forensic analysis or to unplug the network, to hit the reset button or to re-boot systems if all else fails, is not available either. The usual administrative access levels may not be available, as those may be retained by the CSP. Network connections may also be affected. To address some of these issues, a secure channel (VPN) connection to the organization's systems to analyze problems and communicate is needed, as well as network or application monitoring capabilities, and some forensic analysis and collection of alerts and logs.

- *Difficulty in fully testing the breach response procedures.* As with an incident response process, from the smallest misconfiguration to a full-blown disaster, it is vital to go beyond the paper design and actually test the procedures under at least a mock incident occurrence scenario. This is the only way to understand how well the procedures will work and how well the various participants understand their roles. With a data breach when the data in hosted by a CSP, this may not be easy to do. For data under the SaaS model, resource constraints may not allow the CSP to be able to participate in each customer's data breach response exercises. For data under the IaaS model, the CSP may not feel any obligation to do so, assuming it has made reasonable efforts to provide appropriate security in the areas for which it remains responsible. As such, the organization may have to perform such exercises with a surrogate acting for the CSP, hopefully based on its incident response procedures.

6.3 Cyber Insurance

To address the risk of unauthorized data disclosure through data breach or other method, appropriate risk treatments beyond controls include accepting the risk, outsourcing the risk, and insuring the risk. Relatively new is insurance that specially addresses data breaches and their costs and damages. There have long been commercial general liability policies that protect against property damage or loss of use of property. Another policy coverage includes reimbursement for intentional torts and the violation of the right to privacy that a data breach may cause. Applicable insurance policies include both the policy of the organization itself and potentially that of the CSP, if the organization is named as an additional insured on the CSP's policy.

Beyond data breach, other attacks on the Internet presence in the cloud can include attempts to bring down an organization's business through distributed denial of service (DDoS) attacks or more traditionally by using malware to wreak havoc on systems (or the threat to do so). Organizations should consider insurance as a viable part of their risk response in all of these situations. There are varying types of insurance products to address this, ranging from the more mature to the very new, so it is best to look for a specific list of coverage items. These coverage items should be part of both the organization's and the CSP's policies, unless it is completely clear where the ultimate liability for a cost or loss lies and there is financial wherewithal to satisfy it in all circumstances.

The following are some of the coverage types needed to reimburse the costs of: notifying affected parties (including data subjects, regulators, etc.); data subject credit monitoring services (the most typical response to a data breach); setting up a call center to assist data subjects; legal services in responding to litigation (often privacy related) and breach investigations; forensic and security investigations to determine the cause and remedy the immediate situation; public relations to repair any brand or other business-related damages caused by the breach; rebuilding the data, equipment, or services, as necessary; and legal services for pursuing/defending applicable indemnities, litigation damage settlements, awards, and regulatory fines. Coverage should also include: errors and omissions (E&O) for missing software code or patches; claims related to intellectual property infringement or libel; fraud or extortion causing loss of monetary assets; revenue lost due to any business interruption caused by the breach or attack (first and third party); and the payments for fines, settlements, awards, and indemnities.

Any exclusions or limitations must be clearly understood, including the applicability to first-party and third-party claims (on its own policy, the organization is the first party and its customers, vendors, and employees are third parties, while for a CSP's policies, the CSP is the first party and its customers i.e., the cloud consumers, vendors, and employees are the third parties). As an example, data breach cost reimbursement could be limited if caused not by actions of an unauthorized outsider (e.g., hacker) but instead by an authorized insider (e.g., IT employee who discloses personal information). Another example would be the limiting of claims of data breach of data subjects to a certain type of remedial service like credit monitoring or to a specified dollar amount per claimed incident. Pre-breach planning service is a very useful coverage to utilize.

Court cases on insurance have helped to shape the insurance market but have not always been in alignment. With their customers' data stored in the cloud, cloud consuming organizations will look to their business interruption insurance coverage if they cannot access their cloud services. One case helped to get data loss excluded from reimbursement under most policies, as data was considered to be tangible property eligible for reimbursement for its loss, in that "physical damage is not restricted to the physical destruction or harm of computer circuitry, but includes loss of access, loss of use, and loss of functionality." [81] Another case held that the cost of re-inputting data lost due to operator error causing data loss was not a physical loss eligible for reimbursement by insurance.[82] A third case allowed for claims based on the loss of revenue from corruption of data in a datacenter caused by a power outage.[83]

For data breaches, the companies who are breached have had to proceed against their insurer to recover the various costs of a breach. Sony, in trying to get insurance reimbursement after its PlayStation breach in 2011, filed suit against its insurer. The insurer claimed that the class action or claims of Sony were not covered under the insurance policies' categories of "bodily injury," "property damage," "advertising injury," and/or "personal injury." Because there was no injury or damage such as covered by the policies, there was no obligation to defend or indemnify Sony.[84] More recently, another organizational victim of a data breach tried to make a claim under its computer fraud coverage for its costs of data breach response. The insurer would not pay the claim, as the costs were not directly related to the data breach, but the court ruled against the insurer, finding that even though the loss may not have been direct, the breach was its proximate cause.[85]

But third party claims from data subjects who have been breached have had a much harder time getting courts to agree that they have a legitimate legal case (thereby impacting both the CSPs and the cloud consumer organization that took custody of the data subject's data). Courts have looked at whether any injury was suffered by the third party from the breach and typically found the claims to not meet the requirements for an injury sufficient for Article III standing[86] or have found standing but that the third party could not state a claim under any of the theories because no sufficient

---

81. American Guarantee & Liability Ins. Co. v. Ingram Micro Inc., Case No. 99-185 (D. Ariz. 2000).

82. Ward General Ins. Services, Inc. v. Employers Fire Ins. Co., Case No. G031624 (Cal. App. 2003).

83. Southeast Mental Health Center, Inc. v Pacific Ins. Co., Ltd., Case No. 04-2513 (W.D. Tenn. 2006).

84. Zurich American Ins. Co. v. Sony Corp. of America, Inc., Case No. 11-cv-1369 (Sup. N.Y. Jul. 2011).

85. Retail Ventures, Inc., DSW, Inc., and DSW Shoe Warehouse, Inc. v. National Union Fire Insurance Company of Pittsburgh, Pa.., Case Nos. 10-4576/4608 (6th Cir. Aug. 2012).

86. Katz v. Pershing LLC, Case No. 11-1983 (1st Cir. Feb. 2012).

injury had occurred.[87] But in other cases, they have found sufficient injury had occurred (was not speculative or remote) as required to proceed to trial or class certification analysis.[88]

That is not to say that organizations or CSPs can escape liability for data breaches, as regulators are still able to prosecute breaches as violations of state consumer laws[89] and under federal trade[90] and health privacy laws.[91] Organizations need to fully analyze the current legal situation regarding insurance cases in their respective jurisdictions to understand how courts view data loss from a first-party and third-party perspective and ensure that their insurance coverage has the proper wording to match expectations and the organization's accepted risk profile.

6.4 Forensics in the Cloud

The objective of digital forensics is to obtain legally admissible evidence from digital devices (network, servers, PCs, etc.). On a server, capture of information should include the running processes and services, the current logged-in users, network connections/ports, and data in memory. Because in the cloud computing environment there is no longer a one organization to one machine ratio for servers and network devices (at least in a public cloud), there are a number of resulting complications. Besides the issues with the multitenant environment, there must be sufficient controls of the

---

87. Low v. LinkedIn Corporation, Case No. 11-cv-1468 (N.D. Cal. Jun. 2012); In re Sony Gaming Networks and Customer Data Security Breach Litigation, Case Nos. 11cv2119/2120 (S.D. Cal. Oct. 2012).

88. Anderson v. Hannaford Bros. Co., Case Nos. 10-2384, 10-2450 (1st Cir. 2011); Burrows v. Purchasing Power, LLC, Case No. 12-cv-22800 (S.D. Fla. Oct. 2012); Resnick v. AvMed, Inc., Case No. 11-13694. (11th Cir. Sep. 2012).

89. See e.g. Commonwealth of Massachusetts v. Briar Group, LLC, Case No. 11-1185, Final Judgment by Consent (Mass. Sup. Ct. 2011); Insurance Commissioner Fines Health Net of Connecticut for Information Security Lapses, State of Connecticut Insurance Dept. News Release (Nov. 8, 2010); State of Indiana v. WellPoint, Inc., Case No. 49D06-1010-PL-47381 (Ind. Super. 2011).

90. See e.g. In the Matter of Lockout Services, Inc., FTC File No. 102-3076 (2011); In the Matter of Ceridian Corporation, FTC File No. 102-3160 (2011).; In the Matter of SettlementOne Credit Corporation and Sacket National Holdings, Inc. FTC File No. 082-3208; In the Matter of ACRAnet Inc. FTC File No. 092-3088; In the Matter of Fajilan and Assoc. Inc. also d/b/a Statewide Credit Services and Robert Fajilan, FTC File No. 092-3089.

91. See e.g. State of Minnesota v. Accretive Health Inc., Case No. 12-145 (D. Minn. June 2012); Dept. of HHS OCR and BlueCross BlueShield of Tennessee, Resolution Agreement (Mar. 2012).

CSP environment to perform a forensic data capture. If a forensic capture of the CSP environment can be performed, can it be done on live or only dead systems, which utilize different techniques? And each of the popular virtualization server operating systems, such as Citrix Xen and VMware ESX, have a series of unique files that must be known by the forensic examiner, such as log files, swap files, image snapshot files, paging files, configuration files, user profiles, and the registry files. There are many issues involved in utilizing forensics in the cloud, which this section will discuss, after giving a brief overview of the basics of forensics.

Forensic Basics

The capture of forensics information from IT resources may be required for reasons of litigation, criminal or regulatory investigations, or to be able to identify the work of unauthorized individuals, as in the case of a data breach. To capture such digital evidence, the police organizations in the United Kingdom operate under the following principles.[92] These include: not changing data on a computer or storage media that will subsequently be used in court, ensuring that access to original data must be explainable as to relevance and implications in court, and that an audit trail of all computer-based evidence should be maintained and preserved so that a third party can replicate the results. Specific instructions include not turning on a powered-off device or removing the power source from a powered-on device, and labeling all ports and cables on the device. Collection of volatile data is important, including running processes and services, network connections, logged-in and registered users, unencrypted data, passwords, registry information, and other data that may be in memory.

To ensure organizations have a viable forensic analysis capability, NIST recommends a four-phase process of data collection, examination, analysis, and reporting, while "preserving the integrity of the information and maintaining a strict chain of custody for the data."[93] This is based on the four main sources of electronic forensic data: files (file systems, deleted files, free space, slack space, and hidden files), operating systems (in the file system:

---

92. *Good Practice Guide for Computer-Based Electronic Evidence*, ver. 4.0, ACPO UK.
93. NIST, SP 800-86, *Guide to Integrating Forensic Techniques into Incident Response* (2006).

configuration, application and data files, logs and swap, dump and temporary files and in RAM: slack space, free space, network connections, open files, logged in users, and running processes), network traffic, and applications. The four phases transform the data on media into extracted data through the examination phase process into information through the analysis phase process and finally into evidence through using the information in the reporting phase.

Beyond collecting information from PCs and servers, the cloud's ubiquitous network access implicates the use of all types of mobile devices. The forensic capture and analysis process for mobile devices, while having the same ultimate objective as with more stationary devices, differs in the techniques used. This is due to the different hardware, firmware, and software used in the mobile devices, as well as the more proprietary architectures found in these devices. Some complications include the need to leave the mobile device on to capture information but at the same time not connect to any wired or wireless networks, and to avoid overwriting of existing information in memory. According to one source,[94] the steps to undertake on a standard mobile phone include verification of whose device it is via the Subscriber Identity Module SIM card, getting the system description, acquiring evidence by dumping memory, accessing the file system, and utilizing "AT" commands. This evidence includes address books, calendars, text messages, call history, web browsing history, and information resident therein. As with PCs and Internet service provider (ISP) information that exists outside the device for its network connections, there will be a network connection for the mobile device but in addition to ISP connection information, there may be wireless network connection information from that provider. The data collection from such mobile devices may need to take into account emerging privacy standards, such as for data created by or collected directly or indirectly from the mobile user.[95]

According to one recent survey, malicious data breaches were "most often discovered through the use of forensic methods and tools."[96] Forensics after

---

94. SANS Institute, *Mobile Device Forensics* (2009).

95. GSM Association, *Privacy Design Guidelines for Mobile Application Development* (2011).

96. Ponemon Institute, *The Post Breach Boom* (Mar. 2013).

a data breach will involve looking for certain kinds of information, such as the footprints of unauthorized intruders into a system, in addition to the vulnerabilities in a system that were exploited by the intruder. A primary source for analyzing the cause of a data breach is the various system logs. To utilize these logs, they must be set to capture all necessary information and must be protected from being overwritten (some hackers attempt to cover their tracks by modifying logs of their activities). When negotiating with a CSP, the organization needs to understand what information a CSP captures in its various detection and system logs and how the CSP will protect the logs against the intruder being able to modify the logs to cover its tracks. In dealing with forensics when involved in solving a data breach, the use of anti-forensics must understood. After the breach, the attacker may often try to cover its tracks by covering up much of the evidence of its unauthorized entry. In addition to modifying records in system and other logs, this includes activities such as data wiping and data hiding (even using encryption). In the Verizon data breach report, at least one-third of the reported cases involved some use of anti-forensics.[97]

Cloud Specifics

Chapter 4 explained the security risks of virtualization techniques used in cloud computing. One reason virtualization causes a problem for forensics examination is that many of the components collected and analyzed in the process above are no longer available for collection and analysis in the multitenant environment. For example, the deleted files, the free space, and slack space are actually part of the physical file system. When the data storage resources are virtualized and so abstracted from the user, the organization may no longer have access to the physical device, only the virtual device's view of the physical storage, which likely would not include, for example, hidden files. On the server, the memory again is virtualized, so while an IaaS service would provide access to a virtual view of memory, not the total contents of physical RAM, the ability to map it completely for the items listed

---

97. *2012 Data Breach Investigations Report*, Verizon Risk Team, Australian Federal Police, Dutch National High Tech Crime Unit, Irish Reporting and Information Security Service, Police Central e-Crime Unit, and United States Secret Service.

above is lost. Abstraction narrows the possible scope of the forensic data collection and the follow-on analysis.

Contemplating forensic analysis in the cloud environment raises at least these issues that organizations should consider during negotiation of the CSP agreement:

- If forensics analysis is required, who will do it, the organization or the CSP?
- If forensics analysis is the CSP's responsibility, how do they ensure data integrity (e.g., hashing) and chain of custody?
- If forensics analysis is the organization's responsibility, are there APIs or other techniques available for such access?
- What system files may the organization access or not access in performing its analysis?
- Which operating system and related analysis tools does the CSP utilize?
- How will the CSP ensure confidentiality of data of other organizations during a forensic exam?
- How frequently and of what does the organization takes snapshots?
- Are there forensics analysis capabilities of live VMs?
- Are deleted files belonging to the organization still available for analysis?
- Can all copies of the organization's data, including live, mirrored, backup, and deleted be identified at a point in time, including metadata?
- Can all copies of the organization's VMs, including live, mirrored, snapshot, imaged, stopped, decommissioned, and deleted be identified at a point in time?
- What logging is performed by the CSP?
- Is virtualized disk, memory, and network information available for analysis?
- Is there identity and access management log information available for analysis?
- What type of access user ID is required to perform forensic examinations and is the use of these user IDs itself logged?
- What is the use of encryption and what type(s) are deployed?
- Are any keys managed by the CSP necessary for the forensic analysis available to the organization?
- Is federated identity management used and is there an external identity provider?

- Does the CSP have forensic expertise available both for technical assistance and to testify in court as needed?
- Does the CSP have a separate incident investigation environment to utilize for analysis?

The answers to these questions are going to depend not only on the individual CSP and its implemented architecture but also on the service model and deployment model selected by the organization. Access to low-level data will be much more freely available in private clouds than in public clouds and in IaaS environments than in SaaS environments. Taking physical servers or disks offline for imaging is not likely to be allowed in a multitenant environment, so the ability to utilize tools originating from the virtualization management system are key in capturing sufficient valid data. At the lowest level (IaaS), organizations will have access to their own virtual machines and disks but may not have access to the virtual-to-physical interfaces or devices. Images of VMs will be limited to file system ISO images[98] instead of bit-stream images, which would include free and slack space (which may show any deleted files).

ISO/IEC 27037 issued guidance in 2012 on dealing with the initial steps of finding, collecting, and preserving digital forensic evidence.[99] This document provides guidelines on the steps to identify, gather, collect, acquire, handle, and protect and preserve digital forensic evidence. It is related to a series of other ISO/IEC publications including: ISO/IEC 27035,[100] ISO/IEC 27041,[101] ISO/IEC 27042,[102] and ISO/IEC 27043[103] that address security incidents, including how to interpret and analyze such incidents and the appropriate practices to utilize. CSA recently published a brief document that ties these guidelines to the cloud for different device types.[104]

---

98. Based on the ISO/IEC DIS 9660 (1999) standard for volumes/file systems.

99. ISO/IEC 27037:2012 — Information technology — Security techniques — Guidelines for identification, collection, acquisition, and preservation of digital evidence.

100. ISO/IEC 27035:2011 — Information technology — Security techniques — Information security incident management.

101. ISO/IEC CD 27041 — Guidance on assuring suitability and adequacy of incident investigation methods.

102. ISO/IEC CD 27042 — Guidelines for the analysis and interpretation of digital evidence.

103. ISO/IEC CD 27043 — Incident investigation principles and processes.

104. CSA, Mapping the Forensic Standard ISO/IEC 27037 to Cloud Computing (June 2013).

Chapter 7

NEGOTIATING THE CSP AGREEMENT

With the statutory, risk, information security, privacy, and litigation concepts as explained in the previous chapters, lawyers can now begin to bring these together with the needs of the organization for incorporation into the agreements negotiated with CSPs. Chapter 9 lists some of the steps that lawyers will need to undertake to prepare for this. This chapter will first bring together those suggestions for contractual provisions discussed in previous chapters and then discuss additional provisions that should be included. In the second section, several real cloud contracts will be analyzed using examples of leading offerings from each of the three services models: Salesforce.com (SaaS), Google App Engine (PaaS) and Amazon EC2 (IaaS). For organizations with negotiating leverage, the federal government's model agreement is discussed next. Then the negotiated cloud agreements between the City of Los Angeles and its cloud outsourcers are analyzed and the negotiated agreement between Google and the University of Cambridge is considered. Organizations may find that they can negotiate only limited or no changes with large CSPs offering standard agreements (or for click-through service contracts). It is important to note not just what is in the CSP's terms of service and SLAs but where these are silent as to certain provisions and metrics, and thus further negotiating possibilities may exist for the organization to get an agreement that better reflects its requirements. Chapter 8 will discuss practical applications of these contractual provisions.

Executive Takeaways

- How to determine the key contractual provisions to negotiate with a CSP
- How to determine appropriate SLA metrics and reporting schemes
- Understanding of example standard CSP agreements in different service models
- Understanding possible revisions based on negotiated agreements

7.1 Contractual Provisions

Contract Provisions Discussed So Far

In prior chapters of the book, a number of contractual provisions were explained. These are shown by chapter as follows, with additional insights for negotiating with the CSP.

Foreword

- *Choice of law*: When the organization and CSPs are located in different countries, states, provinces or territories, as they inevitably will be, then it becomes imperative to determine which body of substantive law will govern the agreement and any disputes that may arise between the parties. CSPs will likely want to utilize the law of their place of incorporation and unless these local laws are contrary to the way the organization operates or if they are hard to gain knowledge about, then the organization can acquiesce to the CSP preference.
- *Jurisdiction*: For the same reason of geographic diversity, the question of which jurisdiction has the ability to exert control over the parties (and

any necessary third parties) can be resolved (at least as to the parties) in the agreement by both parties agreeing to submit to the jurisdiction of a certain national/local court system.

- *Mandatory arbitration*: Many service providers prefer to require arbitration as the medium in which to resolve any dispute. This potentially reduces both some of the biggest legal expenses (e.g., discovery) and provides for a hopefully less adversarial way to resolve any disputes. Organizations may have a pre-existing policy for handling this provision in vendor contracts but will likely want to retain the ability to litigate in certain circumstances, especially when there may be large liability exposures.

- *Changing the terms of a standard agreement via website posting*: While smaller organizations may have to accept this, organizations with more leverage will require any of: advanced notice, participation in the policy change discussions, emailed copies of the changed policy, or notice after the change.

- *Data integrity*: Depending on which service model is being used, ensuring data integrity may be increasingly important. In an IaaS offering, where the organization controls all transactions and access to the logical systems, there may be little to ask of the CSP. But where a CSP provides the application as a SaaS offering or offers a database in a PaaS offering, especially in a multi-tenant environment or where disparate locations are used for database storage, data integrity assurance is vital. Organizations will want to understand how the CSP ensures data integrity across transactions in its SaaS and PaaS offerings. Loss of data integrity due to corruption by CSP systems or other loss (e.g., hardware failure leading to unrecoverable data loss) should be compensated based on the impact to the cloud consumer.

- *Deletion of data at termination*: At termination of the services, which may be initiated by the organization or possibly the CSP (likely involuntary), there needs to be a clear plan as to what will happen to the data of the organization. This includes not only data content, but metadata, VM images, backup, business continuity, and mirrored copies and systems, transaction, and audit logs. The methodologies for physical as well as logical deletion should be specified.

- *Responding to compelled disclosure*: Because CSPs may receive requests/orders from opposing parties or third-parties involved in litigation or from government investigators, it is essential that the organization have pre-described the actions it expects the CSP to take (and not take), and in what order, upon receipt of such a request.
- *Data location transparency*: As was fully described in the preceding chapters, the principle of data mobility under the cloud may implicate new laws and procedures for the organization to understand and implement. This also becomes a serious issue during litigation discovery, for government investigations or surveillance, and during insolvency of the CSP or any of its subcontractors. As such, the organization needs to insist on up-to-date transparency of what locations their data is stored in and applicable prohibitions thereof. In addition, the ability to view cloud consumer personal data by CSP support staff, which may be located outside a preferred storage region or country, must be accounted for.
- *Limitation of liability*: As with any agreement, there is going to be a negotiation concerning how liability of the two parties is capped. The organization, as the likely plaintiff in any legal action, would prefer that there are no limitations while the CSP will likely offer either a per incident amount or a percentage of revenue received over a limited time period. Organizations with leverage are going to want to ensure, at a minimum, that liability for any conduct based on so-called "gross" negligence is not capped. Organizations may want to also ensure that certain actions that have potentially large costs, such as data breaches leading to violations of privacy laws or regulatory fines, the systemic impacts of malware introduction, or the malicious acts of CSP insiders, are specifically excluded from any limitations. Given the large size of these potential liabilities, the organization needs to ensure the CSP can financially handle such a liability, both by reviewing its financial situation and its insurance coverage.
- *Warranties*: It is likely that the CSP will try to exclude every warranty that it can, express and implied, as limited only by local law. It may be difficult to get a CSP to change this provision and may not be necessary, if due care is given to those provisions addressing the adverse conduct an organization expects is most likely to happen.

Chapter 1

- *Scope of services*: Perhaps the most important initial action is to ensure that the scope of the services is properly defined. This includes not only the cloud service model and cloud deployment model, but systems, data, data owners and custodians, countries, and organizational divisions that are part of the planned outsourcing. The timing of the implementation and the phases of the project must also be clarified.

- *Confidentiality*: All of the work carried out under the CSP agreement, including perhaps the agreement itself, needs to remain confidential. It should include all information and knowledge transferred to and gained by the CSP during the life of the agreement. It must apply to all CSP employees, contractors, subcontractors, vendors and customers. The effectiveness of the confidentiality provisions should extend for a period of years beyond the termination of the CSP agreement.

Chapter 2

- *Compliance with applicable data protection statutes*: Chapter 2 covers data protection laws and regulations in the United States that the CSP must agree to both comply with itself and those statutes that the CSP will assist the organization in complying with. This will require the gathering of sufficient evidence and presentation of appropriate documentation as required to prove compliance to regulators and various auditors.

- *Business associate/subcontractor agreements*: Statutes and regulations such as HIPAA in the United States, many international data protection statutes, and U.S. state information security laws require that any contractors/subcontractors used to process protected data comply with the same level of standards as the organization. This agreement must typically be in writing and is subject to verification through audits. Examples of these agreements should be exhibits in the CSP agreement.

Chapter 3

- *Compliance with data protection statutes for all hosting countries*: For each country where data is hosted or potentially about whose citizens data is processed, the organization and thus its CSP(s) must comply with local data protection statutes. As explained previously, it is easiest to synthesize all of these laws into a single super statute to more easily ensure global compliance. These include the various blocking statutes in certain countries.

- *EU-Specific Compliance:* An agreement that implicates any of the EU countries as a CSP could involve the use of the model contract clauses, binding corporate rules and/or safe harbors. Each of those specialized provisions must address the role the CSP must play in complying with it or in gaining the necessary approvals from EU or other authorities. This includes the CSP as data processor and/or data controller and any sub-processors.

Chapters 4 and 5

- *Vendor bankruptcy*: The potential bankruptcy/insolvency of a CSP or any of its contractors must be protected against for several reasons, beyond just the disruption this will cause to the organization's business. One issue is that the organization's data may become difficult to recover. Another issue is that the data, software programs, or hosting hardware may be considered an asset that the bankruptcy trustee can/must sell to pay off creditors, and is not protected by typical privacy provisions.

- *Risk assessments (statutory and best practice)*: Organizations must ensure that the CSP performs regular risk assessments, to process new threats and vulnerabilities, as discussed in detail in Chapters 4 and 5. This is both to comply with various statutory and regulatory requirements and because it is the appropriate best practices approach for all businesses. The organization will want to receive copies of such assessments.

- *Information security and privacy policies (statutory and best practice)*: Organizations must ensure that the CSP has rigorous information security and privacy policies that set the tone for how the organization views security and privacy and informs the appropriate standards and procedures. This again is both to comply with various statutory and regulatory requirements and because it is the appropriate best practices approach for all businesses. These policies should be thoroughly reviewed, as they form the basis for the CSP's commitment to information security and privacy.

- *Information security and privacy controls (statutory and best practice)*: Organizations must ensure that the CSP has rigorous information security and privacy controls, as discussed in detail in Chapter 5, that follow the information security and privacy policies. This again is both to comply with various statutory and regulatory requirements and because it is the appropriate best practices approach for all businesses. These controls should include both standard and cloud-specific controls and should be appropriately certified.

- *Monitoring of controls for effectiveness*: The design and implementation of controls is not a one-time process. The CSP must have a process for constantly reviewing its existing controls for effectiveness and if found lacking, appropriate remediations should be undertaken. The operating effectiveness of these remediations must then be reviewed and checked for impacts on other related controls. The organization will want to be a recipient of these effectiveness reviews.

- *Incident response*: How CSPs respond to incidents of various types (e.g., breakdown of equipment, hackers, malware, data breaches) with varying degrees of severity (temporary loss of a network, a disaster hitting a major hosting location) will have a direct impact on the organization's business. The CSP agreement and related schedules must definitely describe how, with what response time, and with what type of personnel the CSP will respond to each type of incident that may have an impact on its operations.

- *Right to audit*: For its own statutory compliance needs, to be able to obtain information for financial audits, to determine compliance with the CSP agreement, and for its own peace of mind, the organization needs to be able to audit the CSP. A right to audit may not be something that the CSP offers, due to being constantly invaded by armies of auditors, and may instead offer its customers the ISAE 3402 reports described in Chapter 5. It may also not allow on-site visits or interviews with its employees. Organizations then may want to insist on at least receiving answers to audit questions of its own making, in addition to any standard audit reports the CSP provides. Audits of subcontractors whose controls may have a material impact on the organization need to be considered as well.

- *Right to assess*: Related to the right to audit is the right to either run or receive the results of vulnerability assessments and to perform penetration tests or receive the results of such tests. Because of the number of requests, CSPs may do this once and then provide copies to all interested customers. It is important that these tests are performed by independent third-party experts. The types of tests will vary based on the service model. For example, SaaS applications should be tested for (Structured Query Language) SQL injections and cross-site scripting vulnerabilities, while this may not apply to IaaS level file storage.

- *Ownership of data*: In all cases, the organization needs to require that it is recognized as the owner of all data that it transfers to or creates in the cloud. While for content data this should be clear, it becomes less clear with metadata, log data, backup data and the like. This should also apply to any software programs implemented or designed in the cloud and any related intellectual property rights, including all derivative works.

- *Data disposal procedures*: When a piece of CSP equipment is decommissioned or CSP service is terminated, the organization's data needs to be completely removed from the device, with no chance that a subsequent owner or unauthorized user can recover the information. There are a number of secure data disposal laws, as explained in Chapter 2, and also secure disposal procedures, such as one on media sanitization from NIST.[1]

- *Venue*: The venue should be where it is convenient for the parties to handle a dispute, which for a larger organization may be almost anywhere but for a smaller organization may not be. Inappropriately, it is the smaller organization that may have less leverage to change the venue to a location more convenient for its purposes.

- *Cross-border insolvency*: There are a series of specialized procedures when the organization gets involved in a cross-border insolvency. Given that the cloud may frequently involve multiple smaller CSPs located in disparate countries, the need to understand cross-border rules will

---

1. NIST, SP 800-88 rev. 1, Guidelines for Media Sanitization (Sept. 2012).

only increase. For more on the rules involved, see the cited article which introduces the topic in an international context.[2]

- *Export controls*: Organization have to comply with various export controls, including those on types of encryption and distribution to certain restricted countries. These rules vary widely by the originating country. The CSP should be aware of any export limitations the organization must comply with. While CSP cloud services are generally not subject to export controls in the United States ("The service of providing computational capacity would not be subject to the EAR as the service provider is not shipping or transmitting any commodity, software, or technology to the user"),[3] each country's current export control situation must be evaluated. Three points that organizations must understand are: that they, not the CSP, would be considered the exporter of regulated data sent outside the country through the cloud that the cloud-based data does not have to leave the country, as the disclosure of the data for a non-U.S. resident (e.g., CSP IT personnel) is considered an export and that encrypting the data does not protect it from export control violations.

- *Bribery controls*: The U.S. Foreign Corrupt Practices Act (FCPA)[4] is the most well-known statute addressing behavior of a country's citizens when dealing in business with foreign governments. But it is by no means the only such statute, as other nations also try to control bribery.[5] Again, the CSP must be aware of and also comply with these same restrictions. Penalties for violations of the FCPA and similar statutes in other countries can be quite severe, so accurate reporting is essential.

- *Conflict of laws*: Because multiple sets of laws, perhaps involving far more than just two countries, may be implicated in any cloud-related dispute between the CSP and the organization, the rules for resolving these conflicts should be determined in advance. This may fall back on the conflict of law rules in one of the principal countries or may follow another negotiated course.

---

2. Thomas Shaw, *Asia/Pacific Insolvency Law – Cross-Border Rules for Creditor Corporations*, Asia Law News (newsletter. of the ABA Section. Intl. Law) Vol. 1 Issue 1 (Winter 2010).

3. U.S. Dept. of Commerce Bureau of Industry and Security (BIS), Advisory Opinion (Jan. 13, 2009); BIS Advisory Opinion (Jan. 11, 2011).

4. 15 U.S.C. § 78m.

5. *See e.g.* U.K., Bribery Act (2010).

- *Breach notification*: For reasons both of statutory compliance with breach notice statutes and for its own business reputational interests, organizations must clearly work out in advance how the CSP is going to notify and work with the organization in the case of a data breach. The statutory requirements are somewhat different in each jurisdiction but the general rules for how and how quickly to notify the organization, the affected parties, regulatory agencies and law enforcement must be worked out before a data breach actually occurs. In addition, it is important that organizations and the CSP have the same definition of a data breach that would trigger the breach response procedures. The organization may want a breach to be defined as any unauthorized access, while a CSP may look to the statutory definitions or the actual disclosure of personally identifiable information from a breach.
- *Data retention requirements (statutory and contractual)*: To carry out its requirements to retain (or delete) data of varying degrees of sensitivity, organizations will likely need the assistance of the CSP. The CSP, especially as the service model moves toward the SaaS model, must have specific retention schedules and media migration and preservation parameters.
- *Data preservation*: For civil or criminal litigation, government investigations, and due diligence activities (e.g., M&As), data must be preserved for later use. When using the cloud for any kind of data storage, organizations must be able, upon receipt of orders or in anticipation of litigation or investigations, to freeze their information. Given that the scope of the freeze (a "litigation hold" in lawsuits) may not be known until the request arrives, organizations must work out in advance how they are going to react and how the litigation hold procedures will be maintained in the face of updates as they occur.
- *Data searches*: In U.S. civil litigation, the producing party must be able to search the in-scope data to find the information relevant to its case. The organization and the CSP must work out in advance how access to this data will be made available, especially at the SaaS level, because the CSP does not typically allow access by individual tenants in the multitenant environment. Issues of additional charges, hours available for searches, and other limitations must be worked out in the agreement.

- *Data custodians*: In civil litigation, when authenticating the data, as discussed in Chapter 6, the data custodian may be required to testify or to otherwise authenticate the data (e.g., via affidavit) or the chain of custody during the data collection process. As such, the CSP agreement needs to address how such data custodians will be made available, at what rates, and what knowledge and expertise they are expected to have.

- *Accounting for all copies of a backup:* One of the biggest concerns has to be that the organization's confidential, employee, or customer data will be disclosed to unauthorized entities. One method for this leakage to occur is through the creation of multiple copies of databases, VMs, and transaction logs for purposes of backup, development testing, portability, and fault tolerance. Any of these copies can be lost or improperly disposed of. CSPs must agree to a complete and frequently updated inventory of all copies of the organization's data.

- *Business continuity/Disaster recovery*: The integrated procedures, the testing and the escalation triggers involved with a disaster, from the loss of a device to the loss of a site, must be worked out well in advance of any such incident. The respective roles of the CSP and the organization must be clearly delineated and the contact lists made available.

- *Knowledge of subcontractors*: With the ability to add capacity in the cloud model, multiple CSPs may be involved as the default model in most cases. As such, for many of the other reasons discussed above, the organization must have advance knowledge of the use of such subcontractor CSPs and the legal relationships between the principal CSP and the subcontractor CSP. Organizations with leverage are going to want to insist on pre-approval of any new subcontractor CSP.

- *Exposure to surveillance laws*: In the same manner that organizations can prepare themselves for compliance with data protection statutes globally, they need to also be aware of which surveillance laws their data may become exposed to and how a CSP will respond to such requests. Depending on the nature and sensitivity of the information, the organization may choose to not utilize a CSP that puts its data at risk of unwanted surveillance, as discussed in Chapter 2.

- *Encryption levels used and permitted by law*: Because in the cloud encryption may be the single most important technology control utilized in data protection, the encryption algorithms used, when they are used (at rest, in transit and in use), and the key management techniques should be part of the CSP agreement. And although easing in recent years, many countries have limitations on the types of encryption that are allowed to be used, so any restrictions on import (or export) of such techniques must be fully understood.

- *Digital certificates source*: Related to the encryption types and key management is the issuance and management of digital certificates. Because the process of issuance of digital certifications is done under differing regimes around the world, not all certificate-issuing authorities (CAs) have the same level of credibility. So the CAs used by the CSP, if they are going to be relied upon by the organization, should be specified in the CSP agreement. For best practices on certificate policy, consult the new document from NIST.[6]

- *Identity management/authentication including federation*: The other key control in the cloud is the ability to identify and authenticate users and systems. So it is vital that the organization reaches an agreement with the CSP on what identity management and authentication techniques and standards will be utilized and who will be in control. This includes the role of federated identity management capabilities, which may be connected to or separate from the organization's identity management and authentication systems, and which third party credential issuers and authenticators will be involved.

- *Legal integrity and authentication*: When data is extracted and brought before a court, it must be demonstrated that its integrity has not been violated through the extraction process or in its handling by demonstrating a valid chain of custody. Also, it must be authenticated under local court rules to show it is what it purports to be. The CSPs role in fulfilling these legal requirements for integrity should be determined in advance.

- *Limitations on processing by CSP under statute*: Under various data protection statutes, there are limitations on what data processors are able to do with personal information, besides not disclosing it. This includes restrictions such as not utilizing the data for any secondary purposes not

---

6. NIST, Draft NISTIR 7924, Reference Certificate Policy (Apr. 2013).

envisioned at the time of collection and not selling the data for marketing purposes, even if anonymized. As such, these additional restrictions should be clearly stated in the CSP agreement.

- *Consistency of data breach, data retention and data disposal rules across subcontractors*: These three types of procedures need to be not only established and synchronized under applicable statutes and contractual requirements with the primary CSP but also all secondary CSPs will need to agree to (and be capable of) following the same procedures in the same timelines, including the requirements of any additional local statutes.

- *Virtualization isolation*: In the cloud, the third key control revolves around the use of isolation techniques in the virtualized environment. This is important enough, as with encryption and identity/authentication, to specify in the contract how these isolation techniques will operate, especially those that affect the production system where there may be multi-tenant environments.

- *Notice to data subjects*: Various data protection statutes give data subjects the right to notice of how their data is being processed. While this responsibility remains with the organization, there are roles for the CSP to assist in this process, including the actual notification delivery.

- *Cloud standards*: As explained at length in Chapter 5, cloud standards are evolving but there are several already well accepted. Those standards should be specified and a periodic review of all standards bodies should be undertaken and applicable new standards of revisions need to be added to future revisions to the agreement.

- *Security certification*: Security certifications are one of the most important devices by which a CSP can communicate to its customers that it is committed fully to information security best practices. A requirement to maintain an ISO 27001 certification plus other applicable certifications in privacy and specialized industry security certifications should be a minimum requirement of any CSP agreement.

Chapter 6

- *Choice of procedural rules*: In addition to substantive rules, in a multijurisdiction scenario, the procedural rules need to be determined. This would include the arbitration rules if arbitration is an option and the discovery rules, if discovery requires data in multiple countries.

- *Forensic analysis*: The need for forensic analysis is complicated by the fact that the organization likely has no direct access to the physical devices that would need to have the forensic data capture done. While the analysis can be performed later offsite, it is important that the capture is done correctly and so the organization should specify the roles, procedures and the notification process required.

- *Control of data*: The issue of who has control of the data is critical in the litigation context in the United States, when the possession and custody is with the CSP. As such, a positive statement that the control of the data remains with the organization may ultimately allow the CSP to avoid responding positively to requests for compelled disclosure. In addition, cloud consumers want to ensure that the CSP, which may be involved in other Internet businesses, does not utilize the customer's data for marketing or other purposes.

- *Right to metadata, logs, backup tapes, VM images*: Upon contract termination, in addition to ensuring all organization data is securely disposed of, the organization may wish to be able to extract data beyond content data. This includes the metadata, logs, data backup tapes, VM images and the like, which will make portability to a new CSP much easier. The CSP agreement should specify what types of data can be extracted. In addition, the organization may want to extract data regularly, for its own purposes of business continuity or analysis and the agreement should allow for that.

- *Insurance (CSP and organization)*: One way to alleviate at least the financial concerns related to a CSP going out of business after a serious incident like a major data breach is to have appropriate insurance. The various types of insurance that the CSP should maintain need to be specified in the CSP agreement and the organization would then need to be sure its insurance is complementary to that. Beyond errors and omission insurance, network security and privacy insurance is appropriate to address costs incurred after data breaches and also for fines arising from regulatory non-compliance.

Additional Contractual Provisions

In addition to this long list of contractual requirements, there are several others that need to be discussed during negotiations with the CSP, such as indemnification and the standard miscellaneous contractual terms that may now take on additional significance in the cloud.

- *Indemnification*: The parties will want to be indemnified for the acts of the other party. Given that the acts of the CSP are more likely to generate legal actions, the organization may not want a completely mutual indemnification clause. In any case, the organization may want to specify indemnification in the case of data breach related costs incurred by the organization. This could include legal damages or regulatory fines, breach notification expenses, legal costs and expenses and direct expenses like having to cover credit monitoring services for affected data subjects. Other acts where indemnity should be possible include acts of CSP gross negligence, violations of the law, acts resulting in death or injury, infringement of intellectual property rights, and introduction of malware into the cloud consumer's systems or data.

- *Changes to services*: It is typical for CSPS to be able to modify or even remove completely a service or certain functionality. Depending on the importance of the service to the organization, it may be necessary to require advance notice of any modifications that impact the functionality of a service and certainly a longer advance notice period in the case of the termination of a certain type of service offering.

- *Assignment or delegation of the agreement*: Although it is typical for contractual language to require that CSPS seek approval for assigning their agreements or delegating their responsibilities, it is also typical that such approvals are not unreasonably withheld. The organization might want to require not only a lengthy advance notification period, but also to insist that any successor must satisfy the criteria of a due diligence exercise for approval to be granted and that failure to pass such an exercise will not be considered unreasonably withholding approval.

- *Remedies*: Besides seeking money damages, the organization may want to have the ability to get a CSP to act in a manner appropriate to the organization's view of an event, which may differ from the CSP's. An example would be the situation in which cloud consumer data in a shared, multi-tenant database used by a SaaS application was lost due to some intervening event. While the CSP can within its normal procedures recover all but five minutes of the lost data, the cloud consumer requires a complete restoration (e.g., the cloud consumer was processing real-time customer financial transaction orders). This complete restoration may require the CSP to take extraordinary steps, including recalling data on tapes in off-site locations, providing temporary disk storage space for the data rebuilding, assigning specialists to recover the data, and other specialists to reinsert the data into the database without re-keying. As the CSP would naturally resist, if the CSP agreement had specified that any transactional data loss was an "irreparable harm," then the cloud consumer could seek a legal injunction requiring performance of the complete data restoration.

- *Force Majeure*: Service providers typically do not want to be held liable for service outages due to "acts of God" and other events over which they have no reasonable control. The occurrence of such events typically provides an exception to having to meet the availability requirements in CSP agreements (e.g., "we will be available 99.999% of the time, except for a period of downtime caused by the following"). But with the cloud architecture, it is not clear that such exceptions are still necessary, with vendors moving to almost no downtime.[7] Also, while there is no reasonable control over certain events like earthquakes, tsunamis, and floods, they may be more common in certain areas and so the exclusion of service outages due to an earthquake occurring in an area lying in a known fault zone may not make sense. In other events, such as labor disputes, it is questionable whether there is reasonable control. The list of events in this clause should be scrutinized for reasonable control and any activities from business continuity plans should be required to be exhausted before this clause can be utilized.

---

7. See Google Enterprise Blog Destination: Dial Tone - Getting Google Apps to 99.99% (Jan. 14, 2011), removing the SLA clause that allows for scheduled downtime.

Service Level Agreements

Besides the contractual terms, the other key document in the CSP agreement is the service level agreement (SLA), which may contain just operational metrics, performance, and reporting requirements or may be used to also contain certain contractual terms. The organization must set the appropriate performance levels that it deems essential and compare these to what is offered by the CSP. It must also ensure that its definition of what constitutes each metric (e.g., availability) matches with that used by the CSP. The frequency of measuring and reporting is important, as well as the independence of the party doing the measuring and reporting. There should be both stated penalties for not meeting specified service levels and an enforcement mechanism to ensure receipt of service credits or refunds.

With all SLA metrics, definition is critical. For example, in a study of European public entities,[8] "availability" was variously defined as: service is reachable by all clients (50 percent of respondents), service responds to requests within x time period (speed) (12 percent of respondents), undefined (10 percent of respondents), basic functions are available (9 percent of respondents), don't know (4 percent of respondents), and other (15 percent of respondents). Thirty-seven percent of the respondents defined their availability requirements as just 99 percent, 19 percent as 99.9 percent and only 8 percent as 99.99 percent. These results are surprising in that three-fourths of the respondents had high or very high security requirements. Besides availability, other commonly-used SLA metrics were scalability, time-to-provision resources, and reporting security incidents within a certain amount of time.

The study listed the following as the key cloud SLA issues to consider:

- Parameter definition
- Monitoring methodology
- Independent testing
- Incident/alerting thresholds
- Regular reporting of service levels
- Response thresholds set by organization risk profile

---

8. ENISA, *Survey and analysis of security parameters in cloud SLAs across the European public sector*
   Public Sector (Dec. 2011).

- Penalties for non-compliance and enforcement

A recent ENISA document[9] listed SLA areas and considerations, with the organization tasked with finding the impact of each on organizational risk and how the various metrics are defined, measured, reported, and penalized for failure to meet:

- Service availability (what functions covered, how to define, how to measure)
- Incident response (type of incidents, minimum allowable response times, incident severity classification)
- Service elasticity and load tolerance (definition, which resources, testing)
- Data life-cycle management (monitoring of backups, export, and recovery testing)
- Technical compliance and vulnerability management (definition of security-related configuration options, SW (software) patching, vulnerability testing)
- Change management (notice periods, notification for critical events such as loss of security or other certification)
- Data isolation (what to monitor, failure definition, testing)
- Log management and forensics (definition, testing, cross-checks with other logs)

7.2 Example Agreements

The provisions from these example CSP agreements have been selected to highlight specific areas of concern for an organization negotiating CSP services. The first three represent the three service models, the fourth a government view on cloud contract revisions, and the fifth and sixth negotiated agreements. While these are the actual words of the respective service agreements, each provision is used only for illustrative purposes and must be read in the proper context and using the current version when organizations begin their CSP evaluations. The editing of the provisions consisted only of

---

9. ENISA, *Procure Secure - A guide to monitoring of security service levels in cloud contracts* (Apr. 2012).

eliminating language not needed for illustration. Only provisions that contain material differences are shown after the first example agreement. The agreement provision numbering is the CSP's. Note the last update dates for each.

Saleforce.com[10]

This SaaS application is for customer relationship management (CRM). The selected clauses highlight several of the illustrated points concerning: force majeure, data protection and return, compelled disclosure and warranties, indemnities, and limitation of liability.

1. Force Majeure

4.1 Our Responsibilities: We shall:…(ii) use commercially reasonable efforts to make the Purchased Services available 24 hours a day, 7 days a week, except for: (a) planned downtime …, or (b) any unavailability caused by circumstances beyond Our reasonable control, including without limitation, acts of God, acts of government, floods, fires, earthquakes, civil unrest, acts of terror, strikes or other labor problems (other than those involving Our employees), Internet service provider failures or delays, or denial of service attacks.

2. Data

4.2. Our Protection of Your Data. We shall maintain appropriate administrative, physical, and technical safeguards for protection of the security, confidentiality and integrity of Your Data. We shall not (a) modify Your Data, (b) disclose Your Data except as compelled by law in accordance with Section 8.3 (Compelled Disclosure) or as expressly permitted in writing by You, or (c) access Your Data except to provide the Services and prevent or address service or technical problems, or at Your request in connection with customer support matters.

5.2. Non-Salesforce.com Applications and Your Data. If You install or enable Non-Salesforce.com Applications for use with Services, You acknowledge that We may allow providers of those Non-Salesforce.com Applications to access Your Data as required for the interoperation of such Non-Salesforce.com Applications with the Services. We shall not be responsible for any

---

10. Salesforce.com Master Subscription Agreement (last updated Jan.7, 2013).

disclosure, modification or deletion of Your Data resulting from any such access by NonSalesforce.com Application providers. The Services shall allow You to restrict such access by restricting Users from installing or enabling such Non-Salesforce.com Applications for use with the Services.

7.4. Your Data. Subject to the limited rights granted by You hereunder, We acquire no right, title or interest from You or Your licensors under this Agreement in or to Your Data, including any intellectual property rights therein.

8.3. Compelled Disclosure. The Receiving Party may disclose Confidential Information of the Disclosing Party if it is compelled by law to do so, provided the Receiving Party gives the Disclosing Party prior notice of such compelled disclosure (to the extent legally permitted) and reasonable assistance, at the Disclosing Party's cost, if the Disclosing Party wishes to contest the disclosure. If the Receiving Party is compelled by law to disclose the Disclosing Party's Confidential Information as part of a civil proceeding to which the Disclosing Party is a party, and the Disclosing Party is not contesting the disclosure, the Disclosing Party will reimburse the Receiving Party for its reasonable cost of compiling and providing secure access to such Confidential Information.

12.5. Return of Your Data. Upon request by You made within 30 days after the effective date of termination of a Purchased Services subscription, We will make available to You for download a file of Your Data in comma separated value (.csv) format along with attachments in their native format. After such 30-day period, We shall have no obligation to maintain or provide any of Your Data and shall thereafter, unless legally prohibited, delete all of Your Data in Our systems or otherwise in Our possession or under Our control.

3. Warranties/Indemnification/Limitation of Liability

9.3. Disclaimer. EXCEPT AS EXPRESSLY PROVIDED HEREIN, NEITHER PARTY MAKES ANY WARRANTIES OF ANY KIND, WHETHER EXPRESS, IMPLIED, STATUTORY OR OTHERWISE, AND EACH PARTY SPECIFICALLY DISCLAIMS ALL IMPLIED WARRANTIES, INCLUDING ANY WARRANTIES OF MERCHANTABILITY

OR FITNESS FOR A PARTICULAR PURPOSE, TO THE MAXIMUM EXTENT PERMITTED BY APPLICABLE LAW.

10.2. Indemnification by You. You shall defend Us against any claim, demand, suit or proceeding made or brought against Us by a third party alleging that Your Data, or Your use of the Services in breach of this agreement, infringes or misappropriates the intellectual property rights of a third party or violates applicable law.

11.1. Limitation of Liability. NEITHER PARTY'S LIABILITY WITH RESPECT TO ANY SINGLE INCIDENT ARISING OUT OF OR RELATED TO THIS AGREEMENT (WHETHER IN CONTRACT OR TORT OR UNDER ANY OTHER THEORY OF LIABILITY) SHALL EXCEED THE LESSER OF $500,000 OR THE AMOUNT PAID BY YOU HEREUNDER IN THE 12 MONTHS PRECEDING THE INCIDENT, PROVIDED THAT IN NO EVENT SHALL EITHER PARTY'S AGGREGATE LIABILITY ARISING OUT OF OR RELATED TO THIS AGREEMENT (WHETHER IN CONTRACT OR TORT OR UNDER ANY OTHER THEORY OF LIABILITY) EXCEED THE TOTAL AMOUNT PAID BY YOU HEREUNDER.

Google App Engine[11]

This PaaS service provides the platform and tools (e.g., Java) for users to develop and host their web applications. The selected clauses highlight several of the illustrated points concerning: data location and security, intellectual property and licensing rights, and limitation of liability.

1. Data Location and Security

2.2 Facilities and Data Transfer. All facilities used to store and process an Application and Customer Data will adhere to reasonable security standards no less protective than the security standards at facilities where Google processes and stores its own information of a similar type. Google has implemented at least industry standard systems and procedures to ensure the security and confidentiality of an Application and Customer Data, protect against anticipated threats or hazards to the security or integrity of an

---

11. Google App Engine, Terms of Service (last updated Apr. 1, 2013).

Application and Customer Data, and protect against unauthorized access to or use of an Application and Customer Data. Google may process and store an Application and Customer Data in the United States or any other country in which Google or its agents maintain facilities. By using the Service, Customer consents to this processing and storage of an Application and Customer Data. The parties agree that Google is merely a data processor.

2.3 Data Storage Selection. a. Data Storage. Customer may select via the Service whether the Core App Engine End User Data will be stored permanently, at rest, in either the United States or the European Union, and Google will store it accordingly ("App Engine Data Location Setting"). If no selection is made, Core App Engine End User Data will be stored permanently, at rest, in the United States. b. Transient Storage. Core App Engine End User Data may be stored transiently or cached in any country in which Google or its agents maintain facilities before reaching permanent storage. c. Limitations. No App Engine Data Location Setting will apply to Core App Engine End User Data copied in another location or used with other Google products and services (including any other Google Cloud Platform services). If so, the Core App Engine End User Data will be processed and stored pursuant to Section 2.2 of this Agreement.

2. Intellectual Property and Licensing Rights

1.1 License From Google to Customer. Subject to this Agreement, Google grants to Customer a worldwide, non-sublicensable, non-transferable, non-exclusive, terminable, limited license to (a) use the Service, (b) integrate the Service into any Application and provide the Service, solely as integrated into the Application, to users of the Application and (c) use any Software provided by Google as part of the Service.

6.1 Intellectual Property Rights. Except as expressly set forth herein, this Agreement does not grant either party any rights, implied or otherwise, to the other's content or any of the other's intellectual property. As between the parties, Customer owns all Intellectual Property Rights in any Application and Customer Data, and Google owns all Intellectual Property Rights in the Service.

3. Limitation of Liability

13.1 Limitation on Indirect Liability. TO THE MAXIMUM EXTENT PERMITTED BY APPLICABLE LAW, NEITHER PARTY, NOR GOOGLE'S SUPPLIERS, WILL BE LIABLE UNDER THIS AGREEMENT FOR LOST REVENUES OR INDIRECT, SPECIAL, INCIDENTAL, CONSEQUENTIAL, EXEMPLARY, OR PUNITIVE DAMAGES, EVEN IF THE PARTY KNEW OR SHOULD HAVE KNOWN THAT SUCH DAMAGES WERE POSSIBLE AND EVEN IF DIRECT DAMAGES DO NOT SATISFY A REMEDY.

13.2 Limitation on Amount of Liability. TO THE MAXIMUM EXTENT PERMITTED BY APPLICABLE LAW, NEITHER PARTY, NOR GOOGLE'S SUPPLIER'S, MAY BE HELD LIABLE UNDER THIS AGREEMENT FOR MORE THAN THE AMOUNT PAID BY CUSTOMER TO GOOGLE DURING THE TWELVE MONTHS PRIOR TO THE EVENT GIVING RISE TO LIABILITY.

13.3 Exceptions to Limitations. These limitations of liability do not apply to breaches of confidentiality obligations, violations of a party's Intellectual Property Rights by the other party, or indemnification obligations.

Amazon Web Services[12]

This Amazon agreement covers many different types of cloud services, including Elastic Compute Cloud (EC2), Amazon Simple Storage Service (S3), Amazon CloudFront, Amazon Relational Database Service (RDS), Amazon Virtual Private Cloud (VPC), and Amazon Simple Queue Service (SQS). The selected clauses highlight several of the illustrated points concerning: security and privacy, responsibilities of the customers, changes to the agreement, and uptime service commitments.

1. Security and Privacy

3.1 AWS Security. We will implement reasonable and appropriate measures designed to help you secure Your Content against accidental or unlawful loss, access or disclosure.

---

12. Amazon Web Services Customer Agreement (last updated Mar. 15, 2012).

3.2 Data Privacy. We participate in the safe harbor programs described in the Privacy Policy. You may specify the AWS regions in which Your Content will be stored and accessible by End Users. We will not move Your Content from your selected AWS regions without notifying you, unless required to comply with the law or requests of governmental entities. You consent to our collection, use and disclosure of information associated with the Service Offerings in accordance with our Privacy Policy, and to the processing of Your Content in, and the transfer of Your Content into, the AWS regions you select.

2. Your Responsibilities

4.1 Your Content. You are solely responsible for the development, content, operation, maintenance, and use of Your Content. For example, you are solely responsible for:

(a) (a) the technical operation of Your Content, including ensuring that calls you make to any Service are compatible with then-current APIs for that Service;

(b) (b) compliance of Your Content with the Acceptable Use Policy, the other Policies, and the law;

(c) (c) any claims relating to Your Content; and

(d) (d) properly handling and processing notices sent to you (or any of your affiliates) by any person claiming that Your Content violate such person's rights, including notices pursuant to the Digital Millennium Copyright Act.

4.2 Other Security and Backup. You are responsible for properly configuring and using the Service Offerings and taking your own steps to maintain appropriate security, protection and backup of Your Content, which may include the use of encryption technology to protect Your Content from unauthorized access and routine archiving Your Content. AWS log-in credentials and private keys generated by the Services are for your internal use only and you may not sell, transfer or sublicense them to any other entity or person, except that you may disclose your private key to your agents and subcontractors performing work on your behalf.

4.4 End User Support. You are responsible for providing customer service (if any) to End Users. We do not provide any support or services to End Users unless we have a separate agreement with you or an End User obligating us to provide support or services.

3. Agreement Changes

12. Modifications to the Agreement. We may modify this Agreement (including any Policies) at any time by posting a revised version on the AWS Site or by otherwise notifying you in accordance with Section 13.7. The modified terms will become effective upon posting or, if we notify you by email, as stated in the email message. By continuing to use the Service Offerings after the effective date of any modifications to this Agreement, you agree to be bound by the modified terms. It is your responsibility to check the AWS Site regularly for modifications to this Agreement. We last modified this Agreement on the date listed at the beginning of this Agreement.

4. Service Levels (EC2)[13]

Service Commitments: AWS will use commercially reasonable efforts to make Amazon EC2 available with an Annual Uptime Percentage of at least 99.95% during the Service Year. In the event EC2 does not meet the "Annual Uptime Percentage" commitment, you will be eligible to receive a Service Credit.

Annual Uptime Percentage: is calculated by subtracting from 100% the percentage of 5 minute periods during the Service Year in which Amazon EC2 was in the state of "Region Unavailable," i.e., more than one Availability Zone in which you are running an instance, within the same Region, is "Unavailable" to you, i.e., your running instances have no external connectivity during a five minute period and you are unable to launch replacement instances.

Exclusions: Annual Uptime Percentage measurements exclude downtime resulting directly or indirectly from any Amazon EC2 SLA Exclusion, [as follows]. The Service Commitment does not apply to any unavailability, suspension or termination of Amazon EC2, or any other Amazon EC2

---

13. Last updated Oct. 23, 2008.

performance issues: (i) that result from a suspension described in Section 6.1 of the AWS Agreement; (ii) caused by factors outside of our reasonable control, including any force majeure event or Internet access or related problems beyond the demarcation point of Amazon EC2; (iii) that result from any actions or inactions of you or any third party; (iv) that result from your equipment, software or other technology and/or third party equipment, software or other technology (other than third party equipment within our direct control); (v) that result from failures of individual instances not attributable to Region Unavailability; or (vi) arising from our suspension and termination of your right to use Amazon EC2 in accordance with the AWS Agreement (collectively, the "Amazon EC2 SLA Exclusions"). If availability is impacted by factors other than those explicitly listed in this agreement, we may issue a Service Credit considering such factors in our sole discretion.

U.S. Government[14]

The U.S. federal government has created a standard template to use when agencies are contracting for cloud services with private CSPs. It includes a number of waivers to the CSP's standard terms of service (TOS). The selected clauses highlight the use of the waivers covering several of the illustrated points and also data security.

1. Waivers

E. Indemnification, Liability, Statute of Limitations: Any provisions in the TOS related to indemnification and filing deadlines are hereby waived, and shall not apply except to the extent expressly authorized by law. Liability for any breach of the TOS as modified by this Amendment, or any claim arising from the TOS as modified by this Amendment, shall be determined under the Federal Tort Claims Act, or other governing federal authority. Federal Statute of Limitations provisions shall apply to any breach or claim.

   G. Changes to standard TOS: Language in the TOS reserving to Company the right to change the TOS without notice at any time is hereby

---

14. General Services Administration, Amendment to Terms of Service Applicable to Governmental Users/Members.

amended to grant GSA at least three days advance notice of any material change to the TOS.

K. Modifications of Agency content: Any right Company reserves in the TOS to modify or adapt Agency content is limited to technical actions necessary to index, format and display that content. The right to modify or adapt does not include the right to substantively edit or otherwise alter the meaning of the content.

L. Limitation of liability: The Parties agree that nothing in the Limitation of Liability clause or elsewhere in the TOS in any way grants Company a waiver from, release of, or limitation of liability pertaining to, any past, current or future violation of federal law.

2. Data Protection

U. Security: Company will, in good faith, exercise due diligence using generally accepted commercial business practices for IT security, to ensure that systems are operated and maintained in a secure manner, and that management, operational and technical controls are employed to ensure security of systems and data. An SAS 70 Type II audit certification will be conducted annually, and Company agrees to provide Agency with the current SAS 70 Type II audit certification upon the agency's request. Recognizing the changing nature of the Web, Company will continuously work with users to ensure that its Site and Services meet users' requirements for the security of systems and data.

City of Los Angeles (Negotiated) Agreement[15]

This agreement, unlike those shown above, was a negotiated agreement for up to 30,000 users. There are actually two agreements, one between the organization (here the city government) and the CSP (Google),[16] which is then included as an exhibit to the system integration (SI) agreement. The services in the agreement, which has been made public as it involves a local government as the organization, is for the implementation, training on, and provision of SaaS email and collaboration tool services. For many organizations, this

---

15. City of Los Angeles Information Technology Agency, Professional Services Contract Regarding: SAAS E-Mail & Collaboration Solution (SECS) (Nov. 10, 2009).

16. Google Apps Premier Edition via Reseller Agreement (City of Los Angeles, Cal.).

type of agreement may actually become rather common, with SIs and cloud service aggregators and brokers acting as intermediaries between the cloud consumer organizations and the CSPs. Again only the contractual provisions that are different from those shown above are highlighted. The selected clauses highlight several of the illustrated points concerning: e-discovery, security, confidentiality, right to audit, types of internal control audits, audit remediations, data location, fines for data breach, breach notification, uptime and scheduled downtime.

1. Requirements

1.1.4. e-Discovery requirements must have the following functionality: Ability to search based on the following criteria: Content; Sender and/or recipient; Date range; and Metadata; Ability to store search results with any metadata; Ability to add and delete from search results to create an e-Discovery set and Ability to retrieve or e-Discover archived data based on content, sender, recipient, and/or other metadata with different archival periods.

1.1.10. Security requirements must have the following functionality: 1) Ability to provide segregation of City data from other data; 2) Ability to log access to all City data by City staff; 3) Ability to log access to all City data by non-City staff; and City email and Google Message Discovery (GMO) data remaining within the continental United States.

11. Information Security. Contractor acknowledges that City has implemented an information security program (the City Information Security Program, as the same may be amended) to protect City's information assets, such information assets as further defined and classified in the City Information Security Program (collectively, the "Protected Data"). Where Contractor or its subcontractors have access to the Protected Data, Contractor acknowledges and agrees to the following.

11.1 Undertaking by Contractor. Without limiting Contractor's obligation of confidentiality as further described herein, Contractor shall be responsible for establishing and maintaining an information security program that is designed to: (i) ensure the security and confidentiality of the Protected Data; (ii) protect against any anticipated threats or hazards to the security or integrity of the Protected Data; (iii) protect against unauthorized access to or use of the Protected Data; (iv) ensure the proper disposal of Protected Data; and, (v) ensure that all subcontractors of Contractor, if any, comply with all of the foregoing.

11.2 Right of Audit by City. City shall have the right to review Contractor's information security program prior to the commencement of Services and from time to time during the term of this Contract. During the performance of the Services, on an ongoing basis from time to time and with reasonable notice, City, at its own expense, shall be entitled to perform, or to have performed, an on-site audit of Contractor's information security program. In lieu of an on-site audit, upon Contractor option, Contractor shall complete, within forty-five (45 days) of receipt, an audit questionnaire provided by City regarding Contractor's information security program.

11.3 Audit by Contractor. No more than annually, Contractor, at its own expense, shall conduct a SAS-70 or equivalent audit of Google's information security program and provide such audit findings to City upon formal written request.

11.4 Audit Findings. Contractor shall implement any required safeguards as identified by City or information security program audits.

2. CSP Services Agreement

1.7 Data Transfer. Google agrees to store and process Customer's email and Google Message Discovery (GMD) data only in the continental United States. As soon as it shall become commercially feasible, Google shall store and process all other Customer Data, from any other Google Apps applications, only in the continental United States. Google shall make commercially reasonable efforts to advise Customer when such data storage capability is made available. Notwithstanding the foregoing, Google may store and process Login Data in any country in which Google or its agents maintain facilities.

7.1.1 Confidential Information. The Customer and Google agree that in the event of Google's breach of its nondisclosure or confidentiality obligations under Section 7 with respect to Customer Data, the Customer's damages may be difficult to determine. Therefore, the Customer and Google agree that in the event of Google's breach of its nondisclosure or confidentiality obligations under Section 7 with respect to Customer Data, Google shall pay Customer $10,000 (ten thousand dollars) as liquidated damages for each such incident. For purposes of this provision, the term "incident" shall mean all disclosures of Customer Data to unauthorized recipients arising from the same specific cause or causes. This Section 7.1.1 shall not apply to breaches by CSC or its subcontractors.

Notwithstanding the above, the Customer shall have the right, at any time and in its sole discretion, to waive its right to liquidated damages provided for herein, and to seek actual damages. The Customer and Google agree that should any part of this Section 7.1.1 be deemed unenforceable, then the entire Section 7.1.1 shall be unenforceable. This provision applies only to contract damages.

7.5 Security Breach. To the extent a state or federal security breach law applies to a Security Breach, Google will comply with the applicable law. To the extent no such law applies to a Security Breach, Google will notify Customer of a Security Breach, following the discovery or notification of such Security Breach, in the most expedient time possible under the Circumstances, without unreasonable delay, consistent with the legitimate needs of applicable law enforcement, and after taking any measures necessary to determine the scope of the breach and restore the reasonable integrity of the system. Google will send any applicable notifications regarding a Security Breach to the Notification Email Address.

"Security Breach" means an actual disclosure, or reasonable belief that there has been a disclosure, by Google of Customer Data to any unauthorized person or entity.

14.3 Exceptions to Limitations. These limitations of liability do not apply to breaches of confidentiality obligations, violations of a party's Intellectual Property Rights by the other party, or indemnification obligations.

Google Apps Service Level Agreement: During the Term of the applicable Google Apps Agreement, the Google Apps Covered Services web interface will be operational and available to Customer at least 99.9% of the time in any calendar month. If Google does not meet this, and if Customer meets its obligations, Customer will be eligible to receive the Service Credits.

Definitions. The following definitions shall apply to the Google Apps SLA.

"Monthly Uptime Percentage" means total number of minutes in a calendar month minus the number of minutes of Downtime (means, for a domain, if there is more than a five percent user error rate. Downtime is measured based on server side error rate) suffered from all Downtime Periods (means, for a domain, a period of ten consecutive minutes of Downtime. Intermittent Downtime for a period of less than ten minutes will not be counted towards any Downtime Periods) in a calendar month, divided by the total number of minutes in a calendar month.

"Scheduled Downtime" means those times where Google notifies Customer of periods of Downtime at least five days prior to the commencement of such Downtime. There will be no more than twelve hours of Scheduled Downtime per calendar year. Scheduled Downtime is not considered Downtime for purposes of this Google Apps SLA, and will not be counted towards any Downtime Periods.

University of Cambridge (Negotiated) Agreement[17]

This agreement was between Google and the University of Cambridge for the provision of Google Apps to the end-users at the university.

1.3 Modifications. a. To the Services. Google may make commercially reasonable modifications to the Service, or particular components of the Service, from time to time. Google will use commercially reasonable efforts to notify Customer of any such changes. b. To Applicable Terms. If Google makes a material change to the URL Terms, then Google will notify Customer by either sending an email to the Notification Email Address or alerting Customer via the Admin Console. If the change has a material adverse impact on Customer and Customer does not agree to the change, Customer must so notify Google via the Help Center within thirty days after receiving notice of the change.

1.5 Privacy Policies. Google will comply with the Customer Privacy Notice and the End User Privacy Notice. Changes to these notices will be made as stated in the applicable notice.

1.6 Ads. a. Default Setting. The default setting for the Services is one that does not allow Google to serve Ads. Customer may change this setting in the Admin Console, which constitutes Customer's authorization for Google

---

17. Google Apps Education Edition Agreement between Google, Inc. and The Chancellor, Masters, and Scholars of the University of Cambridge (Oct. 8, 2010).

to serve Ads. If Customer enables the serving of Ads, it may revert to the default setting at any time and Google will cease serving Ads.

1.7 Data Transfer. As part of providing the Service, Google may store and process Customer Data in the United States or any other country in which Google or its agents maintain facilities. By using the Services, Customer consents to this transfer, processing and storage of Customer Data.

1.8 Safe Harbor. During the Term, Google will remain certified to and comply with the U.S. Safe Harbor Privacy Principles of Notice, Choice, Onward Transfer, Access, Security and Data Integrity and Enforcement issued by the U.S. Department of Commerce ("Safe Harbor") or a comparable framework for cross-border data transfers agreed with the European Union. If during the Term, Google has failed to maintain its Safe Harbor certification or should the United States and the European Union cease to engage in Safe Harbor or a comparable framework, Customer will have the right to terminate the Agreement pursuant to Section 11.1 herein.

1.9 Security Breach. To the extent a state or federal security breach law applies to a Security Breach, Google will comply with the applicable law. To the extent no such law applies to a Security Breach, Google will notify Customer of a Security Breach, following the discovery or notification of such Security Breach, in the most expedient time possible under the circumstances, without unreasonable delay, consistent with the legitimate needs of applicable law enforcement, and after taking any measures necessary to determine the scope of the breach and restore the reasonable integrity of the system. Google will send any applicable notifications regarding a Security Breach to the Notification Email Address.

1.10 Use of Customer Data. Other provisions of this Agreement notwithstanding, Google may scan or index Customer Data for the following purposes only: (i) to allow End Users to search for information in their End User Accounts; (ii) to allow Google to perform spam filtering, virus detection, and/or similar security tasks; (iii) to allow Google to respond to Customer's and/or an End User's request for assistance; (iv) to allow Google to meet its legal obligations; or (v) otherwise to allow Google to provide the Services. Google's scanning and indexing procedures shall be automated and involve no human interaction with Customer Data, except to the extent necessary to respond to Customer's and/or an End User's request for assistance or to meet Google's legal obligations. Unless Customer enables the Services to serve Ads, Google will not use any Customer Data for advertising purposes.

1.11 Instructions. Customer, as data controller, instructs Google, as data processor, to provide the Services in accordance with the Agreement.

10.2 Disclaimers. EXCEPT AS EXPRESSLY PROVIDED FOR HEREIN, NEITHER PARTY MAKES ANY OTHER WARRANTY OF ANY KIND, WHETHER EXPRESS, IMPLIED, STATUTORY OR OTHERWISE, INCLUDING WITHOUT LIMITATION WARRANTIES OF MERCHANTABILITY, FITNESS FOR A PARTICULAR USE AND NONINFRINGEMENT. GOOGLE MAKES NO REPRESENTATIONS ABOUT ANY CONTENT OR INFORMATION MADE ACCESSIBLE BY OR THROUGH THE SERVICE. THE SERVICE IS NEITHER DESIGNED NOR INTENDED FOR HIGH RISK ACTIVITIES. CUSTOMER ACKNOWLEDGES THAT THE SERVICES ARE NOT A TELEPHONY SERVICE AND THAT THE SERVICES ARE NOT CAPABLE OF PLACING OR RECEIVING ANY CALLS, INCLUDING EMERGENCY SERVICES CALLS, OVER PUBLICLY SWITCHED TELEPHONE NETWORKS.

Chapter 8

PRACTICAL APPLICATION

Organizations ready to move to the cloud must now take all of the techniques described in the previous chapters and apply them to the actual situations they are facing. This includes the financial analysis described in Chapter 1, the U.S. statutes and regulations and the surveillance laws described in Chapter 2, the international laws in three global regions described in Chapter 3, the information security and privacy risk management techniques described in Chapters 4 and 5, the discovery preservation and disclosure requirements and data breach response and insurance topics discussed in Chapter 6, and the contractual provisions and example CSP agreements in Chapter 7.

In this chapter, the focus is on utilizing these techniques to understand the legal, compliance, information, business, and technology risks in assessing CSPs, the appropriate risk treatments for those assessed risks, and then negotiating the agreement for cloud computing services with the selected CSP. The chapter's first section starts with a comprehensive approach to utilize in selecting and negotiating cloud agreements. The second section presents two example scenarios that should encompass small, medium, and large organizations. The third section applies the comprehensive approach to those example scenarios.

Executive Takeaways

- How to assess internal risks before outsourcing
- How to assess information security, privacy, and other risks of the CSP
- Analysis and negotiation of CSP agreement provisions
- Application of assessment and negotiating techniques in typical organizational scenarios

8.1 Comprehensive Approach

When preparing to evaluate the use of cloud computing services, organizations will need a repeatable and stable approach that can be utilized each time that the use of cloud computing services is considered. The migration to the cloud could happen all at once, organization-wide, but it is much more likely for larger organizations that it occurs in several iterations, project-by-project and division-by-division. This repeatable approach will utilize the same set of evaluation criteria. For those criteria that have been previously assessed with the same CSP, only incremental updates to the assessments may be required. There may be revisions to the evaluation criteria, for example when new standards are released. With cloud computing in its early stages of maturity, it is best to revisit the current state of the detailed criteria before using them to evaluate candidate CSPs and cloud workloads. But the high-level approach should remain constant over time. The steps in this approach are:

A. Defining the *scope* of which applications, data, platform tools, or infrastructure that will potentially be moved into or acquired from the cloud
B. Defining the organization's specific *use* of the cloud (i.e., what service models and which deployment models are most appropriate)
C. Determining the organization's current ability to outsource to the cloud and its own security profile through a *self-assessment*

D. *Assessing* the candidate CSPs against the pre-determined evaluation criteria

E. *Negotiating* with the selected CSPs on the required terms and conditions and service level agreements

Scope

It is unlikely that the definition of scope will include all IT functions in all regions for all divisions, except in the smallest of organizations. More likely, organizations will utilize, especially in the early days, the cloud for specific purposes (e.g., business continuity, backup, supply chain applications, developmental tools, etc.). And it may be on a national, regional, or divisional basis instead of global and organization wide. As such, defining the scope of not only what is but what is not included is a key first step.

It is then vital to understand the relationships between systems, data, and infrastructure that are in scope for the cloud and those that are not in scope (at least at this time). It is all too common to fail to fully investigate or understand the linkages to data, APIs, processes, and infrastructure that remain outside of the outsourcing scope. The interfaces, dependencies, and relationships must be clear, so existing data, system and network inventories, mappings, and data flows are of great benefit here. A new set of linkages may need to be built as part of the outsourcing to the cloud system, depending on what is migrated to the cloud and what is utilized in the cloud (e.g., new SaaS applications will need new inter-system data flow diagrams). This could be a relatively simple process, if the organization and the CSPs utilize standard APIs and make interoperability a key feature of their service offerings. If there are significant non-standard APIs, proprietary linkages, or legacy systems, then the migration to the cloud may be more difficult to understand, implement, and maintain.

Cloud Use

The prospective cloud usage requires knowing which features in what mixture will be acquired. Although not always necessary at the beginning when pilot projects may be the initial step into the cloud, it is best if, thereafter, each use of the cloud is part of a strategic plan. For example, a migration plan moving the organization through different phases from pre-cloud virtualization to a private cloud to a public cloud or an approach that allows the organization to use the cloud for bursting or for specific purposes like application development, data mining, research, or business continuity. In each use of the cloud, the service model to be used must be determined. For example, will the application in question be replaced entirely with a cloud application (SaaS), be developed with cloud-based tools or use cloud-based middleware or data storage (PaaS), or will the existing application be moved onto a server hosted by another organization (IaaS)? The deployment model must also be determined. Is the organization attempting to utilize its own cloud infrastructure (private cloud), will it be utilizing a public cloud, or will it be utilizing a combination of both in some type of hybrid configuration?

The drivers for these decisions will be business-strategic, financial, technical, legal, and organizational, and the appropriate combination(s) of service model and deployment model will be input into the following phases. An approach to this was introduced in Chapter 1. How the organization uses technology to compete, its business growth plans, the remaining economic life of IT assets, IT staffing resource capabilities and availability, headcount limitations, statutory and regulatory compliance issues, legal liability exposures, capital versus operational budget availability and flexibility, the degree of interoperability and standardization of IT systems and infrastructure, its assessment of the business and other risks of outsourcing, its governance structure, and the organization's overall risk tolerance are just a few of the many criteria that must be part of the analysis to make these determinations.

Organization Self-Assessment

Determining the organization's ability to outsource involves understanding the obligations organizations have under the statutes and regulations as discussed in Chapters 2 and 3 and any contractual commitments it has made. The organization must also assess its information security and privacy programs and its own abilities to manage the risks covered in Chapters 4–6, including the governance capabilities to oversee the outsourcing relationship. It cannot be emphasized enough that moving to the cloud may help organizations address a specific need, such as a lack of technical infrastructure or a specialized skill set, but it is not a panacea for those organizations that do not have a full understanding of their legal, compliance, business, and technology obligations and risks. Except possibly for smaller organizations, the cloud should address at most a handful of gaps that an organization has assessed. In any case, the organization always will retain the ultimate liability and responsibility, so it must have strong oversight functions. Outsourcing to the cloud should not be viewed as throwing something over the wall but more like passing something to your neighbor situated close by.

The organizational self-assessment should be no less rigorous than that which the organization will perform on the candidate CSPs. A strong internal look will identify those areas that must be first addressed before outsourcing, and other areas that could possibly be outsourced currently. It is best to utilize the same standards-based approach described in Chapters 4 and 5, after perhaps starting with a baseline IT assessment utilizing such methodologies as ISO 27005,[1] NIST's Risk Control Framework (RCF),[2] and ISACA's Risk IT.[3] The requirements for and actual results of statutory, regulatory and contractual compliance must also be assessed and so must the outsourcing governance capabilities of the organization, both technical and legal. The results of independent audits and assessments of the organization will also provide an unbiased interpretation of current gaps and required remediations in the risk treatment and compliance approaches used.

CSP Assessment

Assessing the candidate CSPs involves the information security and privacy risks, controls, and standards explained in Chapters 4 and 5 and the various additional cloud-specific preservation and disclosure requirements detailed in Chapter 6. It also involves the ability to meet the compliance needs described in Chapters 2 and 3. This assessment may be split into several phases and could come before, during or after receiving replies to any of the following outsourcing initiation techniques: requests for information (RFI), requests for quotations (RFQs), or requests for proposal (RFPs). It may also be the case that the organization is performing the assessment on

---

1. ISO/IEC 27005, Information Technology—Security Techniques—Information Security Risk Management (2008).

2. NIST, SP 800-37, rev. 1, *Guide for Applying the Risk Management Framework to Federal Information Systems* (2010).

3. ISACA, *The Risk IT Framework* (2009).

its own, not having the leverage to be able to command tailored responses from the CSPs. If using one of "RFx" techniques, the assessment process may be appropriately split into two phases, one a higher level assessment of a field of CSPs and then a more detailed assessment of a narrowed field of CSPs that survived the first phase.

Assessing potential CSPs includes not only getting the answers to specific questions, perhaps using one of the methods outlined in Chapters 4 and 5, but even more importantly checking their external security certifications, their externalized audit reports on CSP internal controls, and the organization's own description of their security controls. For example, Amazon provides a white paper description of its security processes that should be a minimum expectation of CSPs.[4] ISO 27001 certification and a clean ISAE 3402 SOC-3 report are other minimum standards that organizations should expect to find at leading CSPs. The more third-party, standards-based vetting that a CSP can produce, the more credible its offerings.

CSP Agreement
Negotiating with the selected CSP involves the techniques and provisions discussed in Chapter 7. This includes not only reaching agreement on the various legal and business issues but also the service-related issues contained in the SLA. The starting point is likely to be a standardized contract or terms of use provided by the CSP to which variances will be agreed. The degree of flexibility provided to the organization by the CSP is one of the criteria to be evaluated in the previous step. When negotiating with larger CSPs or for organizations without significant leverage, getting changes may not be easily accomplished, so such organizations will want to prioritize those items that they absolutely must have before being able to sign any agreement to outsource to the cloud.

Because they have likely been requested from so many different prospective customers, some of the (especially more established) CSPs are now beginning to incorporate certain terms into their agreements. As shown in Chapter 7, for example, with some CSPs it is possible to limit the geographic location of the data stored with them, thereby limiting a number of risks. To

---

4. Amazon Web Services, *Overview of Security Processes* (2010).

be competitive, CSPs may likely incorporate more of these must-have provisions into their standard agreements, so organizations will need to determine this each time they intend to outsource to the cloud. Some terms will clearly be negotiable, while other terms will be somewhere in the middle, not clearly negotiable but potentially so. By looking from the perspective of the CSP and the cloud market, organizations will understand which terms will likely not be negotiable, such as one-way indemnity clauses or significantly higher liability caps on acts of ordinary negligence, and will avoid wasting negotiating cycles on unreasonable demands. And as previously mentioned, it is important to see what terms are silent or missing and to see if such terms can be added by negotiating them in as part of a clarification process.

One other point to look for as the cloud market matures is that the negotiations may not occur directly between the cloud consumer and the CSP. Instead, a variety of intermediaries may contract with the cloud consumer. These include cloud brokers who can consolidate many cloud services, systems integrators who can provide not only cloud services but also other IT services not directly related to the cloud, and telecom providers who can provide both cloud network access and cloud services. These intermediaries may be able to take on more risk than CSPs and/or agree to more flexible terms than CSPs. Back-to-back provisions may be required.

8.2 Example Scenarios

To demonstrate how this comprehensive approach process should work, the following two simplified scenarios will be utilized:

- A large multinational organization wants to use the cloud for its payroll applications and wants to outsource its general file servers to hosting in the cloud. This scenario will look at both the IaaS and SaaS service models and the public and private cloud deployment models.
- A domestic-only small or medium sized enterprise (SME, which may also be called a small or medium sized business—SMB) wants to use the cloud to be able to build and execute web applications for its organization and its suppliers. This scenario will look at the PaaS service model and the public cloud deployment model. Because it has a limited budget

for IT staff, it wants to implement Security as a Service (SecaaS) for any applications that it develops.

Multinational Organization

A multinational organization will typically have expertise in helping to evaluate cloud use and prospective CSPs but also potentially will have negotiating leverage over most CSPs, in being able to get contractual and SLA terms that it requires. Given its legal obligations and large number of stakeholders, it is important that it both understand and negotiate into these agreements those terms that allow it to remain in compliance with its varied obligations.

Security Situation of the Organization

The organization has an information security policy and it performs regular risk assessments. The information in the payroll application contains sensitive and personally identifiable information. The information in the payroll system is encrypted but the information on the general file server is not. The remote network authentication techniques use the OpenID protocol, with some attempts at federation under SAML. Server virtualization has been implemented but no other features or functions of a private cloud are yet in use.

Security Situation of the CSP

The CSP is ISO 27001-certified in its information security program and posts a privacy policy on its website. It offers SaaS (certain applications), PaaS (certain development tools) and IaaS (hardware, network and virtual machines with standard OS under hypervisor and virtualization management system) service models but has not implemented any cloud-specific standards. It generates encryption keys for authentication purposes for each unique active user but may reuse them after service termination. Resources and users can be authenticated using SAML federation techniques. Vulnerability scans and threats are assessed annually and controls reevaluated and, if necessary, remediated or added. The data is uploaded to the SaaS application's shared proprietary database. Annual ISAE 3402 audits and penetration tests are performed and the reports are made available to all current customers. Organizations are provided their own virtual machines and virtual storage, network and computing resources as needed, all of which may be located on the same respective physical devices. Virtual machines are provided to all co-tenants based on a common security profile. All security events are logged but the logs contain information about all co-tenants. Backups are made daily of all databases and logs and electronically stored in a separate location, with a tape backup sent offsite from the remote site daily on a regular rotation. The ability to host systems in two different locations/resource groupings is available.

Standard Terms of CSP's Services Contract and SLA

The terms of the contract limit the liability of the CSP to actual payments received in the last twelve months for conduct for which it is primarily liable. There is mutual indemnification for third party intellectual property rights violations. The jurisdiction and venue are in the global headquarters of the CSP, which is in a different country from where the service will be initiated. The agreement specifies that the CSP may utilize subcontractors at its own discretion to provide the virtual resources. The organization owns all its data stored on the CSP's site(s) and any programs generated therein. Organization data is confidential only if so designated in writing and is to be protected with reasonable care. The CSP may disclose the organization's information if legally compelled to do so. Upon termination, the CSP will return copies of the organization's data in the desired format. No independent audits are allowed. The SLA specifies an aspiration of 99.999 percent uptime availability for applications and infrastructure.

Domestic SME

A small or medium sized enterprise typically does not have the leverage to negotiate many of the terms of a CSP's standard agreement. As such, is important to focus on ranking its requirements to ensure that it gets at least the must-have issues addressed in the CSP agreement. While it does not have the same concern about international issues as multinationals, given the data mobility of the cloud, it may also be required to understand the laws of any location where its data may be hosted.

Security Situation of the Organization

The organization has an information security and privacy policy that it purchased but has not been able to customize it to its business, although it does try to follow it. Risk assessments were done initially when implementing these policies. The organization's IT resources have been used primarily for development of applications instead of information security risk analysis in recent years. There is no business continuity plan but regular backups are performed. The data used in its applications is considered a trade secret. It is required under its supplier agreements to ensure complete deletion of all supplier records within two years of any transaction.

Security Situation of the CSP

In addition to the first CSP, a second CSP is being considered to provide the PaaS. The second CSP does not have a security certification. It utilizes other cloud providers in other countries to process some of its elastic resource capabilities. It provides PaaS services for development tools and for its own databases accessed with its own proprietary API. A third CSP, a regional firm specializing in security services including remote security management functions is being considered to provide the Security as a Service, as is a well-known international brand name in malware protection software.

Standard Terms of CSP's Services Contract

The second CSP's standard agreement is similar except that it does not allow negotiation of most contractual terms, including its per-incident maximum liability of $5,000. The terms are silent as to its operational responsibilities in case of a data breach. The third CSP and the international malware protection software company are offering the security services at a standard monthly price based on a standard agreement. The terms do not mention records retention, deletion, or preservation capabilities or responsibilities.

8.3 Applying the Approach to the Example Scenarios

In this section, the methodology explained throughout the book and summarized in the first section will be applied to the two cloud computing usage scenarios described in the second section, providing illustrations which organizations may choose to apply in their approach to the cloud. The first two steps, setting the scope and determining the cloud use (service and deployment models), have already been defined in the scenarios, so this section will focus on the final three steps: organization self-assessment, CSP assessment, and CSP agreement.

Multinational Organization

Organization Self-Assessment

The multinational organization must first consider if it is ready to outsource. This will require not only the initial effort to put the business case together and staff, design, and implement the outsourcing project, but the organization must also have the governance methods, skills, and resources to continue to oversee the outsourcing services. It must also have a rigorous enough information security and privacy program so that it has an appropriate metric by which to assess and later audit the CSP.

Assuming it is ready to outsource, it must consider the legal obligations that it will be under. Assuming that it already is in compliance with its existing statutory, regulatory, and contractual commitments, it must understand first what additional aspects of its existing obligations may be impacted by outsourcing to the cloud. For example, as explained in Chapter 2, under HIPAA, business associates agreements are required when outsourcing protected health information, among any and all subcontractors as well. In addition, due to the data mobility principle, there can be new legal obligations that arise, as the data may be hosted in additional countries.

When the legal obligations have been delineated, then the information security and privacy risks must be understood. The risk assessment and risk treatment processes are essential here. One or more of the methodologies specified in Chapters 4 and 5 should be in place, which starts with one of the standard methodologies, supplemented by at least one of the cloud-enhanced methodologies. The information risk assessment for most organizations can utilize ISO 27005[5] or ISACA's Risk IT,[6] while government agencies can utilize NIST's risk assessment process[7] or one of the ENISA methodologies.

---

5. ISO/IEC 27005, *Information technology - Security techniques - Information security risk management* (2008).
6. ISACA *The Risk IT Framework* (2009).
7. NIST SP 800-30 Rev. 1, *Guide for Conducting Risk Assessments* (Sept. 2012).

These methodologies will all focus on the current and ongoing assessment of threats, the scanning for vulnerabilities, and the impacts and likelihood of losses caused by these risks. Using a ranking of these risks and the organization's tolerance for residual risk, the various treatment options of retain, insure/outsource, avoid or reduce or eliminate the risk are chosen. It is the latter of these treatments that involves the design and implementation of information security and privacy controls, as addressed by ISO 27002, NIST SP 800-53, and COBIT, among others explained in Chapter 5.

Assuming that the organization has properly designed, implemented, and operates its risk assessment and treatment program according to one of these methodologies, in preparation for cloud outsourcing there are several controls that need to be re-visited. Using the ISO 27002 control framework, these controls involve the oversight of outsourcing, including contact with security specialist forums and professional associations (§6.1.7), dealing with external parties (§6.2), responsibility for assets (§7.1), information classification (§7.2), legal compliance with applicable statutes (§15.1), compliance with security policies and standards (§15.2), and audit considerations (§15.3). The cloud controls that apply to the organization will be addressed in the context of the CSP assessment in the next step.

- *The organization has an information security policy and it performs regular risk assessments.* A key requirement before outsourcing is that the organization itself is committed to information security and privacy and has the programs in place to control, monitor, and remediate security issues. When it can control its own house, it is ready to proceed to outsourcing. It must extend its risk assessment process to include those threats and vulnerabilities to which the CSP is exposed.
- *The information in the payroll application contains sensitive and personally identifiable information.* This classification denotes not only an added level of information security and privacy protections but potentially implicates quite a number of statutory obligations. The organization is going to have to take the necessary steps to ensure that at a minimum those controls that it currently has in place work effectively in the cloud computing context. For every country where the payroll application will host personally identifiable data or the organization has

employees, the organization will need to ensure compliance with the data protection laws as discussed in Chapters 2 and 3. In addition, local employment laws must be reviewed for confidentiality, usage, and cross-border restrictions. There must also be an emphasis on the additional controls for sensitive data and the implications under various statutes and in the practices of the CSPs.

- *The information in the payroll system is encrypted but the information on the general file server is not.* Use of encryption needs to be evaluated on an end-to-end basis, for encryption of the data in transmission, physical transport, in storage, and in use. The encryption algorithms used and the management of encryption keys are significant areas that must be discussed in depth with the CSP. Also, if data must be transferred into or retrieved from the cloud-based payroll system, the encryption controls used by the organization need to work seamlessly with those used by the CSP.

- *The remote network authentication techniques use the OpenID protocol, with some attempts at federation under SAML.* While it is beneficial that the organization already is using identity management and remote network authentication federation techniques, it must determine how its authentication process will work with the CSP's identity management and authentication system. For the SaaS application, the organization will want its users to at least be able to avoid signing in again, assuming they have already been authenticated inside the organization. The passing of identity credentials and other required information may utilize a third-party identity provider (meaning an entity that has originally accepted the identity of the user, provided an appropriate credential, and now is verifying that credential) or the CSP may itself function as both the service provider and the identity provider. Federation among differing protocols is usually a non-trivial process, depending upon the federation requirements (single sign-on, single sign-off, etc.). The required authentication tokens (e.g., passwords, one-time passwords, biometrics, software or hardware encryption) and the implications of these technologies for the necessary authentication assurance levels must also be understood.[8]

- *Server virtualization has been implemented but no other features or functions of a private cloud.* For IaaS service models, the internal use of server virtualization possibly implies an easier technical migration to a CSP using computer server virtualization but the institutional understanding of virtualization should allow the organization to more easily assess the potential risks therein, as discussed in Chapter 4. These risks include the lack of use or visibility to the same tools utilized in the non-virtualized environment and issues arising from the multi-tenant architecture. The organization's experiences with server virtualization (and any desktop virtualization) will inform the assessment of the CSP's use of virtualization (e.g., location of intrusion detection capabilities).

CSP Assessment

When assessing a CSP or multiple CSPs, the assessment process may be performed in two phases: first higher-level assessment as part of a broader selection process that narrows it down-to a few CSPs and then to just one CSP for a final in-depth assessment. For purposes of this explanation, it is assumed that only a single phase will be utilized for an in-depth assessment of this CSP. While CAMM may be used to assist the narrowing process in a two-phase approach, in all cases the various risks raised in Chapter 4 must be addressed. This may be done by using these risk questions in tandem with the risk assessment processes described above. Or the risks may be evaluated utilizing cloud-ready tools such as the ENISA Risk Assessment Framework, the CSA Consensus Assessments Initiative Questionnaire, or the BITS AUP delta cloud controls along with the SIG questionnaire. Government agencies (or practically any organization) can use the ISIMC risk manager questions along with the FedRAMP controls, utilizing the methodology laid out in SP 800-53A.[9]

The most important skill in performing these types of risk assessments is knowing when something is satisfactory on its face, when it is unsatisfactory on its face, and when it requires additional investigation to determine

---

8. *See* NIST, SP 800-63 rev. 2, *Electronic Authentication Guideline* (Feb. 2013).

9. NIST, SP 800-53A rev. 1, *Guide for Assessing the Security Controls in Federal Information Systems* (2010).

if it is satisfactory or unsatisfactory. For the multinational organization, on the facts presented, all require analysis and likely additional actions.

- *The CSP is ISO 27001-certified in its information security program and posts a privacy policy on its website.* This is a great start and should give the organization a significant belief in the CSP's commitment to information security and privacy. The ISO 27001 certification requires among other items that the CSP has a risk assessment program, has a viable information security policy, has working information security and privacy controls that are effective, has incident handling procedures that are followed all the way through to the closing of an incident, and that the management and employees have demonstrated a commitment to reviewing and improving security. The privacy policy provides insights into how the CSP will collect, process and dispose of the organization's information and the data handling restrictions that it imposes upon itself. The organization should also look for best practices that may not be part of these standards (which should be viewed as the lower, not the upper limit), such as the SaaS applications undergoing code vulnerability analysis for each significant programmatic revision.

- *It offers SaaS (certain applications),* PaaS *(certain development tools) and IaaS (hardware, network and virtual machines with standard OS under hypervisor and virtualization management system) service models but has not implemented any cloud-specific standards.* Although few cloud standards are widely accepted at this point, the organization should determine the status of the CSP's cloud standardization efforts. There are numerous efforts underway, for example, in cloud portability and interoperability, and de facto standards, for example, in portability and data management, as described in Chapter 5. Commitment to emerging or de facto standards is something that demonstrates a show of strength from a CSP. Some interfaces, such as those that are part of application programs, may be more difficult to modify, so it is essential that these must not change from CSP to CSP. The trust boundaries of the cloud environment must be understood as well as the respective roles of the organization and CSP in maintaining trust.

- *It generates encryption keys for authentication purposes for each unique active user but may reuse them after service termination.* The use of these encryption keys is a good practice, but the organization should insist that there is no reuse of keys. While the likelihood of problems is probably small in a multi-tenant environment, such risks should be minimized. The strength of the encryption algorithm used needs to be clearly understood, as do the techniques for protection and management of keys by the CSP and the key lifecycle.

- *Resources and users can be authenticated using SAML federation techniques.* This is a good practice but care must be taken in the exact deployment techniques, so further inquiry is required. The organization stated that it used OpenID with some attempts at SAML for single sign-on identity federation, while the CSP utilizes SAML. As these identity management federation protocol implementations can be quite complex, the exact implementations must be understood, as well as whether there is a need to utilize OpenID identities within the SAML federation. The groups of resources and users that will participate will also need to be specified. The organization needs to understand how the CSP protects the authentication interface against attack.

- *Vulnerability scans and threats are assessed annually and controls reevaluated, and if necessary, remediated or added.* Annual risk assessments are not sufficient, as they need to occur more frequently. Vulnerability scans should also happen much more frequently and should at best be continuous and automated. While annual reassessment of all controls is probably sufficient, new risks arising from the likelihood of new threats or vulnerabilities manifesting themselves must be continuously assessed and controls or other appropriate risk treatments designed and implemented as necessary. One area that the organization should specifically ask the CSP about is how it monitors potential insider threats. How the CSP protects against external threats is one aspect, but as many security incidents come from the inside, so the CSP must make clear the detection and prevention processes it utilizes to identify and prevent insider threats (e.g., review all uses of privileged accounts, check for suspicious outbound traffic, multiple reviews of all configuration changes, matching all user accounts to a real user).

- *The data is uploaded to the SaaS application's shared proprietary database.* The issue here is not what it seems. Although the data is in a proprietary database, it likely can be extracted as easily as it was uploaded and imported. What is of greater concern is that the database is shared, so the logical and physical data isolation controls must be verified. And there is no mention of either the techniques used to protect the upload process files and transmission, which should be encrypted, or the stored database, which should likely be encrypted.

- *Annual ISAE 3402 audits and penetration tests are performed and the reports are made available to all current customers.* This is another control that should provide much comfort to the organization. What it wants to verify is which type of report will be produced for existing customers and, more importantly for the initial assessment, whether it can, as a prospective customer, review it. A clean audit report and penetration testing without material issues should always be what the organization expects of the CSP.

- *Organizations are provided their own virtual machines and virtual storage, network, and computer resources as needed, all of which may be located on the same respective physical devices.* The concern here is that, in the event of a data breach or system failure, logical isolation controls may fail or that virtual isolation controls may fail during normal operation by rogue virtual clients that are able to escape virtual machines. The isolation controls, for data, processes, and VMs, in both normal operation and in case of unusual events, must be thoroughly investigated. In addition, the organization will want to insist that all VMs are provided in a common file format for portability and that the CSP utilize available standards, such as ISO/IEC 17203:2011 (OVF).

- *Virtual machines are provided to all co-tenants based on a common security profile.* If the security profile is at a high enough security threshold, this is probably a positive. The security details of the VM implementation may not be sufficient for the organization's needs, so it will want to investigate its ability to add additional security safeguards. This is more likely with an IaaS environment where the organization receives pre-built VMs from the CSP. In the best scenario, each VM is provided with malware, firewall, and intrusion detection and prevention capabilities and no

261

keys are embedded therein. Regardless of the service model employed, the organization should insist on the highest level of visibility possible into the virtual environment.

- *All security events are logged but the logs contain information about all co-tenants.* First, the organization will want to understand what the respective meanings of "all" and "events" are. "All" may mean only security events over a certain level of severity, while "events" can have many different meanings (e.g., is occasional external network probing an event?). Once it knows what events are logged, it will want to know how long the log information is retained (some logs fill up quickly and may be overwritten). Then the organization will want to understand its ability to extract the log information, in terms of granularity, timing, and software tool use (e.g., view or export). The organization will need to understand how the logs and the virtual management environment are protected from attack.

- *Backups are made daily of all databases and logs and electronically stored in a separate location, with a tape backup sent offsite from the remote site daily on a regular rotation.* Daily backups of data and transaction logs are a must, as are storage in a second location and offsite copies regularly rotated. But this introduces several issues for the organization to further investigate. One issue is that there is no mention of encryption of the off-site backups. A second issue is the unknown location of both the second site and the off-site storage locations. A third issue is that there will be a large number of copies and how these copies all be accounted for, during the period of the contract and at service termination. A fourth issue is that there is no mention of backups of virtual machines, and for reasons of portability and data deletion, the organization will want to be able to take away all copies of both data and virtual machines. The schedule of not only images of at least production VMs and interim snapshots should be specified and these as well need to follow the migration of backups to mirror and off-site locations. The period that the CSP retains the various backup media and copies should be considered as part of a records retention policy that takes into account all appropriate compliance requirements.

- *The ability to host systems in two different locations/resource groupings is available.* The organization will need to analyze in depth what this option signifies. If the hosting options are in different geographic locations, how disparate are they? In case of a natural disaster, they should not be subject to the same potential source (common earthquake fault lines or exposure to coastal storms or tsunamis). For possible device failures, loss of telecom service, or accidental misconfigurations by the CSP, the single point of failure analysis must be performed. To adequately do so, the organization will need a much better understanding of possible scenarios that could cause a service disruption and design its integrated business continuity plan with these restrictions in mind.

CSP Agreement

The CSP standard agreement has a number of areas that must be addressed.

- *The terms of the contract limit the liability of the CSP to actual payments received in the last twelve months for conduct for which it is primarily liable.* At a minimum, the organization will want to negotiate proportional liability and would want to avoid a cap or ensure a much higher one in the case of a data breach based on the negligence of the CSP. There will be significant costs in settling a data breach, including but not limited to the costs of notification, credit report monitoring, legal costs, and potential fines from regulators, which insurance may only partly address.
- *There is mutual indemnification for third party intellectual property rights violations.* This is a typical provision in agreements and is not usually a cause for concern. But the organization may want to consider the service model it is utilizing to determine if a balanced indemnification clause makes sense. In a SaaS service model, it will be the CSP's software and thus intellectual property that is most in play on the organization's data, while in an IaaS service model, it will be the organization's software and data. Other things to consider include the nature of the software that the CSP is using to run its applications, databases, operating systems, provisioning services, system management capabilities, utilities, and security services. The use of any open source software should be noted, and as much licensing information as possible should be obtained.

- *The jurisdiction and venue are in the global headquarters of the CSP, which is in a different country from where the service will be initiated.* The organization will want the governing law of the agreement to be a law it is completely familiar with or one where it can reasonably get the information if it needs to, in the case of needing to pursue litigation. It also would want the venue in the locale of the likely witnesses (e.g., system administrators and/or data custodians), assuming that location has sufficient judicial protections. With multinationals, this is not often a major issue, assuming it is a jurisdiction where it has a major presence (and therefore local legal staff). But a conflict of laws analysis of the likeliest areas of dispute may be a prudent measure to determine the preferred locations and set of laws.

- *The agreement specifies that the CSP may utilize subcontractors at its own discretion to provide the virtual resources.* The organization needs to insist that all subcontractors are pre-approved and vetted in a manner similar to the CSP. A risk assessment of any CSP is an absolute minimum requirement for any agreement. Any subcontractors must be used only under a written agreement with the CSP. A location awareness API is a key contractual provision that the organization needs to insist upon so that data outside the approved locations will not be written or migrated there. Machine-readable SLAs of all service providers would also be optimal, to ensure that any such subcontractors meet the requirements of the organization. This is further discussed under the domestic SME section.

- *The organization owns all its data stored on the CSP's site(s) and any programs generated therein.* The organization must insist on retaining ownership to all data it transfers to and creates on the CSP's servers, including any metadata. The organization must also insist on retaining all intellectual property rights to all works created on the site by the organization (in the case of PaaS or IaaS models). The CSP should not be given the right to modify the organization's data, except to the extent that its software applications used by the organization modify the data of the organization.

- *Organization data is confidential only if so designated in writing and is to be protected with reasonable care.* All data should be considered confidential, whether deemed so or whether it reasonably should be expected to be confidential. Classification of organization data according to different levels (secret, confidential, limited distribution, public) makes it easier to apply access rules but CSPs may or may not be interested in that level of detail. CSP access will differ depending on the service model employed but the confidentiality requirements should apply to data in use, in memory, in transit, in physical transport, and on physical media.

- *The CSP may disclose the organization's information if legally compelled to do so.* The organization should insist that it be notified before any compelled disclosure is acted upon. While possibly legal, there should be no voluntary disclosure of organization data allowed. In addition, if forensic data capture services are required, the CSP must state how it would go about performing such a procedure or if it will allow the organization to perform such (most likely for IaaS models). And the CSP must explain how it will respond in the case of the seizure of a physical device that is not related to the activities of the organization but on which it is a co-tenant.

- *Upon termination, the CSP will return copies of the organization's data in the desired format.* The organization should insist on an accounting of all copies of the data and secure disposal of all such copies, including all VM copies and slack space. The return of data must be in an agreed upon format. The CSP may allow the organization to retrieve its own data within a limited window and possibly could allow the export of VMs. The concern is that all copies are completely deleted, including those on subcontractor servers and those that may be on business continuity tapes off-site.

- *No independent audits are allowed.* If the organization cannot conduct its own audits, then it must insist on receiving copies of ISAE 3402 reports, similar to the SOC-2 reports described in Chapter 5. It would be best if the internal audit department of the organization would be allowed to at least provide questions that the CSP would respond within a specified period of time. In all cases, the organization must be able to collect sufficient evidence to meet its audit and compliance needs and how these records will be preserved and made available should be agreed to well in advance.

- *The SLA specifies an aspiration of 99.999% uptime availability for applications and infrastructure.* The organization should insist that this is a minimum threshold, after clearly understanding that its definition of "uptime" and the CSP's are the same and clarifying what is excluded from it. It is worth remembering that this should be from the user's perspective, in that the consumer of cloud services will be concerned with the availability of the service it is acquiring from the CSP, not the availability of any particular devices (e.g., network, hosts). In addition, the organization will want to specify penalties for failure to meet this minimum benchmark, perhaps in the form of service credits.

Domestic SME

The domestic SME is going to have to conduct the same analysis as the multinational organization in determining whether it is ready to outsource or not, but can do so in a scaled-down manner. It may have lesser compliance obligations due to exposure to a lesser number of countries where it does business, but it is also likely to have fewer legal and IT resources with which to undertake the analysis of the CSPs. It would be appropriate to focus its resources on the areas it sees as the source of the highest risks in cloud use.

Organization Self-Assessment

- *The organization has an information security and privacy policy that it purchased but has not been able to customize it to its business, although it does try to follow it.* The fact that the policies have been purchased actually is a benefit, as it likely means that they are more standardized and based on specific security expertise. The problem is that the organization has not customized it to reflect its specific needs. This needs to be remedied before it considers outsourcing. In addition, regular monitoring and reporting on compliance, follow-up actions, and required training all must be in place.
- *Risk assessments were done initially when implementing these policies.* It is not clear if risk assessments are still performed periodically and what happens to the findings. Again, this must be remedied before outsourcing. All organizations must understand how information, which is likely to be their most valuable assets (be it proprietary business techniques,

intellectual property, customer or market knowledge, etc.), is put at risk in an ever-changing threat and vulnerability landscape and so be able to apply appropriate risk treatments, even if this means just knowing and accepting these risks.

- *The organization's IT resources have been used primarily for development of applications instead of information security risk analysis in recent years.* The SME's desire to outsource is based on being able to redeploy its IT team resources away from doing so much application development and possibly being able to use other application development resources located elsewhere to fill that gap, while applying its higher-skilled people to address the security situation. This type of resource realignment is a typical reason for outsourcing and should help address these two IT skill issues. It will also help to reduce exposure to resource attenuation, so that the SME retains sufficient expertise to be able to appropriately govern the cloud outsourcing threats, responses, incidents, and resolution.

- *There is no business continuity plan but regular backups are performed.* This is a valid reason for outsourcing to the cloud: to gain the technical infrastructure to implement a BCP. But it must be clearly understood that such technical infrastructure is only a component of a BCP (e.g., what happens if the organization's primary office location is destroyed by an earthquake or flood?). A BCP plan must still be developed based on asset identification and valuation, RTOs and RPOs, and must be scripted and tested, as described in Chapter 5.

- *The data used in its applications is considered a trade secret.* Organizations should move such sensitive data to the cloud with extreme care. Significant protections are required, as a breach of such information could eventually put the organization in jeopardy as a going concern. In addition, the organization must be aware of the trade secret law protections of any jurisdiction where such data would be stored or otherwise processed. The potential implications of such data being put into the cloud and losing its trade secret protection due to a lack of true confidentiality or lack of reasonable expectations of being able to safeguard it must be fully explored first.

- *It is required under its supplier agreements to ensure complete deletion of all supplier records within two years of any transaction.* The organization currently does this by manually monitoring the results of a monthly report on last update dates of records stored in the file system. The organization will want to understand whether the CSP provides any similar types of reports on database record life and how the CSP is able to help comply with its records retention/deletion policies and commitments.

CSP Assessment

- *In addition to the first CSP, a second CSP is being considered to provide the PaaS. The second CSP does not have a security certification.* The lack of a security certification should be a red flag to the organization, both of a possible lack of commitment to security by the second CSP and of the extra due diligence work that will have to be done by the organization to assess the second CSP's controls. Only under exceptional circumstances should such a CSP be considered.

- *It utilizes other cloud providers in other countries to process some of its elastic resource capabilities.* While not in itself a problem, this does trigger the need to further investigate which countries are being used. The organization should insist on pre-approval before any data is hosted or otherwise processed outside the contracting country. It should also determine how to account for the security practices and data copies of these other CSPs, in addition to how to hold them legally liable if need be. The data protection statutes in Chapter 3 must be reviewed, not only for compliance with the privacy, information security, and data breach provisions identified but also to understand what restrictions are placed upon the transfer of cross-border data. This involves any cross-border data transfers involving personal or sensitive information as well as the impacts of any blocking statutes. In addition, the surveillance laws identified in Chapter 2 must be taken into consideration based on the countries that could potentially host the data.

- *It provides PaaS services for development tools and for its own databases accessed with its own proprietary API.* The utilization of proprietary APIs would require the organization to re-code its application if it changes CSPs. The organization must discover if the CSP will use cloud standard-based APIs as they emerge. Also, as it will be utilizing the cloud for application development purposes, the organization must understand how easily it can provision new VMs for each development phase in the application lifecycle, customized for the application code and data applicable to that SDLC phase. The methodology and timing of development tool revisions is also vital.

- *A third CSP, a regional firm specializing in security services including remote security management functions is being considered to provide the Security as a Service, as is a well-known international brand name in malware protection software.* The lack of security skill sets and up-to-date security software is a common issue in SMEs and an appropriate reason to turn to the cloud. The organization does need to maintain a strong security posture and threat-awareness program, even if this service is outsourced. The choices that the SME has are between the regional firm that can provide additional skilled resources to handle services such as monitoring for security incidents and the international brand name firm that provides a product that provides many of the detection functions but leaves the follow-up activities to the organization to address. Both choices may be valid, depending on the role the SME wants to take on.

CSP Agreement

- *The second CSP's standard agreement is similar except that it does not allow negotiation of most contractual terms, including its per incident maximum liability of $5,000.* The definition of an "incident" must be investigated more fully, as an incident may be what happens on a record level or on a database level and in the case of a data breach, should be clearly specified in the agreement. A data breach as defined by the CSP may only be as defined by local law (e.g., when users are materially affected), so clarity of that term is important.
- *The terms are silent as to its operational responsibilities in case of a data breach.* The CSP must have incident response, escalation, remediation, review, and reporting requirements, in addition to potential statutory compliance requirements under law, all of which should be clearly spelled out in the agreement. The organization should be immediately notified when there is a breach of any kind (as previously discussed, there must be agreement on what constitutes a breach) and there must be a process that clearly identifies who notifies affected users, law enforcement,

and government agencies, in what order, and under what specific circumstances.

- *The third CSP and the international malware protection software company are offering the security services at a standard monthly price based on a standard agreement.* While both firms are offering monthly pricing, this may mask what is actually being offered. The regional firm, without the brand recognition, may be more flexible in its pricing and may include the malware protection and incident notification and resolution services, in addition to more insight as to potential risks for this type of application profile. The brand name firm may have a stronger threat detection capability and be able to resolve most threats automatically without the need for human intervention but without the customization for the organization's particular application. In either case, the organization will want to be able to perform application penetration testing to ensure there are no vulnerabilities in its web applications and related network defenses and it will need the concurrence of both the CSP and its Security as a Service provider.

- *The terms do not mention records retention, deletion, or preservation capabilities or responsibilities.* Every organization will need to continue to meet its compliance responsibilities for records retention and deletion arising from statutory, regulatory, and contractual commitments when the data is in the cloud. While IaaS customers would be expected to handle these responsibilities themselves, SaaS customers would not and if certain records will need to be maintained for or deleted after a specified time, the CSP will need to assist the organization with deletion or retention of records that it may not be able to completely control. In the event of litigation or investigation, the preservation duties of the CSP must be clearly spelled out under the agreement, based on communications from either the organization or third parties, including government entities. The ability to search preserved data and the types of data that may be searched must be specified.

Both Agreements

In addition to the provisions discussed above, the organization will need to ensure that at least the following provisions are also given the appropriate consideration in negotiating CSP agreements, as discussed in Chapter 7.

- Choice of law
- Jurisdiction
- Mandatory arbitration
- Changing the terms of a standard agreement via website posting
- Warranties
- Confidentiality
- Vendor bankruptcy
- Venue
- Cross-border bankruptcy
- Export controls
- Bribery controls
- Conflict of laws
- Names of data custodians
- Procedural rules
- Data integrity/chain of custody process
- Insurance
- Forensic data capture process
- Indemnification
- Changes to services
- Assignment or delegation
- Remedies
- Force majeure
- Critical success factors, key performance indicators, and metrics

Chapter 9

LAWYERS AND THE CLOUD

With a firm understanding of the applicable statutes and regulations, information security and privacy risks and risk treatments, and contractual provisions
and negotiating points, lawyers are almost ready to address cloud computing
for their organizational clients. But first there are a few other areas to consider,
which are covered in this chapter. The first is the legal ethical implications of
lawyers using the cloud in support of their practice. The second is gaining
an understanding of the issues related to cloud use by individual consumers
who may become clients individually or as part of organizations. The final
section presents the types of knowledge that the lawyer must acquire before
undertaking the many steps in supporting clients' migration to the cloud as
outlined in the previous chapters.

Executive Takeaways

- Understanding the ethical issues of cloud use by lawyers
- Understanding the differences in supporting individual cloud consumers
- Organizational knowledge and skills needed to assess and negotiate with CSPs
- How to get started in the cloud

9.1 Legal Ethics and Cloud Use

The use of the cloud by lawyers would seem to be no more of an issue than it would for any other service business. After all, lawyers have been using the variety of outsourced services for as long as other businesses have. But due to the confidentiality requirements in the attorney-client and work product privileges, use of the cloud by lawyers actually raises a number of potential ethical concerns. These concerns have so far been addressed and documented, and guidance has been provided in white papers and legal ethics opinions, by both the ABA and state bar associations. The use of the cloud by lawyers is still gaining trust, as a majority of legal IT professionals recently surveyed at law firms did not yet favor moving their own key applications to the cloud, although storage, email, and HR were viewed as suitable cloud apps by a majority of the respondents, with (Electronic Data Discovery) EDD, CRM, and litigation support close to a majority.[1]

The software and services that lawyers use in the cloud are subject to the same types of risks documented in the previous chapters, with the added caveat that law firms seem to have become a target for bad actors on the Internet, due in large part to the fact that lawyers have significant amounts of confidential documentation containing non-public information but weak

---

1. Legal IT Professionals, *2012 Global Cloud Survey Report* (Nov. 2012).

cybersecurity profiles.[2] Conversely, law firms are hired by organizations who have suffered data breaches to gain the benefit of the attorney-client privilege for activities like internal investigations of the breach that they do not want to become part of future litigation.[3]

When considering cloud services like storing files with client information, lawyers should analyze the implications of the terms of service. For example, here is part of the privacy policy for a leading cloud storage provider: "Compliance with Laws and Law Enforcement Requests; Protection of Dropbox's Rights. We may disclose to parties outside Dropbox files stored in your Dropbox and information about you that we collect when we have a good faith belief that disclosure is reasonably necessary to (a) comply with a law, regulation or compulsory legal request; (b) protect the safety of any person from death or serious bodily injury; (c) prevent fraud or abuse of Dropbox or its users; or (d) to protect Dropbox's property rights. If we provide your Dropbox files to a law enforcement agency as set forth above, we will remove Dropbox's encryption from the files before providing them to law enforcement. However, Dropbox will not be able to decrypt any files that you encrypted prior to storing them on Dropbox."[4]

ABA

The ABA Commission on Ethics 20/20 published an issues paper in September 2010, drafted by the commission's Working Group on the Implications of New Technologies. Called "Client Confidentiality Issues,"[5] the working group listed a number of potential security threats arising from use of cloud computing, including:

- Unauthorized access to confidential client information by CSP's employees or hackers

---

2. *See e.g.* FBI E-Scams and Warnings, *Spear Phishing E-mails Target U.S. Law Firms and Public Relations Firms* (Nov. 17, 2009); *China-Based Hackers Target Law Firms to Get Secret Deal Data*, Bloomberg (Feb. 1, 2012).

3. *Law Firms Tout Cybersecurity Cred,* Wall Street Journal (Mar, 31, 2013).

4. Dropbox Privacy Policy (last updated Oct. 15, 2012).

5. ABA Commission on Ethics 20/20 Working Group on the Implications of New Technologies, *For Comment: Issues Paper Concerning Client Confidentiality and Lawyers' Use of Technology* (Sept. 20, 2010).

- Storage on servers located in countries with fewer legal protections for ESI
- CSP's failure to back up data adequately
- Unclear ownership policies for stored data
- Ability to access the data using easily accessible software after termination of the CSP relationship (voluntarily by the lawyer or involuntarily because of the CSP's bankruptcy)
- CSP's procedures for responding to government requests for access to information
- Policies for notifying customers of security breaches
- Policies for data destruction when a lawyer no longer wants the relevant information available or for transferring the data if a client switches law firms
- Insufficient data encryption
- The extent to which lawyers need to obtain client consent before using cloud computing services to store or transmit the client's confidential information

The working group made the important point that "there may be a gap between technology-related security measures that are ethically required and security measures that are merely consistent with 'best practices.'" For example, in cloud computing while it might be "inadvisable" for a lawyer to utilize a CSP that does not comply with industry encryption standards, it is "not necessarily unethical" to do so.

The working group also referenced as an example the information security and privacy requirements in the new Massachusetts statute that applies to lawyers with confidential information on Massachusetts residents. The working group also believed that because cloud computing is arguably a form of outsourcing, the procedures outlined in a prior ethics opinion on outsourcing may be applicable.[6] This opinion describes a lawyer's obligations when outsourcing work to lawyers and non-lawyers.

---

6. ABA Comm'n On Ethics and Professional Responsibility, Formal Op. 08-451 (2008).

In addition, the commission wanted to understand if Model Rule 5.3[7] on supervision of non-lawyers needs to be revised to include cloud computing. The commission was trying to determine which cloud computing security and privacy practices should be deemed "essential for lawyers" and whether they should be required to negotiate these practices into any agreements with CSPs. It also discussed confidentiality issues with mobile input devices accessing or storing confidential information and asked for input on "cyberinsurance and cyberliability insurance."

The ABA Commission on Ethics 20/20 created several resolutions for the Model Rules that were passed in August 2012 by the ABA House of Delegates and that touch on cloud computing. One resolution[8] changes Model Rule 1.6(c), requiring that "[a] lawyer shall make reasonable efforts to prevent the inadvertent or unauthorized disclosure of, or unauthorized access to, information relating to the representation of a client." A second resolution[9] involved Comment 3 on Model Rule 5.3, Responsibilities Regarding Nonlawyer Assistance. Titled NonLawyers Outside the Firm, the Comment stated in part that "[a] lawyer may use nonlawyers outside the firm to assist the lawyer in rendering legal services to the client. Examples include …using an Internet-based service to store client information. When using such services outside the firm, a lawyer must make reasonable efforts to ensure that the services are provided in a manner that is compatible with the lawyer's professional obligations."

State Bar Associations

The state bar associations have also been weighing in on this subject. The New York State Bar Association's Committee on Professional Ethics has issued an opinion on storage of confidential data with CSPs.[10] The opinion states that it is ethical to do so if the lawyer takes "reasonable care" to stay in compliance with their confidentiality requirements. This does not signify a guarantee that "the information is secure from any unauthorized access."

---

7. ABA Model Rules of Professional Conduct 5.3.

8. ABA Comm'n. on Ethics 20/20, Resolution 105A, Lawyer use of technology and confidentiality (Aug. 2012).

9. ABA Comm'n. on Ethics 20/20, Resolution 105C, Ethical implications of retaining lawyers and nonlawyers outside the firm to work on client matters (i.e., outsourcing) (Aug. 2012).

10. N.Y. Bar Ethics Op. 842 (2010).

In addition, lawyers are required to stay abreast of technological changes to ensure that the storage system continues to protect the confidential data. And the lawyer is to monitor the law of privilege, to ensure that online storage "does not cause a loss or waiver of privilege."

The opinion states that lawyers are responsible, if there has been a data breach at the CSP, for determining whether their client's confidential data was breached, stopping use of the CSP until the effects of the breach are remedied, and notifying his or her clients appropriately.

"Reasonable care" includes:

- Ensuring that the online data storage provider has an enforceable obligation to preserve confidentiality and security and the provider will notify the lawyer if served with process requiring the production of client information
- Investigating the online data storage provider's security measures, policies, recoverability methods, and other procedures to determine if they are adequate under the circumstances
- Employing available technology to guard against reasonably foreseeable attempts to infiltrate the data that is stored
- Investigating the storage provider's ability to purge and wipe any copies of the data, and to move the data to a different host, if the lawyer becomes dissatisfied with the storage provider or for other reasons changes storage providers.

Other states have also issued ethical guidance. Arizona has stated that lawyers must take reasonable measures to "protect the security and confidentiality of client documents and information,"[11] which should include "firewalls, password protection schemes, encryption, anti-virus measures, etc." It calls for a competent review of the security measures and periodic reviews thereafter and cautions lawyers to recognize the limitations of their competence in this area. Arizona had previously determined that it was "not unethical" to electronically store client information on systems connected to the Internet, as long as the lawyer took reasonable steps to ensure that the information

---

11. Arizona Bar Ethics Op. 09-04 (2009).

was not disclosed to third parties, lost, or destroyed.[12] This included assessment and treatment of risks and the use of external expertise if the lawyer did not possess those skills.

Maine's Board of Overseers of the Bar addressed the question of whether it was unethical to utilize third party vendors to process and store client information, including the use of a backup facility.[13] More specifically, if there was an issue with the vendor's technicians, outside the lawyer's direct supervision and control, having access to this client data. The opinion said this was permissible, if the lawyer took reasonable steps to ensure that the firm performing the storage services had sufficient safeguards that the "conduct of these individuals is compatible with the professional obligations of the lawyer." Again, the lawyer needs to ensure that the storage firm has a "legally enforceable obligation to maintain the confidentiality" of the lawyer's client data.

California's state bar looked not directly at cloud computing but more generally at whether the duties of competence and confidentiality were violated when lawyers used technologies to store or transmit client information if "the technology may be susceptible to unauthorized access by third parties."[14] The opinion directs lawyers to go through a six-step evaluation before utilizing such technologies. These steps include an assessment of: the level of security possible with this technology; the sensitivity of the client's data; the impacts to the client if the data is disclosed; the client's instructions not to use the technology and personal security situation (e.g., can others access the information if the technology is used); the legal ramifications for unauthorized access or interception (i.e., the more severe the ramifications the greater the expectation of privacy); and the urgency of the situation (e.g., exigent circumstances).

A more recent California bar opinion discussed the cloud in the context of a virtual law office (VLO).[15] It said that "[w]hile an attorney may maintain a VLO in the cloud where communications with the client, and storage of and access to all information about the client's matter, are conducted solely

---

12. Arizona Bar Ethics Op. 05-04 (2005).
13. Maine Bar Ethics Op. 194 (2008).
14. California Bar Ethics Op. 2010-179 (2010).
15. California Bar Ethics Op. 2012-184 (May 2012).

279

via the internet using a third-party's secure servers, Attorney may be required to take additional steps to confirm that she is fulfilling her ethical obligations due to distinct issues raised by the hypothetical VLO and its operation. Failure of Attorney to comply with all ethical obligations relevant to these issues will preclude the operation of a VLO in the cloud as described herein.

Nevada's state bar had previously answered the question of whether it was unethical to store confidential client information and/or communications without client consent, in an electronic format on a server or other device that is not exclusively in the lawyer's control."[16] In likening this to storing client's paper documents in a third-party warehouse, the opinion states that a lawyer acting competently and reasonably is not in violation of ethics rules, even if an unauthorized or inadvertent disclosure should occur."

Citing both the Nevada and Arizona ethics opinions, Alabama's bar association has stated that electronic documents should be protected at least as well as paper documents, ensuring reasonable methods are in place to protect their confidentiality, security and integrity.[17] Firewalls, intrusion detection, and backup are all mentioned as security measures. The opinion specifically addresses cloud computing: "lawyer may use 'cloud computing' or third-party providers to store client data provided that the attorney exercises reasonable care in doing so." Reasonable care includes knowing the CSP's processes for securing the data and compliance with a confidentiality agreement, in addition to staying abreast of changes in technology.

Iowa's state bar association issued its opinion about the use of SaaS.[18] Quoting previous guidance, it said that "[a]ccess to stored data and data protection should be taken into consideration when performing due diligence. Whatever form of SaaS is used, the lawyer must ensure that there is unfettered access to the data when it is needed. Likewise the lawyer must be able to determine the nature and degree of protection that will be afforded the data while residing elsewhere." The opinion suggested that lawyers identify any legal issues raised by such use (e.g., becoming subject to new legal jurisdictions), find out about financial and service termination considerations, and analyze data protection issues such as password protection and encryption.

---

16. Nevada Bar Ethics Op. 33 (2006).
17. Alabama Bar Ethics Op. 2010-02 (2010).
18. Iowa Bar Ethics Op. 11-01 Use of Software as a Service – Cloud Computing (Sept. 2011).

The Massachusetts Bar Association issued an opinion on using the Internet to store client information.[19] This opinion emphasized that a lawyer must make reasonable efforts to ensure that the provider's "terms of use and data privacy policies, practices and procedures" are compatible with confidentiality obligations and that if a client expressly states that she or he does not want the Internet used for storage or communication, the lawyer must obey that direction. Additionally, sensitive data requires express consent before being stored or communicated via the Internet. The opinion referenced prior guidance on the use of unencrypted emails between lawyers and their clients. It also said that lawyers should be "examining the provider's existing practices (including data encryption, password protection, and system backups) and available service history (including reports of known security breaches or "holes") to reasonably ensure that data stored on the provider's system actually will remain confidential, and will not be intentionally or inadvertently disclosed or lost."

New Hampshire's bar association issued its opinion on cloud computing use.[20] It allows a lawyer to use cloud computing "consistent with his or her ethical obligations, as long as the lawyer takes reasonable steps to ensure that sensitive client information remains confidential." The opinion differentiated email from cloud computing, stating that email "presents unique risks and challenges." It touched on ethics rules for competence, confidentiality of information, informed consent, safekeeping of property, and responsibilities regarding nonlawyer assistance. It noted ten criteria for lawyers to consider when using cloud computing services, including commingling of data, data ownership, data retention, and notification if subpoenaed.

Other state bars, including those in North Carolina, Oregon, and Pennsylvania have recently issued ethics opinions[21] that focus on Internet storage or more specifically on SaaS and cloud computing services. The guiding principle is that the lawyers need to make reasonable efforts to ensure that their clients' information remains confidential even if it is stored in the cloud,

---

19. Massachusetts Bar Ethics Op. 12-03 (May 2012).

20. New Hampshire Bar Ethics Op. 2012-13/4 The Use of Cloud Computing in the Practice of Law (Feb. 2013).

21. North Carolina Bar Ethics Op. 6 (Oct. 2011); Oregon Bar Ethics Op. 2011-188 (Nov. 2011); Pennsylvania Bar Ethics Op. 2011-200 (Nov. 2011).

including understanding the technical and business criteria upon which to assess a CSP, likely utilizing much of what has been presented throughout this book, although probably only using a subset of these processes to conduct CSP assessments would be considered a reasonable effort. Client consent and understanding should also be obtained.

9.2 Individuals in the Cloud

Beyond organizations, lawyers may also be called on by individuals to provide advice in their use of the cloud. While the same statutes in Chapters 2 and 3 apply, there may be additional specialized statutes involved. With only one organizational entity involved, the due diligence activities focus even more heavily on the CSP instead of the consumer of cloud services. In addition, the CSP is going to be providing its standard services under a standard agreement, so the lawyer may need to become more familiar with those standard CSP agreements and terms of use, some of which were reviewed in Chapter 8.

For many consumers, they are already in the cloud and have been for many years. Web-based email systems, file, photo, and video sharing sites, blogs, micro-blogs, and social networking sites, professional and personal reference sites, and online versions of popular desktop applications are within the definition of what makes up the SaaS and even the PaaS service models of the cloud. Many if not most of these applications have been used and terms agreed to without much if any consideration and certainly without the need for legal advice. But as consumers become more aware of the risks involved (as data breaches become well known) and while consumers put more of their information into the cloud (or it is put there for them through organizations), there will be an increasing need to assess the risks and protect the consumers' rights to their data stored in the cloud.

While in most countries the data protection laws apply no matter if it is an organization outsourcing a customer's data to the cloud or if it is the individuals doing it themselves, in many countries there are additional consumer-specific laws. These are often concerned with protection of consumer financial information. For example, in South Korea, there is a consumer financial information statute that requires specific protections of consumer information involved in financial transactions.[22] Statutes that involve specific types of consumers may also be relevant, such as the protection of the information of minors under the Children's Online Privacy Protection Act (COPPA) in the United States.[23] Lawyers will need to have an appropriate understanding of applicable statutes, but may also want to keep an eye out for those statutes that protect the personal information of consumers who are citizens of the jurisdiction (e.g., the Massachusetts security statute discussed in Chapter 2), even though the provision of cloud services occurs in other jurisdictions.

The bigger consideration for lawyers when dealing with the negotiating ability of consumers is the reality that they will have little or no negotiating strength with the CSP. The emphasis then is on how much of a risk assessment can be performed based on the information about the CSP's practices that is publicly or otherwise available to potential customers. The CSP's privacy policy will be clearly displayed on its website, and at least with larger CSPs (e.g., Amazon AWS, as discussed in Chapter 8), so will its information security practices. The following are those recommendations from Chapter 5 that should still be given full consideration, even when an individual consumer is involved:

- *Create a baseline assessment of the individual consumer's current information security and privacy program, including known risks.* Individual consumers should take the time to self-assess those actions that they take that may expose their data in the cloud to unnecessary risks. Examples of this include use of inappropriate passwords (but many sites now provide feedback on the strength of passwords), sharing of equipment or passwords with others, non-secure data disposal techniques, or the non-encrypted use of wireless networks.
- *Determine any incremental risks for systems, data and/or infrastructure that will be placed into the cloud and their interfaces back to systems that*

---

22. Republic of Korea, Electronic Financial Transactions Act (2006).
23. COPPA (1998), 15 U.S.C. §§ 6501–6506.

will not be placed into the cloud. For an individual consumer, this could occur with interfaces such as that between common identity credential providers that are used across multiple SaaS applications or for the formatting and protection of file systems used both locally and in the cloud.

- *Perform a risk assessment of the prospective CSPs utilizing a methodology such as those introduced in Chapter 5.* This should always be done, although the assessment may be a subset of the recommended steps and may focus on looking for established risk assessment and treatment programs and asking a few key questions. Individuals can review posted privacy policies, check news stories for any adverse security information and look for the presence of certifications based on international and national information security and privacy standards.

- *Incorporate the risk treatment plan and the monitoring, measuring, and reporting capabilities into the SLA with the selected CSP.* There will likely be a standard SLA, with the cloud consumer able to choose different service levels. The need for each differing service level (e.g., does an extra 47 minutes of availability per year make any difference to a consumer?) can be explained by the lawyer. The penalties that apply to missed service levels should be understood. How security incidents are investigated and reported, external reviews of the network and applications, and independent audits should be specified and the reports available in some fashion to the consumers.

For the CSP agreement, lawyers must be able to identify the areas of concern in the standard CSP agreements and advise on choosing the proper options when such options are offered. While individual consumers may not be able to modify these standard provisions, they should at least be aware of the implications. As these cloud agreements mature, some of these terms may become more favorable, or at least become negotiable. The following are some of the CSP agreement recommendations from Chapter 8 and how they might be impacted in providing advice to an individual consumer;

- *Limit CSP liability to actual payments received in the last twelve months for conduct where it is primarily liable.* A consumer would want to consider: any exclusions that exist for the costs of a data breach, whether there are limitations per incident and what is considered an incident (e.g., each record or each breach), limitations on consequential damages, and whether gross negligence on the part of the CSP is required for there to be any liability at all.

- *The CSP may disclose the individual's information if legally compelled to do so.* Individuals should insist that they are notified before any compelled disclosure is acted upon and also that there are no voluntary disclosures by the CSP (as allowed for certain requests). Individuals must also insist that the CSP is not making their information available for any type of secondary use, such as marketing, separately or in aggregation.

- *The terms are silent as to its operational responsibilities in case of a data breach.* The CSP's statutory compliance requirements should be clearly spelled out in the agreement. Individuals will need to understand how they are notified and under what circumstances (e.g., only if there is a breach that the CSP believes may impact their information but not if the information is encrypted and the CSP does not reasonably believe the breach caused harm).

- *Upon termination, the CSP will return copies of the individual's data in the desired format.* Individuals will need to look at how long of a window they have to extract their information, what formats the extractions may be in, and any restrictions on the time of day or month the extractions can take place.

9.3 Starting and Concluding

Starting Use of Cloud Services

When a lawyer becomes involved with the possibility of her or his client utilizing cloud computing services, this should trigger a series of actions and expertise that will be part of effectively addressing this area. Besides her or his own personal requirements to become conversant in the areas of risk assessment, technology, information security, privacy, or the applicable statutes, to implement many of the steps outlined in this book, the lawyer will need to acquire organizational knowledge of the following:

- Statutes and judicial decisions in every country where the organization does business or has customers, or where the data is processed that may impact data privacy, information security, government surveillance capabilities, or cloud computing

- Industry-specific regulations that may impact data privacy, information security, or cloud computing
- Contractual obligations that the organization has agreed to regarding privacy, security, or other commitments to customers or vendors
- Local labor laws and restrictions on use and transfer of employee information
- Blocking statutes of any kind in these countries
- Rules of evidence and related rules of procedure in these countries
- Prospective legislation in these countries involving any of these topics
- Legal compliance requirements that may impact cloud computing (e.g., SOX, FCPA, etc.)
- Internal information security and privacy policies and procedures
- Internal risk assessments and treatments
- Audit reports on the organization's internal controls
- Third-party assessments of the organization's controls for networks/web applications
- Information security and privacy certifications held by the organization
- Organization's use of the web, including e-commerce and related privacy policies
- Organization's business continuity/disaster recovery plan
- Organization's data breach notification obligations and response plan
- Organization's insurance coverage related to information security, privacy, and outsourcing
- Inventory of information assets, with valuations and criticality
- Inventory of information by classification and sensitivity levels
- List of trade secrets and other high-value organizational assets
- Current and potential litigation
- Litigation hold procedures
- Forensic data capture techniques
- Digital evidence procedures for maintaining chain of custody
- Procedure for creating authenticated source records
- Records retention policies, procedures, and custodians
- Records retention obligations from statutes and contracts

- Organization's limitations of liability
- Organization's indemnity policy
- Organization's standard outsourcing terms and conditions

With these documents providing a baseline understanding, from there the process as outlined throughout the book and highlighted in Chapters 7 and 8 as the comprehensive approach should begin.

Final Thoughts

While this book has looked at several examples of organizations considering the cloud, to generalize the discussion, the perspective used was one based on a justification of cloud use from the technical and financial viewpoint more than the commercial business viewpoint. But that need not be the case at all. Business needs can (and perhaps always should) be the direct driver behind the move to cloud computing. The need to increase sales, move into new markets, carry out mergers and acquisitions, perform what-if simulations, open new offices, stores or market-facing access points, market new products, increase internal and external reporting and communications, provide new services, deepen supply chain capabilities and facilitate research, or enable consolidation and business synergies, are all drivers that can move organizations to cloud computing services.

Organizations considering the cloud should also have a broad understanding of how quickly it would make sense to move to cloud solutions. SMEs, without the investment in infrastructure and better able to change their processes, may be on a shorter timeframe to obtain the benefits of expertise or infrastructure that they may not have access to, even several years down the road. Larger organizations, with a significant investment in the IT infrastructure and people to staff it, may be less able to quickly change processes and so the steps into the cloud may need to be incremental. These may include pilot projects, outsourcing certain less essential tasks or non-competitive advantage processes or using a cloud bursting bridge to a CSP to handle cyclical (e.g., monthly payroll or annual reporting) processing needs.

The movement from the centralized then decentralized IT models so prevalent these last fifty years to one where IT is a commodity utility that is easily attained and paid for has long been the hope. With the cloud computing model, that hope may finally be matched to an architecture that allows it to happen. In this book, the lawyer's role in dealing with cloud computing has been discussed, with the goal of providing a firm foundation in the global and domestic statutes, information security and privacy risks and controls, the impacts on records management, data breaches, identity management, and litigation and investigation-related duties in the cloud, while trying to keep an eye on the horizon for possible future dangers.[24]

This all leads to the capability of having a fully informed assessment of multiple CSPs and then negotiation of the cloud agreement with the CSP finally selected by the organization. It is this new role of advising their clients about cloud computing that requires lawyers to have knowledge of not only the legal aspects but the technological and financial aspects of this area. The fully informed lawyer has the ability to steer clients through all the marketing buzzwords, technical acronyms, and standardized agreements to ensure that his or her clients are fully protected in their increasingly tight and long-lasting embrace of the cloud.

---

24. Bryan, Ford, Asst. Prof. Yale Univ., *Icebergs in the Clouds: the Other Risks of Cloud Computing* (May 17, 2012).

APPENDIX

CLOUD STANDARDS AND GUIDANCE ORGANIZATIONS

- American Institute of Certified Public Accountants (AICPA)
- Alliance for Telecommunications Industry Solutions (ATIS) Cloud Services Forum*
- Article 29 Working Party (Working Party on the Protection of Individuals with regard to the Processing of Personal Data)
- Association for Retail Technology Standards (ARTS)
- BITS
- Cloud Industry Forum (CIF)
- Cloud Computing Interoperability Forum (CCIF)*
- Cloud Computing Use Cases Group*
- Cloud Security Alliance (CSA)
- Common Assurance Maturity Model (CAMM)
- Distributed Management Task Force (DMTF)
- European Network and Information Security Agency (ENISA)
- European Telecommunications Standards Institute (ETSI)
- Federal Financial Institutions Examination Council (FFIEC)
- Global Inter-Cloud Technology Forum (GICTF)*
- Institute of Electrical and Electronics Engineers (IEEE)
- Internet Engineering Task Force (IETF)*
- Internet Research Task Force (IRTF)*
- ISACA

- International Auditing and Assurance Standards Boards (IAASB)
- International Organization for Standardization/the International Electrotechnical Commission (ISO/IEC) JTC1
- International Telecommunications Union — Telecommunications Standardization Sector (ITU-T)
- Liberty Alliance/Kantara Initiative
- National Institute of Standards and Technology (NIST)
- Network Centric Operations Industry Consortium (NCOIC)*
- Organization for the Advancement of Structured Information Standards (OASIS)
- Object Management Group (OMG)/Cloud Standards Customer Council (CSCC)
- Open Cloud Consortium (OCC)
- Open Cloud Manifesto
- Open Data Center Alliance (ODCA)
- Open Grid Forum (OGF)
- Open Group
- Open Management Group (OMG)
- Payment Card Industry Security Standards Council (PCI)
- Storage Networking Industry Association (SNIA)
- TeleManagement (TM) Forum
- Trusted Computing Group

* = Not discussed in this book

TABLE OF AUTHORITIES

INDEX

Model Rule 5.3, 277
MP. *See* Media protection (MP)
Multinational organization, 252–253, 255–256
Multi-organization projects, 11
Mutual Legal Assistance Treaties (MLATs), 48

N
NARA. *See* National Archives and Records Administration (NARA)
National Archives and Records Administration (NARA) guidelines, 45–46
National Institute of Standards and Technology (NIST), 2, 41, 44, 168
National Security Letters (NSLs), 49–51
Navarro v. Verizon Wireless, LLC, 39
Nevada Bar Association, 280
New Hampshire Bar Association, 281
New Zealand, 85–86, 90
NIST. *See* National Institute of Standards and Technology (NIST)
Non-standard services purchases, 23

O
OASIS. *See* Organization for the Advancement of Structured Information Standards (OASIS)
Object Management Group (OMG), 165
OCC. *See* Open Cloud Consortium (OCC)
ODCA. *See* Open Data Center Alliance (ODCA)
OGF. *See* Open Grid Forum (OGF)
OMG. *See* Object Management Group (OMG)
On-demand self-service, 3
Open Cloud Consortium (OCC), 163–164
Open Cloud Manifesto, 168
Open Data Center Alliance (ODCA), 167
Open Grid Forum (OGF), 164
Organization for the Advancement of Structured Information Standards (OASIS), 165
Outsourcing
  cost analysis of, 19–21
  impediments to, 15
  international, 58–59
Ownership, data, in contract with cloud provider, 218

P
PaaS. *See* Platform as a Service (PaaS)
PATRIOT Act, 48, 49–51
Payroll, 256–258

Made in the USA
Coppell, TX
12 February 2020